Integral Emotional Intelligence

KEYS TO CREATING AN EXTRAORDINARY LIFE

Endorsements for
Integral Emotional Intelligence:
Keys to Creating an Extraordinary Life

"Integral Emotional Intelligence: Keys to Creating an Extraordinary Life is a work of art, providing us with profound truth, stated clearly and concisely. The material can be understood at many levels and the more we engage with it, the more we can appreciate its depth."

—Ilene Val-Essen, PH.D., author of
Bring Out the Best in Your Child and Your Self: Creating a Family of Mutual Respect

"This book is not about fixing or repairing what's broken. It is about helping already fully functioning and healthy human beings learn to embody their authentic self and gain access to previously unthinkable levels of love, joy, fulfillment, and satisfaction. It offers professionals in the field of human behavior a comprehensive blueprint for empowering individuals to achieve true self-mastery.

"The word 'breakthrough' is often overused and under deserved. But in this case, it is the most appropriate way to describe the impact this work will have on our ability to support people to live fuller, happier, and more joyous lives."

—Neal Rogin, author of *Delightenment*

SHANNON M. HOWARD
AND LONNIE GREEN, PH.D.

Integral Emotional Intelligence

KEYS TO CREATING AN EXTRAORDINARY LIFE

Volume I
The Mastery of Integral Emotional Intelligence Program

Highest Ground Institute
Novato, California
highestgroundinstitute.org

Publishing Management: Ruth Schwartz, TheWonderlady.com

Ordering Information:
Quantity sales: Special discounts are available on quantity purchases by schools, colleges, universities, and study groups, as well as corporate and nonprofit organizations. For details, contact the authors at inquiries@highestgroundinstitute.org.

Integral Emotional Intelligence: Keys to Creating an Extraordinary Life / Shannon M. Howard and Lonnie Green, Ph.D. —1st ed.
979-8-9868406-0-4 paperback edition
979-8-9868406-1-1 ebook editions
Library of Congress Control Number: 2022923262

Table of Contents

Dedication

This work is dedicated to our daughters, Rachel Greenspan and Julia Tate, beautiful souls who are confident, funny, loving, and wise women. We have learned so much from them and are beyond blessed to have them in our lives.

Additionally, this material is dedicated to all individuals who are on a path of awakening and self-mastery and have chosen to make their personal growth and spirituality a priority.

Appreciations

Collaborating with Lonnie for more than a decade on the research and development of this material has been an enormously fulfilling experience, for which I am deeply grateful. We have been fortunate in that while we have many shared areas of interest, we also have complementary areas of strength and varied fields of expertise to draw from. All our interactions are based on win-win and mutual benefit, and she is an absolute joy to have as a partner and co-conspirator for all things good.

Between us, this material reflects more than nine decades of experience working to empower others, and by a happy convergence, ourselves. Lonnie's experience has been primarily through her work as a counselor and therapist, while mine has been as a life coach and a social activist working on the issues of ending hunger, conflict transformation, contemplative spirituality, and social and economic justice. Additionally, we have drawn upon our shared interest and experience as holistic health and parenting mentors while crafting this program.

If I were to fully appreciate and acknowledge everyone who has made a difference in the development of this knowledge, then the list itself would be a book. Following is a partial list of my teachers and cohorts, to whom I am deeply grateful:

- Gordon Davidson, Corinne McLaughlin, Gillian Wright, Emily Baumbach and the Michael teachings, Tara Lemasters, Lynne Twist, Lewis Gibson, Oz Garcia, Landmark, Shamil Idriss and my colleagues at Search for Common Ground, and the folks at the Shalem Institute for their metaphysical and spiritual guidance.

- Jach Pursel and Lazaris for their loving presence and the vast body of onto-logical distinctions they have made available over the past many decades. Their wisdom has greatly empowered the development of this material.

- My sisterhood of friends: Jane Shaw, Jennifer Wood, Sarah Gold, Marie Case, Cheryl Buck, Jerri Binder, Janeen Koconis, and my UK metaphysical group, to mention a few. You have kept faith with me through life's challenges—always loving, always supportive, and never judgmental.

- Joan Holmes, who mentored me and gave me the opportunity to work as a global citizen at a very young age.

- Gail Allen and Ilene Val-Essen, my incredible parenting mentors. Thank you for all your wisdom and guidance.

- My clients, who have done me the great honor of allowing me to partner with them on their journey of unfoldment. Each of you has contributed to the refinement of this material.

- My beta readers, who have engaged with this material in its various iterations and have given me invaluable feedback and support (some of whom I have mentioned previously but deserve additional appreciation for their time and effort): Rachel Greenspan, Walter Wright, Ted Howard, Neal Rogin, Greg Callahan, Ilene Val-Essen, Allan Henderson, Cheryl Buck, Kate Amunrud, Marie Case, Janeen Kokonis, and David Helvarg.

Shannon M. Howard

The information in this book has taken a lifetime to accumulate. I thank all my graduate school professors, who taught me so much about human behavior and motivation as well as what it takes to keep intimate relationships thriving.

I have learned even more outside my academic schooling, mainly by following my ever-expanding interest in emotional intelligence and its many facets. It has been my good fortune to be exposed to the work and wisdom of countless experts in the fields of holistic health, integral studies of human nature, spirituality, emotional expression, and personal evolution. I am grateful beyond words for everything I have learned from them.

I am thrice blessed in my partnership with Shannon Howard, a true soulmate and fellow traveler on the path of making a difference in the human condition. She is an exquisitely articulate scholar, a generous human being, and a fabulously fun friend. I will forever appreciate her inspiring me to participate in this integral emotional intelligence project with her.

Lonnie Green

Highest Ground Institute

Mission

The mission of The Highest Ground Institute is to facilitate the emergence of an integral approach to emotional intelligence that

- encompasses a holistic and heart-centered view of being human;
- fosters self-mastery, internal emancipation, and the ability to bring about everyday transformation; and
- provides individuals with the keys to empowering and accelerating their personal growth and evolution on a sustainable and ever-expanding basis.

Vision

We envision a world in which having a holistic understanding of how to be emotionally intelligent is commonplace. This integral emotional intelligence approach to personal development encompasses all four domains of human expression and how they interact: mind, body, emotions, and spirit or consciousness.

Our aim is to provide individuals with the knowledge, tools, and coaching necessary to empower them to be their best selves. In other words, to enable individuals to empower themselves to develop self-mastery, cultivate an unshakeable sense of their inner being, and operate more fully from their personal highest ground.

Just as humans need to acquire reading literacy, so too must we make the effort to become emotionally literate—it is a knowledge base that is necessary for navigating life with ease, success, and joy. Our goal is to have this knowledge be as practical, accessible, and empowering as possible.

We envision working collaboratively with like-minded individuals and organizations to make integral emotional intelligence education and coaching more widely available. This includes expanding the community of people who are committed to fostering emotional intelligence and empowering them with practical ways of generating co-creative, "you *and* me" outcomes in their lives and in the world.

Intended Outcomes

Gaining emotional literacy and practicing the principles of integral emotional intelligence in a thoughtful and committed way creates the opportunity to accomplish the following outcomes:

- Achieve greater self-mastery and freedom from old, unhelpful beliefs and habitual modes of operating that no longer serve you.

- Navigate relationships with greater success and increase the amount of love flowing in your life.

- Enhance the experience of emotional safety, trust, intimacy, love, and enjoyment in your significant relationships.

- Discover and cultivate your inner emancipated adult.

- Master the ability to consistently turn problems, challenges, and breakdowns into breakthroughs and opportunities for growth.

- Lower your overall level of emotional reactivity, increase your resilience, and become more at ease with the discomfort of vulnerability in a way that allows for greater well-being, peace, happiness, and fulfillment.

- Enhance your ability to heal and integrate emotional wounds and fulfill unmet needs by learning self-therapy processes and techniques.

- Increase your ability to work with challenging emotions in ways that have positive impacts, such as creating greater freedom from fear and anxiety; reducing pain, suffering, guilt, and shame; and expressing anger more constructively.

- Understand healthy ego development and relax the hold of your negative ego and inner critic.

- Be more present to what is occurring in your life while cultivating an expanded sense of equilibrium, also known as unshakable presence, in the face of life's challenges.

- Create greater freedom from the influence of your past and have your present experience be shaped by your future and who you are becoming.

- Accelerate your personal growth, build a stronger foundation for your life, and increase your sense of agency and ability to manifest the life you want.

- Cultivate the art of everyday transformation by choosing to own your reactions and author your responses in ways that shift dysfunctional, reactive, and adversarial dynamics to functional, respectful, and mutually beneficial ones.

- Increase your ability to make positive impacts in your work by cultivating transformative leadership and communications skills, and by developing your ability to generate partnership dynamics.

- Empower yourself to be a resource and support for others on their journey of personal growth and inner emancipation.

Preface
Working With This Material

This book is the first part of The Mastery of Integral Emotional Intelligence Program. This curriculum is organized into three volumes, each with an overarching theme or themes. The material is presented, as concisely as possible, as a series of textbooks, which include both theory and practice. The other two volumes are currently in various stages of research, writing, and review.

This overall program is designed to be an owner's manual for being human and a reference guide for how to live a life of extraordinary well-being and fulfillment. This volume contains distinctions that illuminate what makes each of us think and act the way we do and offers practical steps for gaining self-mastery and living a happier, more joyous life. Self-empowerment is the basic operating principle that informs this work of inner emancipation and is the criterion against which all theory and practices are measured.

A highly practical and rewarding way of approaching this material is by creating goals for your personal growth and applying these concepts to your real-life challenges. This could be any issue or breakdown you are experiencing that you want to evolve into something more positive, or it could be any area of life where you simply wish to grow and become more self-actualized.

Everyone has their own learning style and moves through this information at their own pace. A chapter a week is a good tempo for some, as it takes time for self-reflection and integration. Some people prefer to work with an integral emotional intelligence coach or counselor so that they have assistance in applying these principles to their lives, thereby accelerating their process.

A general suggestion as you work through this material is to keep a companion notebook or journal for recording your reflections and insights. You are also encouraged to mark up your textbook if you find that helpful.

All of the diagrams included in this volume are available online to download. Videos and podcasts are being developed to support visual and auditory learning. These can also be used as resource material for individuals who want to facilitate a book club or study group.

The Highest Ground Institute is responsible for the creation and content of The Mastery of Integral Emotional Intelligence Program. A full program description is available online.

CREATING A FOUNDATION FOR SELF-MASTERY

Building Block of Emotional Literacy

Understanding what it means to embody emotional intelligence in an integral way.

Core Competencies of Emotional Intelligence

Being self-reflective and practicing the art of self-empowerment and self-advocacy, which means being a firm advocate for your best self and for your personal growth and evolution.

Developing impeccability about reaching for the most conscious, heart-centered, and magnanimous version of yourself that you have access to in any situation.

Chapter 1
Introducing Integral
Emotional Intelligence

What Is the Purpose of This Material?

Overview

The purpose of *Integral Emotional Intelligence: Keys to Creating an Extraordinary Life* is to empower you to gain self-mastery, practice the art of everyday transformation, and consistently live from your best, most authentic self.

Self-mastery is about increasing your power to effect positive change. It involves practicing being present and awake to what is occurring in your life in ways that enable you to shift from negative and dysfunctional dynamics to positive and functional ones. Causing everyday transformation occurs in all the moment-by-moment opportunities you have to make choices and act in ways that are less reactive and more intentional, more heart-centered, and increasingly beneficial to yourself and others.

The path of self-mastery is about acquiring the knowledge base and mastering the skills necessary to enable you to live more and more of your life from your best self. It is about having a practice of responsibility, integrity, respect, and excellence, and is a powerful, authentic, and deeply fulfilling way of living. What being your best self doesn't mean is being perfect or in any way better than anyone else. This isn't about fixing yourself; it is about being your authentic self more fully. Who you are inside is already worthy, competent, and deserving.

Developing integral emotional intelligence is a process of gaining techniques and tools that empower you to reveal more of who you truly are inside and express the qualities of your best self in your daily life. This means cultivating your sense of equilibrium and magnanimity, such that you are able to operate more and more from your personal highest ground.

This first volume in The Mastery of Integral Emotional Intelligence Program is designed to empower you with the knowledge and skills necessary to be able to live from your authentic self on a consistent basis. To help you more fully understand the purpose of this material, some key concepts will be introduced in this section that will be covered in greater depth in later chapters. These concepts are basic areas of emotional literacy needed in order to gain emotional mastery.

The first concept that will be introduced relates to the nature of the inner design of being human that we all share, which is called the psyche. The other concepts relate to understanding how dysfunctional and functional dynamics get played out in life. They illustrate the two basic operating domains of being human that we embody and express on a moment-by-moment basis.

The simplest way to describe the difference between these two operating states is that they are composed of attitudes and approaches to life that are either fundamentally unconscious and adversarial, or conscious and co-creative. The concepts we will introduce that help us identify when and how these two basic operating states are being played out are called the drama triangle (originally developed as part of transactional analysis), and the empowerment dynamic (which was created by David Emerald).

The Psyche

Understanding your psyche and how its components work together in synergistic ways is foundational to being emotionally intelligent. Your psyche is composed of three parts: the conscious self, the superconscious self, and the subconscious self. Each of these parts embodies distinct qualities of consciousness and intelligence. Because we have these three main areas, or ways, that consciousness is expressed through us, we are multidimensional beings. The understanding of how these parts all work together is referred to as multidimensional psychology.

Self-mastery requires strengthening your connection to the part of your psyche that is called your conscious self. This is your sense of your inner being, your personal autonomy and agency, and is also known as your authentic self. Your conscious self is your experience of being in the present; it is your timeless sense of awareness, which stays constant throughout all the moments of your life. Cultivating presence and developing your ability to remain steady in the awareness of your conscious self is one of the most important skills of being emotionally intelligent.

A major focus of this material is learning how to work with your subconscious self to create internal freedom and becoming emancipated from unconscious blockages or barriers that are holding you back. This means learning how to relax the hold of your negative ego, live more fully in the present, and have your present be shaped by future potential rather than dominated and unconsciously driven by past experiences. This is an ongoing process of integration, one that continuously moves you toward happier and healthier states.

The following image is a visual representation of the purpose of this program. It is an illustration of the psyche—the inner design of being human—and symbolizes the path of self-mastery.

The three circles within the larger oval represent the main ways that consciousness moves through your physical body. The bottom circle stands for the subconscious self, which is centered in your solar plexus. The middle circle stands for the conscious self, which is centered in your heart, and the top circle stands for the superconscious self, which is located in the crown of your head. The oval shape they are within symbolizes the totality of your experience of being alive in the present moment.

The two triangles represent the two fundamental types of dynamics that occur in everyday life. These are dynamics that you play out internally toward yourself *and* externally toward others. The top triangle represents the empowerment dynamic, which is composed of dynamics that are conscious, purposeful, functional, and co-creative in nature. The bottom triangle represents the drama triangle, which is composed of dynamics that are unconscious, dysfunctional, and reactive.

Everyone moves back and forth between these two dynamics, from being in a state of equilibrium and calmness to being in a state of disequilibrium and reactivity, and then back again. The path of self-mastery and inner emancipation involves choosing to live more and more of your life from the empowerment dynamic.

The Drama Triangle

The bottom triangle is the drama triangle and originates in the subconscious self, specifically the part of the subconscious that is referred to as the negative ego. It is made up of unconscious losing games (which are also known as zero-sum games), dysfunctional dynamics, defense mechanisms, and negative beliefs and attitudes. The drama triangle is a fear-driven defense structure we learned as children when we felt wounded in some way and needed to protect ourselves.

Our families and other sources of cultural conditioning unwittingly demonstrated and reinforced these dynamics, which we then internalized. This automatic mode of operating became our default strategy when under stress, and we unknowingly became expert at these ways of functioning in life. By the time we became adults, however, many of these defense mechanisms stopped serving us.

The three positions, or roles, of the drama triangle are victim, persecutor, and rescuer. The main characteristics these roles have in common are a lack of responsibility and respect, and a diminished sense of self-esteem. We embody the positions of this triangle when we are reactive and feel put upon or put down, done to, messed with, or are otherwise at the effect of people and life in negative ways.

Sometimes people become so habituated to living in a state of reactivity that they don't realize that's what they are doing—it just becomes their version of normal. They don't recognize how personally destructive it is and that they can make another choice. When this occurs, it can have tragic consequences, especially with close friends, family members, and work relationships.

The roles of the drama triangle are played out incessantly in the world. These dynamics are common, even daily, occurrences, and are mostly invisible until you comprehend how they work. Even when you aren't actively generating them, you will have many opportunities to deal with people who are. They are inescapable, and once you understand them you will see them everywhere.

One of the most empowering things you can do to gain emotional mastery is to become aware of how these destructive and damaging modes of operating are playing out in your life and in the lives of the people around you. Then, building upon this foundation of understanding, you can begin to master the ability to shift these dynamics to more positive, beneficial ones and create transformation in every area of your life.

Being a victim is the central role of the drama triangle and happens when we feel oppressed by, or at the effect of, our lives, and have given up our responsibility and agency to effect positive outcomes. Self-pity, martyrdom, and feelings of being helpless, hopeless, and powerless accompany this role, as well as the attitudes of "Poor me," "They're so mean," and "It's so unfair." Playing the role of being a victim is primarily a mental construct and is a form of internal oppression that is distinct from legitimate, external forms of victimization.

The persecutor role occurs when we are unconsciously driven to control, punish, or win over others, no matter what the cost. When in the persecutor role, we disrespect other people's values, choices, and boundaries, and are in denial about the hurtful impacts we are having on the people around us. The main attitude of the persecutor is, "I'm right and you're wrong."

When we slide into the rescuer role, we unconsciously denigrate and insult others by relating to them as being inferior and incapable. This form of rescuing can be very subtle and isn't the same as offering genuine help when it is requested. Instead, it is an ego-driven way of feeling superior and indispensable to others. The main unconscious attitudes of this role are, "I am more knowledgeable, capable and efficient than you," "I am important because you need me," and "The more you need me, the more important I feel."

One reason we continue to embody the roles of victim, persecutor, and rescuer is that the negative ego is certain the interim payoffs that come from engaging in these dynamics are essential to survival. These are payoffs such as being right, getting attention, being in control, feeling superior or important, and being indispensable. These interim payoffs work to make us deny the multiple devastating costs that always accompany the playing of any losing game.

Whenever you are operating from any of the roles of the drama triangle, you are giving away your personal power and will feel like you are losing in some way. *No one* wins when they are caught up in the drama triangle—not you or the people you are interacting with. When people deny this sense of losing, it is often just a coping mechanism for avoiding all the bad feelings that come with engaging in any losing dynamic.

The Empowerment Dynamic

The top triangle originates in the conscious self and represents the empowerment dynamic. The positions on this triangle are creator, challenger, and coach. Respect, responsibility, and a strong sense of your authentic self are the key aspects of these roles. This triangle represents winning games, which are also known as infinite games, and are composed of functional dynamics and positive beliefs and attitudes. It is a self-aware, heart-centered way of approaching life and is based on principles of co-creation and partnership.

When you are embodying the roles of the empowerment dynamic, you are cultivating and operating from your inner adult—the wisest and most mature part of yourself that you have access to. These dynamics are the expression of your conscious self in action, and when you function in this way both your inner being and your outer expression in life are congruent in a positive way. Although we are all, to some degree, unintentional experts at the roles of the drama triangle, the roles of the empowerment dynamic are ones that usually require work to develop.

Being a creator is the central role of the empowerment dynamic. It is the conscious role that replaces the unconscious role of being a victim. It is an orientation toward life that is one of acceptance and ownership. When you are operating from this role, you have taken back your personal power and agency. You have taken responsibility and are willing to be "at cause," or in charge of, your life. You are expressing your personal agency, rather than just complaining about the way things are.

Being a challenger replaces being a persecutor and is based on self-advocacy. First and foremost, this means challenging *yourself* to be the best, most magnanimous, version of yourself that you can be. Only then will you be able to successfully challenge others to be their best selves.

Being a coach replaces being a rescuer and is based on respect. Coaches provide assistance only when there is a request or permission for it, and any advice they give is with the intent to empower others to be more self-reliant, self-expressive, and successful.

Living Above or Below the Line

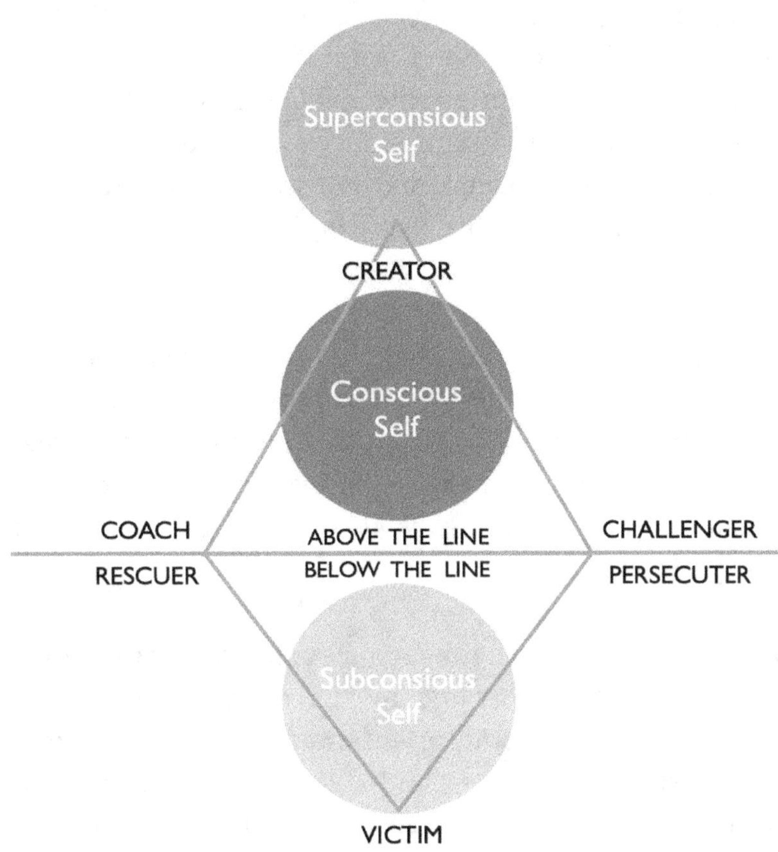

There is a line between the bottom of the conscious self and the top of the subconscious self where the two triangles join. This line is the demarcation of the domains of life that are called above the line and below the line. This concept has its roots in ancient wisdom traditions, in which it is called the altar of sacrifice or renunciation. What this refers to is the understanding that you need to be willing to sacrifice, or give up, the interim payoffs you're getting from unconscious, losing games and dynamics. These interim payoffs are the false sense of winning you replace, as you rise above the line, with the greater benefits of taking a heart-centered, conscious approach to life.

A relatively straightforward example of this is when you are holding a grudge and want to punish or get revenge on someone for something they did. A lot of your energy goes into perpetuating negative thoughts and feelings, but there is also a certain amount of excitement or intensity that is being generated. This is an interim payoff of feeling enlivened, even though it costs you by trapping you in bad feelings. There is a lot of drama and a false sense of power in this below-the-line approach.

Instead, giving up the negative excitement and desire for retribution allows for being heart-centered, and you can then practice forgiveness and be assertive about setting healthy boundaries. You can empower yourself by getting disentangled from the negativity of the person or situation, processing your emotions, completing the past, integrating lessons learned, and moving on with your life. As you can see from this example, when you are operating above the line, there is very little drama.

When you are willing to take full responsibility for yourself and how you show up in life, you are operating above the line. This requires practicing self-acceptance and embracing, rather than denying, what is occurring in your reality. It means actively choosing to be functional by moving your inner orientation from your subconscious self in your solar plexus to the wisdom and maturity of your conscious self in your heart.

Operating above the line requires taking a co-creative, partnership stance in life and adopting a key attitude of "you *and* me." In contrast, operating below the line usually means defaulting to a victim orientation. This is when we feel powerless and reactive, at the effect of our lives, with a limited sense of personal autonomy or agency. This is a profoundly defensive, adversarial state, and a key attitude is "you *or* me" or "you *versus* me."

Practicing self-mastery and causing everyday transformation requires a commitment to reaching for the most magnanimous version of yourself that you can access in any situation. It requires being self-reflective and a firm advocate for your best self and your personal growth. It involves taking a conscious, mindful, heart-centered approach to life, one in which you own your reactions and author your responses, rather than simply acting out your reactivity. It is a way of showing up that is authentic and powerful, courageous, respectful, empathic, thoughtful, and principled.

What Is Integral Emotional Intelligence?

Overview

The practice of integral emotional intelligence is one of developing self-mastery, that is, cultivating your ability to create everyday transformation and consistently and sustainably live from your best self. To understand integral emotional intelligence, it is helpful to first look at the commonly accepted understanding of emotional intelligence.

The concept of emotional intelligence has been around since at least the early decades of the twentieth century. More recently, emotional intelligence as a psychological theory was developed by Yale president Peter Salovey and his colleague, Professor John Mayer. Journalist and psychologist Daniel Goleman based his book *Emotional Intelligence* on their research and has helped formulate and popularize the commonly held definition of emotional intelligence, which follows.

The simplest and most generally accepted definition of emotional intelligence is

a) the ability to identify and name your emotions,

b) the ability to regulate or manage your emotions, and

c) the ability to recognize and respond constructively to the emotions of others.

Current theory regarding emotional intelligence includes five major areas of competence:

1. Practicing self-awareness.

2. Responding to and engaging with your own and other people's emotions and behaviors constructively.

3. Deepening your empathy toward yourself and others.

4. Motivating yourself from your best intentions.

5. Enhancing your interpersonal and social skills.

Much is known about what the traits of emotional intelligence are, but less is known about how to embody it. It is much easier to study and talk about what emotional intelligence looks like than it is to know how to *be* emotionally intelligent. For example, it is widely agreed that emotionally intelligent people are resilient. There are certain things that they think and do. But how do you go about *being* resilient?

Emotions don't exist in isolation, and the *embodiment* of emotional intelligence requires taking a holistic approach. This means considering all four areas of human expression—mental, physical, emotional, and spiritual (or consciousness)—and understanding how these areas work together in synergistic ways. It is not possible, for example, to become truly emotionally intelligent without also increasing your spiritual intelligence (your knowledge of your inner being and consciousness).

This whole-person (holistic) approach to emotional intelligence is called *integral emotional intelligence*. Although the prevalent understanding of emotional intelligence is not holistic, for the sake of expediency, whenever the term emotional intelligence is used from here on, we mean *integral* emotional intelligence.

This material has emerged from an inquiry into how to *be* emotionally intelligent. By inquiring deeply into the nature of who you are as a conscious self, you can move beyond simply learning the techniques of how to act emotionally intelligent—you can *become* emotionally intelligent. In other words, you move beyond the realm of "what to think and do" into the realm of "how to be."

When you look at emotional intelligence in an integral way, what becomes possible is mastering the art of being transformative: being able to consistently cause enhanced outcomes for yourself and for the people around you.

Recurring Themes

There are four main themes that are woven throughout this material: waking up, growing up, clearing up, and showing up. They are part of integral theory, which was conceived by the philosopher Ken Wilber, and are the four elements of personal development necessary for creating sustainable transformation.[i] These are the main areas of personal growth that require attention and effort if a person is to become self-actualized.

Although our research uncovered these distinctions after most of this volume was written, we believe that they provide an empowering context and way of looking at this material. We have adapted these four elements for our purposes and will be referring to them from time-to-time.

1. *Waking up.* Cultivating being present, self-reflective, and self-aware.

2. *Growing up.* Moving beyond being egocentric and ethnocentric to a more expansive, heart-centered, and integrated sense of self-identification. It means becoming more world-centric (being a global citizen) and cosmic-centric, which means having a reverence for all life and an experience of interconnection. Growing up also means discovering and choosing to cultivate your inner adult, which is also known as your conscious self.

3. *Clearing up (also called cleaning up).* This involves doing the psychospiritual work of healing old wounds, releasing old, self-limiting defense mechanisms, completing the past, and relaxing the hold of your negative ego.

4. *Showing up.* Taking responsibility for your life: your worthiness, purpose, principles, relationships, agency, and impact. It involves choosing to operate above the line on a moment-by-moment basis. Showing up means becoming oriented toward creating the future rather than being driven by the past, stepping up to challenges in ways that are mutually beneficial, and expressing your gifts in the world.

In addition to the four elements of personal development woven throughout this program, this curriculum is primarily composed of two types of information: the building blocks of emotional literacy and the core competencies of emotional intelligence.

This book is divided into four parts, with the building blocks and core competencies that will be covered in each section highlighted at the beginning of each part. This is to provide greater context for what you are about to read. At the end of each chapter there is also a summary of the self-empowerment tools and practices that were covered in that chapter.

1. *The building blocks of emotional literacy.* These building blocks are the conceptual knowledge needed in order to understand how you operate as an emotional being. They are called building blocks because there is a sequence to learning them, with each new area of knowledge building upon and deepening your understanding of the previous ones. This information includes foundational psychological and spiritual distinctions.

2. *The core competencies of emotional intelligence.* These are the self-mastery skills and practices required in order to fully embody emotional intelligence

in your everyday life. Although core competencies are highlighted at the beginning of each section, mastering them is an ongoing practice that is a long-term, even lifelong, undertaking. You will no doubt have many opportunities to practice these in your daily life, and there is virtually no limit to how skillful you can become and how much value you can create for yourself and others.

> "To be emotionally literate is to be able to handle emotions in a way that improves your personal power, and improves the quality of life for you, and equally important, the quality of life for the people around you." —Claude Steiner, *Emotional Literacy: Intelligence with Heart*

> "Spiritual practices help us move from identifying with the ego to identifying with the soul."
> —Ram Dass

One other note about this material. As you will no doubt notice, there are several key concepts in this material that keep being repeated. This is intentional, as it takes repetition to reprogram our subconscious away from old patterns of thinking toward more empowering ones, and to integrate new knowledge so that it becomes habitual and is automatically recalled whenever needed.

Sometimes, if a person is to really understand a distinction, then it needs to be repeated and looked at from different angles and have more of its nuances teased out. Various ways of describing a concept resonate differently with different individuals, depending on their life experience. Being heart-centered, living above and below the line, and dysfunctional versus functional dynamics are among the distinctions that will be referred to frequently. Some, such as being in observer mode and being in your conscious self, are repeated often enough that they become mantras for the program.

Know that when information is repeated, it is not meant to be a comment on your intelligence but rather a way of embedding knowledge more deeply in your subconscious mind. Our goal is to make this information as understandable, as accessible, and as useful as possible.

Why Is Mastering Emotional Intelligence So Critical?

1. *Emotional intelligence is the gateway to sustainable happiness and a fulfilling life.* Quality of life and satisfaction are not achieved solely through knowledge and action, what is referred to as *thinking and doing.* Lasting happiness requires an understanding of who you're *being* and how you're approaching all aspects of your life. It is understanding how to access and express heart, wisdom, and depth of character in your daily interactions.

2. *Emotional intelligence underpins and determines the quality of human relationships.* All of life is about relationships: how you relate to yourself, others, your work, your environment, and your circumstances. Individually and collectively, we all have many unexamined biases about emotions, which hinder our relationships with one another. Becoming more emotionally intelligent enables you to move beyond these biases to create more trust, deepen intimacy, and deal more masterfully with relationships in every area of your life. The greater your understanding and practice of emotional intelligence, the healthier your relationships will be—and the greater your joy and fulfillment.

3. *Emotional intelligence is necessary for successfully navigating your daily life.* Emotions are intrinsic to everything you do, yet it can be difficult to name what you are experiencing, embrace your feelings, and work with them in positive ways. Most of us haven't been educated about how to deal with emotions constructively, particularly the more challenging ones. We often actively suppress or deny them. Or we might be unconsciously acting them out, leaving a trail of damage in our wake, rather than dealing with our emotions in ways that create emotional safety, strengthen trust, and deepen intimacy.

Emotional intelligence is also needed for developing skillful means. This is a concept borrowed from Buddhism, and means timely action based on kindness, respect, truthfulness, wisdom, and compassion. Skillful means are inherently elegant, in the sense that the maximum results are accomplished with minimum effort and application. An example of having skillful means is understanding when it is necessary to flow with the energy of a situation, when to exert energy, and when to withdraw it. Rather than resistance, there is acceptance and responsibility, which allows for greater personal agency.

4. *Facilitating the resolution of conflicts requires emotional intelligence.* All problems have an emotional component. Either they are *caused* by difficult, unresolved emotions, or problems *cause* difficult emotional reactions to arise. Resolving problems skillfully requires accounting for people's feelings and needs, not just what they're thinking and doing. Every time you enhance your ability to handle the emotional aspects of problems, you positively affect your life and the lives of others.

> "Although attempting to bring about world peace through the
> internal transformation of individuals is difficult, it is the only way."
> —His Holiness the Dalai Lama

5. *Emotional intelligence is the key to being resilient, which is the capacity to recover quickly from difficulties.* More specifically, resilience is your ability to recover your sense of self, your equilibrium, and your well-being in the face of challenges. Developing greater resilience is a major theme of this work.

Being emotionally intelligent doesn't mean that challenging situations never occur in your life, but rather that you have developed the necessary skills and strength of character to be able to reclaim your sense of self as quickly as possible. Additionally, being emotionally intelligent helps you gain more value from your breakdowns and integrate a greater degree of learning. You are more adaptable and therefore better able to thrive. You have enhanced your self-efficacy, which means having greater trust in yourself and your abilities. You trust that you can deal with whatever comes up, which in turn leads to greater confidence and less anxiety.

6. *Emotional intelligence enhances self-expression and personal effectiveness.* In the workplace, emotional intelligence has proven to be twice as important for outstanding performance than either technical skill or cognitive ability for jobs at every level.[ii] It is equally important for exceptional performance in every role of life, whether it be parent, teacher, coach, student, athlete, family member, or neighbor.

You were born with an innate aptitude for being emotionally intelligent. Whether you choose to develop that emotional intelligence by committing to your personal growth and development is a fundamental choice that only you can make. This decision depends upon the degree of your inspiration, sincere desire, and calling to create a better quality of life for yourself and others.

You either make this choice consciously or go through life sliding in and out of unconscious states of reactivity and confusion, wondering why things aren't working out as well as you would like. You might even be your own worst enemy, frequently feeling at the effect of your life and circumstances—dissatisfied, unhappy, anxious, lonely, or misunderstood.

Accelerate Your Journey

When you feel called to grow and evolve, it is normal for various forms of emotional resistance to arise, such as avoidance, denial, defensiveness, or procrastination. Following are some keys to success for addressing resistance while learning this material. The following practices are useful in any domain in which you wish to initiate or accelerate personal growth.

These keys to success are attitudes and practices that are self-empowering. You don't have to believe them per se. Instead, adopt them, act "as if," and notice what occurs. As you gain understanding of this material and practice it, you will empower yourself to accelerate your personal growth, discover more of your personal power, and strengthen your connection with who you really are—your authentic self.

You Are Okay Just the Way You Are

There is nothing "wrong" with you. You are not a bad or a wrong sort of person, and this material isn't about fixing yourself. We each have our own foibles, wounds, and areas in which we would like to grow. But who we are inside, our inner being, is already worthy, competent, and deserving. We many *have* issues, but we *are not* our issues. We are so much bigger than our issues; we are the field of consciousness in which they exist.

Integral emotional intelligence is about cultivating and revealing more of who you truly are, your best self, and relaxing the hold of your negative ego. It involves strengthening your connection to your conscious self—your sense of inner being and magnanimity. As you do this, you become stronger, more wholehearted, and increasingly resilient. We are *all* in the process of becoming more conscious, heart-centered human beings, growing and integrating the lessons we've learned in life. This is the entire point of human evolution.

Your relationship to your sense of worthiness and your self-esteem, however that occurs for you, is a topic that will be revisited several times in this program. It is important to understand what these concepts mean. Simply put, self-worth has no prerequisite other than existence. If you are alive, then you are worthy. You have value. The spark of consciousness that animates you, that grants you life, is the same consciousness that infuses every living being.

No one is more or less worthy than anyone else. To believe otherwise is a lie, one that we bought into, usually when we were very young, when we felt wounded and were in pain. We internalized the dysfunction around us and thought that there must be something wrong with us to experience that sort of violation. When we continue to adhere to the lie of unworthiness, we are unconsciously stating that spirit, however we define it, is also unworthy.

Your self-esteem is how you measure what you think about yourself—your inner being and your outer expression in the world—in the present moment. It is like a radar or sensing device that, just like breathing, is always operating.

Your self-esteem comprises several components:

- Your value judgments about who you are as a person.
- Your sense of worthiness as a human being.
- Your evaluation about your right to exist.
- How well you think you are expressing yourself in the world through your actions.

The trance of unworthiness is an affliction that is particularly pernicious in Western culture, and *if* that is a lie you bought into early in life, then it will require some effort to get it to relax its hold on you. This is critical work, as feelings of unworthiness lead to low self-esteem and are a major blockage to being able to give and receive love. Lack of self-worth can lead to depression, loneliness, isolation, addiction, and alienation.

Affirming and owning your innate worthiness is a major milestone on your spiritual path. Until you do, you will have a barrier to giving love and receiving love from others, and to receiving higher frequencies of love and guidance from your superconscious self. Your personal growth is ultimately an infinite, winning game that has no end point; it is an ever-expanding and positive upward cycle. This process works best when you keep remembering your innate value and worthiness and avoid making yourself wrong or negatively comparing yourself with others.

It takes a sense of positive self-esteem, a willingness to be vulnerable, and a healthy dose of humility to accept that wherever you are on your personal journey is *exactly* where you should be. It also takes a willingness to let go of any attachment to negative self-talk or self-punishing behavior.

Exercise Discernment

Developing your discernment is a process of refining your ability to home in on your inner truth. It is being able to zero in on what resonates with and feels right to you. Discernment is the ability to look deeper, beyond the outer appearance of things, to discover the hidden or underlying truths that may be obscured by rhetoric or emotional intensity. Discernment is a process of looking within for guidance while being self-reflective and inquiring into what the source and quality of that internal guidance is.

A key practice for cultivating your sense of discernment is centering in your conscious self and actively listening for the messages from your higher self or soul. It requires being in observer mode and being able to sort through and distinguish between the various voices in your head, for example, the voice of intuition as differentiated from the voice of the inner critic. This aspect of discernment will be gone into more deeply in later chapters.

To create value, it isn't necessary to believe in or agree with everything in this material. What's important is trusting yourself to determine what resonates with you and feels useful to you on your journey and letting go of what doesn't.

Use the Power of Inquiry

Many assertions are made in this material. They are based on years of research and application. You are invited to view these statements as opportunities to inquire more deeply into how you have constructed your life, rather than as beliefs to which you must subscribe. This material casts light upon and challenges many unconscious and commonly held negative beliefs, patterns, and assumptions. These assertions are intended to provoke deeper thinking and empower you in developing your intuition.

We will be examining the nature of beliefs, attitudes, and assumptions more fully. You are encouraged to use self-inquiry and self-reflection to identify unconscious beliefs, attitudes, and assumptions that have been holding you back and no longer serve you. Once recognized, you can then be at choice about adopting more beneficial ones.

Often the path of internal emancipation is a process of learning to ask yourself good questions. Your subconscious is designed to give you answers if you figure out what questions to ask and are patient and persistent about getting a response. It *is* possible to bring your unconscious modes of operating up to your conscious awareness, and in the process develop greater agency and autonomy.

Fear of what we might find lurking in our subconscious can fuel our denial and resistance to practicing self-inquiry. We often have a very adversarial relationship to our subconscious, which only makes it harder for us to grow and evolve. You will discover as you go through this material that these fears are unnecessary, and that there is a much more empowering place to stand regarding working with your subconscious self.

Be Willing to Move Beyond Habitual Patterns

Psychological healing and growth cannot happen without first being willing. Healing old, destructive patterns is an expression of self-love and requires two things. First, you have to be willing for the healing to occur, and second, you have to commit to being healed. Remember that it *is* possible to shift even the most intractable patterns of thinking and behavior that are holding you back to ones that are more beneficial.

There are several distinctions and techniques we will be exploring regarding how to make this shift, including why you might be hanging on to old ways of operating that no longer support you. The first step is being willing to adopt the attitude that you *can* heal, grow, and evolve to happier states and more positive ways of operating in life. Sometimes feelings of discomfort arise when doing this inner work. This is a normal and, thankfully, temporary state.

Develop a Set of Practices

Your journey is unique, and you will have your own take on what distinctions and practices are most empowering to you. A practice can be something that you think or do that replaces an unhelpful pattern of thought or behavior. Practices take many forms and are often tailored to specific goals or situations. Many practices are simply part of your inner conversation. These are things you tell yourself that are empowering, such as, "I can handle this," whenever you are feeling anxious.

Some of your practices might be positive attitudes you are committed to holding, such as, "I can create value for myself out of this breakdown." Or they might be actions, such as remembering to breathe slowly and deeply whenever you feel stressed. Some of your practices can be thought of as little formulas for success, simple ways of operating, or routines that help you navigate your life with greater ease and enjoyment. Sometimes identifying the best practice for a recurring situation requires that you illuminate and unpack the unconscious dynamics that are driving the pattern you want to replace.

A key is to look for what "feels like an opening" for you. Naturally, if your practices don't feel like an opening, then chances are you won't do them. All empowering practices assist you in being more fully present and awake to what is occurring in your reality. They help to invoke the energy of your conscious self and soul and support you in becoming more heart-centered, calm, and composed. They are thoughts, actions, and ways of being that resonate with you, feel authentic and positive, and enhance your experience of feeling okay and being in equilibrium.

Something to note about adopting new beliefs and attitudes is that it can feel awkward or odd when you try on new ones. If you are used to wearing sweatpants and try on a custom-made suit, then it might feel strange at first—but that isn't necessarily a bad thing. Growth can feel uncomfortable as you are integrating new ways of being and operating.

Neural pathways grow through use, and chances are the beliefs or attitudes you want to replace have had years to solidify and create strong neural pathways. Thankfully, there is neural plasticity, which means that we have the ability to develop new neural pathways. There is truth in the adage, "Fake it until you make it." Remember that it *is* possible to create new patterns of thinking and responding; it just takes intention, repetition, and persistence. Therefore it is valuable and necessary to develop a set of practices for yourself.

Be Patient

It can take time for results to manifest, and it is easy to become frustrated when things don't seem to be moving quickly. Mastery takes time and patience. It is said that talent is only 10 percent of what it takes to become a great artist. The other 90 percent is the hard work of learning and practicing your craft. Be patient with yourself, stay present, and be willing to make mistakes and feel awkward while practicing new skills.

Although these concepts may seem abstract at first, as you work with them and they become more deeply ingrained, their value as tools for accelerating personal growth and transformation will become clearer and you will get more traction.

Summary of Self-Empowerment Tools and Practices

Recognize your self-worth and inherent value (self-worth has no prerequisite other than existence).

Develop your sense of discernment.

Expand your point of view by using the power of inquiry to bring unconscious beliefs, patterns, and assumptions up to your awareness.

Be willing to grow and evolve beyond habitual beliefs and ways of operating, and embrace any temporary discomfort that might arise.

Develop and use a set of practices to help you navigate life with greater ease and joy.

Be patient with yourself while learning new skills.

CHAPTER 2
BEING EMOTIONALLY INTELLIGENT

This chapter is divided into two sections: "Embodying Emotional Intelligence" and "Practices for Developing Emotional Intelligence." These are broad categories with some areas of overlap. This material will help ground you in the foundational principles of becoming more emotionally intelligent. By internalizing these distinctions and practices, your trust in your ability to make powerful, positive, and beneficial choices in life will expand.

Embodying Emotional Intelligence

Take an Integral Approach

> "The word integral means comprehensive, inclusive, non-marginalizing, embracing. Integral approaches to any field attempt to be exactly that: to include as many perspectives, styles, and methodologies as possible within a coherent view of the topic."
> —Ken Wilber (philosopher)

The most powerful and transformative way to approach emotional intelligence is from an integral perspective. This means recognizing that all parts of life—the mental, physical, emotional, and spiritual—are interconnected in intimate ways, and each part is truly understood only in relationship to the whole. These four areas of human expression intersect and work together synergistically. When you increase your intelligence in one area, this has a positive impact on your intelligence in every other area.

The field where these four areas of human expression overlap, where you experience their convergence, is your conscious self. Your conscious self is your inner point of awareness, your sense of being present and awake to all areas of your existence. More about what your conscious self is and how to work with it will be covered in the next several chapters.

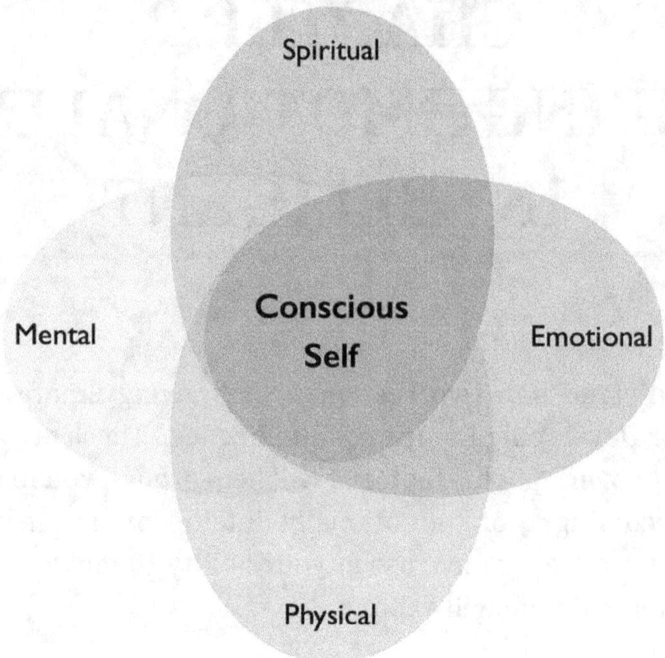

Approaching any issue in life from a holistic perspective means accounting for what is occurring simultaneously in all four of these areas. For example, the holistic treatment of a physical malady means accounting for a person's attitudes and beliefs about their well-being as well as taking into account emotional, environmental, and social factors. It also includes considering the spiritual guidance, or intuition, that is intrinsic to creating a successful healing journey.

Our emotions don't exist in isolation, and to truly be emotionally intelligent we need to adopt a "whole systems" approach. For every emotion we have, we also have a corresponding thought (or set of thoughts), a set of physical sensations, and a greater purpose and context for that emotion. Our mindset, our physical health and body chemistry, and our degree of awareness all impact our emotional state.

By using whole systems theory when looking at our emotions, we can begin to see how our emotions relate to, and are influenced by, all the other areas of human expression. We can discern the most beneficial ways to express and process our emotions. We can develop self-mastery, learn how to cause transformation in our daily lives, and empower ourselves to accelerate our personal growth.

"Becoming a spiritual person requires becoming aware of your emotions. You cannot become spiritually advanced while you are unaware of what you are feeling. Your emotions are the force field of your soul. You can't become a compassionate or caring person and be unaware of your emotions at the same time. It also requires consciousness of your intentions and taking responsibility for your choices." —Gary Zukav, *Soul to Soul*

Own Your Reactions and Author Your Responses

"Between stimulus and response lies a space. In that space lies our freedom and power to choose a response. In our response lies our growth and our happiness." —Anonymous

Fundamentally, emotional intelligence is about self-knowledge. This leads to self-mastery, which allows you to navigate your emotions and behaviors with skill and equanimity and respond constructively to the emotions and behaviors of others. Some elements of self-knowledge, or emotional literacy, include understanding who you are as a conscious being, the nature of your psyche, and your personality's defense structures.

Self-mastery, which is also referred to as self-regulation, is the capacity to take responsibility for your reactions on a moment-by-moment basis and choose your responses. This ability is at the heart of creating personal transformation and can be summed up with this phrase: Own your reactions and author your responses.

Being emotionally intelligent means having trust in your ability to

a) observe and take responsibility for your thoughts, feelings, and emotions;

b) return to your calm, centered self; and

c) author your responses in ways that are for the highest good for yourself and others.

Cause Personal Transformation

The definition of *transformation* is "a thorough or dramatic change in someone's or something's form or appearance"; it is a metamorphosis. Transformation never invalidates the past. Rather, it gives you a new way of making sense of it.

In the context of emotional intelligence, causing personal transformation can be summarized as the following:

> You might not be able to control the circumstances
> of your life or control your reactions to them, but you
> always have the opportunity to author how you respond.

Causing transformation means having dominion over what you say and do and making choices that help integrate your reactions to whatever is occurring in a positive way. When you author your responses, you exercise your personal power and agency. By showing up this way in the present moment, you literally create new possibilities for your future.

Being transformative in your daily life is about strengthening your understanding of who you are as a *self* and strengthening your ability to observe your thoughts and behaviors. It is finding that place of autonomy within, from which you can make real choices, ones that express your highest principles and values.

Causing personal transformation means taking responsibility for your emotional reactivity and strengthening your ability to return to a calm, grounded, and steadfast place—again and again, moment by moment. You build character by gaining greater mastery of your self-regulation and doing that in ways that are consistent with the principles and intentions of your best self.

Becoming more emotionally intelligent does *not* mean that you will never have breakdowns, react intensely, make mistakes, or feel upset. It does not mean that you will never feel betrayed or shamed by another, or experience loss or grief. And it does not mean transcending or repressing your emotions or attaining an idealized state of perfection. It *does* mean learning how to name, own, and process your challenging emotions in positive and constructive ways. It *does* mean bringing your best self to, and gaining value from, whatever is occurring

It bears repeating that becoming emotionally intelligent isn't about fixing yourself: your inner being is already just fine. It is about revealing and expressing more of who you are as a conscious self. This self can't be developed; it can only be revealed. You do this by pulling back any layers of woundedness or defensiveness you might have that are obscuring it. This is the process of individuation, in which you gradually become more and more aware of your authentic self by doing the clearing up work of healing the disintegrated, or wounded, parts of yourself.

Becoming emotionally intelligent isn't about trying to force yourself to change because you are somehow wrong; rather, it is about revealing and understanding more deeply who you are and how to bring forth your best self, the part of yourself that is inherently emotionally intelligent.

Emotional self-mastery means being awake and present to life in all its rough-and-tumble glory and becoming more fully alive, grounded, and resilient in the process. It means developing the strength of character to become less defended and more vulnerable, open, authentic, and available. It is both a humbling and a liberating experience.

Move from Dysfunctional to Functional States

A key skill of being emotionally intelligent is developing the ability to move from dysfunctional states of operating to more functional ones. To be in a state of dysfunction means to be experiencing bad feelings and negative, unworkable outcomes, which in turn create more bad feelings and negative outcomes. In other words, you are caught in a downward spiral, which is also called a vicious circle. Similarly, to be functional is to experience good feelings and positive, workable outcomes, which lead to more good feelings and positive outcomes. You are then in an upward spiral, which is called a virtuous cycle.

In addition to owning your reactions and authoring your responses, practicing self-mastery also means you have access to your personal power and agency so that you can shift dysfunctional behavior patterns and circumstances to more functional ones. It also means you have developed the skills necessary to work with and evolve these dysfunctional, disintegrated parts of yourself toward greater states of functionality and integration.

For example, a dysfunctional approach of seeking reprisal can increase bad feelings, escalate violence, and create negative results. Working toward forgiveness and reconciliation, which is a functional approach, can lead to greater healing and resolution and create positive outcomes. Even when external reconciliation with others or with the situation isn't possible, becoming reconciled internally, practicing self-care, and setting healthy boundaries can create a sense of greater personal well-being.

Everyday transformation occurs when you are able to shift unconscious, unhealthy, and unworkable dynamics to ones that benefit everyone involved. In other words, you choose to move away from states of disintegration toward greater states of integration. Your ability to cause transformation is determined by the ground of being from which you relate to your life. Your fundamental ground of being is your sense of self, that heart-centered place of autonomy and loving awareness from which you observe and hold all aspects of your life.

Acquire Self-Knowledge

"We only see what we have names for." —Garrett Hardin (ecologist)

"The eye sees only what the mind is prepared to comprehend."
—Henri Bergson (philosopher)

Being emotionally intelligent requires becoming literate in a set of concepts called distinctions. Whereas information is about content, distinctions are the abstractions that help you sort out and organize the content of what is occurring in your reality. Distinctions are the concepts you use to create and frame your worldview. The specific type of concepts used in this material are called ontological distinctions. Ontology is the study of the science of existence, of being and becoming. It inquires into the nature of consciousness and reality.

A distinction creates a boundary around where something starts and where it stops. Distinctions illuminate how something is different from everything around it. A distinction allows something to show up that seemingly wasn't present before, that wasn't distinguishable or knowable. Distinctions alter how you see the world in ways that content information cannot. How often have you had the experience of learning something new and then seeing it everywhere? It is staggering to think about how much is occurring that we don't, or can't, see in our reality because we don't yet understand it as a distinction.

Once you have fully understood a distinction, it "uses you" at least as much as, if not more than, you use it. You don't need to consciously remember distinctions. In fact, they are often hard to hang onto, because they can be abstract and have several parts that need to be understood to grasp their totality. Once you have internalized an ontological distinction, it will show up as needed during your life. It goes into both your mind and your conscious self, where it gets imprinted and becomes integrated into your ground of being. It begins to condition and influence your life.

The ability to own your reactions and author your responses is a distinction. Taking a holistic approach to life is a distinction. Transformation is a distinction. Racism and gender inequality are distinctions: you can't recognize or name racist or misogynist behavior or oppression without these distinctions.

You will find that throughout this material, there are certain distinctions that are revisited several times and looked at from various perspective. This is because the understanding of a distinction keeps getting deeper the more you work with it and the more you learn other, related distinctions.

The more a person lacks empowering ontological distinctions, the more ineffectual that person will be. Self-mastery requires learning a new set of distinctions, ones that can positively influence and shape what is occurring in your present reality and create new possibilities for being and action.

Practices for Developing Emotional Intelligence

The following are practices that, when done in concert with the elements of embodying emotional intelligence just discussed, will empower you to express your best self in any circumstance. These practices are part of the component of personal development called waking up. Even in the face of apparent mistakes and failures, these practices will empower you to get back in charge of your life as quickly as possible.

Be Self-Reflective

A prerequisite for developing emotional intelligence is a commitment to being self-reflective, or self-aware. The amount of satisfaction people experience in their relationships with others is directly correlated with their ability to be self-reflective. This is even more important when there is conflict or upset present.

To be self-reflective is to be self-examining and have a commitment to self-discovery. Self-examination requires taking a somewhat neutral, detached, nondefensive attitude toward yourself. This is referred to as being in observer or witness mode. In this state of being, you can find the nonattachment and flexibility necessary to widen your current frames of reference.

Being self-reflective is sometimes referred to as being awake to who you are and your underlying needs. It requires being open-minded. This means being willing to examine your thoughts, beliefs, attitudes, emotions, reactions, deeper needs, and deeper motivations in a nonjudgmental way. Self-reflection *requires* that you slip into observer mode so that you can witness how you are operating in life.

Neurobiologists refer to this state of witnessing yourself as metacognition, in which you become aware of your awareness and can observe your thoughts and reactions, rather than automatically acting them out. You are designed, as are all human beings, to be able to hold these two levels of consciousness simultaneously. This attitude of awareness objectifies your subjective experience. The philosopher and spiritual teacher George Gurdjieff referred to this state as self-remembering. When you are in observer or witness mode, you automatically shift your focus so that you are centered in your inner, conscious being.

Self-reflection is not a new concept. The ancient Greeks coined the maxim *Know thyself.* Although it is an innate skill we all have, not everyone is ready or willing to be self-reflective. It's a paradox: you must have a certain degree of self-awareness before you can become truly self-aware.

There are two main ways to be self-reflective. One way is to act as your own mirror by developing your ability to be in observer or witness mode. Another is to allow your relationships to function as a mirror for you. You can discover aspects of yourself when another person reflects them back to you through their observations or reactions to you. Often, as uncomfortable as it might feel, the only way to discover our blind spots are when someone points them out to us.

Self-reflection requires courage, humility, and a commitment to being relentlessly honest with yourself while letting go of any self-righteousness. It also requires slowing down and sometimes even calling a timeout, especially when something isn't working. There is a paradox with regard to self-reflection, in that you need to slow down in order to accelerate your growth. What it doesn't require is being perfect or changing who you really are; rather, being self-reflective is about discovering and expressing your authentic self more fully.

Recognize When You're Feeling OK or Not OK

This distinction was first made in transactional analysis in the 1960s and was abbreviated and capitalized as OK and not OK. Because so many people are familiar with this concept, we have chosen to use this format as well.

There are two basic categories into which people sort their life experiences: either they feel OK, or they feel not OK. A core competency of emotional intelligence is knowing whether you are in a state of feeling OK (in equilibrium) or feeling not OK (in disequilibrium) at any given point in time.

You have a finely tuned internal radar that tells you, moment by moment, whether something feels "on" or "off." If you are paying attention, then you instantly know when you have a need that is not being met or when something feels inappropriate or out of place. Feeling OK or not OK is the main way you have of gauging whether your needs are being met and if the circumstances you are engaged with are beneficial to you.

Feeling OK is shorthand for being in a state of equilibrium: you feel good inside or worthy. Feeling OK is having a sense of being all right or on, of being whole and thriving. Some other words that describe how this state feels are *secure, calm, happy, focused, optimistic, confident, enthusiastic, connected, fulfilled, enlivened,* and *well.*

Feeling not OK is shorthand for being in a state of disequilibrium: you feel bad inside or unworthy, somehow not right or off, broken, or damaged. Some other words that describe how this state feels are *insecure, disconnected, wrong, pessimistic, irritable, impatient, defensive, doubting, ashamed, unfulfilled, unsettled, unhappy,* and *failing.*

Sometimes being in a state of disequilibrium is not necessarily an indicator that something is wrong. When you're working on mastering a skill, you might need to pass through a stage of disequilibrium while you're struggling with integrating something new. This sort of disequilibrium can result in positive growth. For example, the terrible twos are often a time when children are frustrated and struggling with being able to express themselves verbally. This gets resolved as they become more articulate.

But being caught in a state of *consistently* feeling not OK can be very destructive. It's at the core of most compulsive, addictive behavior patterns. While in this state of discomfort, people tend to self-medicate and go for instant gratification, desperately attempting to make themselves feel OK inside and find some relief from their bad feelings of being not OK. Choosing to take the path back to equilibrium is an essential aspect of self-mastery.

Employ Self-Scrutiny

Employing self-scrutiny means questioning any emotional or mental reactivity or resistance that arises. It requires digging deeper to uncover what is underneath and driving any automatic, limiting self-defense structures and habitual, self-defeating patterns. Some useful questions to ask yourself are, "What is my motive?" "Where am I coming from?" "What is really going on with me?" and "What needs are driving my behavior?"

One of the main things that impedes personal growth, being happy, and having fulfilling relationships is our habitual, unconscious self-defense mechanisms. We all have them—they are a basic part of the design of being human. We developed these defensive coping mechanisms when we were very young as a way of protecting ourselves from harm.

Examples of common, everyday defense mechanisms include *denial, avoidance, blaming, judging, repressing, resistance, rationalization, cynicism, distortion, neediness, projection,* and *passive-aggressive behavior.* These unconscious behavior patterns helped us to feel separate from unpleasant, overwhelming thoughts and feelings and from scary situations.

These defenses were useful, even necessary, tools for our survival when we were young. As we became more mature, these self-protective mechanisms often became unnecessary and stopped serving us. Fortunately, you don't need to hang onto defensive strategies that have been holding you back or keeping you stuck in reactive patterns. The first step is to become aware of them. Name and own them so that you can stop using them as unconscious ways of reacting and acting out. You can be grateful for how they have served you, make the choice to release them, and replace them with attitudes and practices that produce more positive outcomes.

Understanding how to work with your defense mechanisms and cultivating a genuine, even if reluctant, willingness to be with any discomfort that might arise can open the door to substantive personal breakthroughs. For the emotionally intelligent person, being uncomfortable is not the litmus test for whether life is working and can be a positive sign of growth and increased authenticity.

Use Self-Advocacy and Self-Empowerment

The generally accepted meaning of self-advocacy is the ability to communicate your needs and make requests for having them met. It is about being assertive in speaking up for yourself and letting others know what you are thinking and feeling. Although this is an accurate definition, there is a deeper meaning of self-advocacy that is used in this material, one that gives you greater access to your personal power and agency.

This type of self-advocacy means being a firm proponent of your authentic self. It is a commitment to being centered in your heart and your awareness of who you are as a conscious being. It is a commitment to showing up in your best self. How you can achieve this is by being in observer mode and adopting beliefs, attitudes, and practices that are empowering. It can be helpful to think of self-advocacy as a muscle that needs to be strengthened through use: we get better at it the more we do it.

Being self-empowered *requires* being a firm advocate for your conscious self and for your personal growth and evolution. Self-empowerment starts with a commitment to reach for the most magnanimous version of yourself possible in a situation. It's about striving for excellence. It's not about trying to be perfect or better than others: it's about being committed to authentically expressing your inner being. Self-advocacy is about choosing to show up above the line in the present moment.

Self-abandonment is the opposite of self-advocacy. Self-abandonment happens when you slide below the line into thinking that your needs don't matter and that ultimately you are unworthy and don't matter. You stop being in observer mode and abandon your conscious self. This leads to jumping onto the drama triangle and playing losing games, such as trying to please or rescue others or have them approve of you. You might even become a persecutor toward yourself, which leads to self-punishment and self-sabotage and will cause you to feel like a victim, albeit a self-inflicted one.

When you abandon yourself, both you and everyone you interact with start losing. You cannot get off the drama triangle from within it, attempting to win by playing at it harder or better than everyone else. You must use self-advocacy to transcend it, waking up to who you are as a conscious self and to your innate self-worth. There is nowhere to go; there is only waking up.

There is a growing body of literature on empowerment, the definition of which can vary, depending on the context in which it is used and whether the focus is on an individual or a group. Empowerment is a concept that in recent years has often been co-opted for commercial use. For example, companies might make the claim that their merchandise will be empowering to women if they purchase it. Despite this appropriation, empowerment is an important concept and worth reclaiming.

To empower a person is to give power or authority to them and to facilitate or give them the means to achieve something. In this material, the focus is on self-empowerment, as opposed to collective empowerment, and on the process of gaining skillful means for self-initiated growth and personal development.

The purpose of self-empowerment is internal emancipation. This means having your hands firmly on the levers and dials of your personal evolution, with your conscious self at the controls. This allows for greater autonomy and self-determination. When equipped with the necessary tools, you can become more and more liberated from internal oppression in your daily life. By understanding internal oppression, it is possible to gain greater insight into what is driving collective oppression and structural violence.

Internal oppression occurs primarily when your present experience is being overshadowed and driven by your past. This is when the unconscious and fear-based thoughts, beliefs, attitudes, feelings, and behaviors you adopted as defense strategies earlier in life are playing out in current time. This includes unconscious beliefs and attitudes that are part of your enculturation. These unconscious dynamics are usually not in your best interests and do not reflect your most authentic self.

This program offers tools and techniques to empower you to become more and more fully emancipated from your past, from internal oppression, self-limitation, and self-sabotage. When you are self-empowered, you consciously align your internal and external life with the values, principles, and intentions of your best self. These principles are *always* consistent with mutual respect and benefit for all.

Be Present

Emotional intelligence is not a destination: it's a moment-by-moment practice of constantly bringing yourself back to your most centered, grounded, conscious self. It requires acceptance of who you are and whatever is occurring. Rather than being in denial or fighting with the way things are, you are present to what is happening in a way that allows for you to work more masterfully with what is so.

When you are present—observing and owning your reactions—you have the wherewithal to author how you wish to respond to a situation. When approached this way, *everything* that occurs in your life becomes a chance to practice and gain more personal agency, autonomy, and freedom. Staying awake to your moment-by-moment experience of living becomes your meditation. Breakdowns in life become opportunities for breakthroughs and transformation.

Becoming emotionally intelligent means cultivating the courage and compassion to own and embrace *all* your experiences in present time, even the challenging ones. In the process of this, you become more and more fully alive. Being emotionally intelligent includes the inevitability of becoming upset and being in a state of reactivation, invalidating yourself and potentially feeling like a failure. No matter how skillful you are, life is not something you can control, and it will always find ways of throwing you off-center.

Achieving a high degree of self-mastery means cultivating the depth and strength of character necessary to continually look within, connect with your best self, and be guided by your highest principles. It doesn't mean being naive or idealistic. Rather, it is about having the skills to successfully navigate the challenges and difficulties of real life, becoming ever more awake to the underlying dynamics that drive your interactions.

In summary, these practices of self-empowerment are part of building the bridge between where you are now and where you want to be in life: having increased well-being, flourishing relationships, and greater happiness and fulfillment.

"Happiness cannot be traveled to, owned, earned, worn, or consumed. Happiness is the spiritual experience of living every minute with love, grace, and gratitude." —Denis Waitley (motivational speaker)

Summary of Self-Empowerment Tools and Practices

Take a holistic approach to life by considering how mind, body, emotions, and spirit all work together.

Practice everyday transformation by owning your reactions and authoring your responses.

Be in observer mode (use metacognition) and practice being present.

Acquire self-knowledge and become literate in self-science, also known as ontological understanding.

Recognize when you are feeling OK or not OK, and what that might be telling you about yourself and the situation.

Be self-reflective and use self-scrutiny to relax the grip of old defense structures.

Make your personal growth a priority, and advocate for your best self and your personal evolution.

Be present and practice bringing yourself back to your most centered, grounded, conscious self on a moment-by-moment basis.

UNDERSTANDING YOUR MULTIDIMENSIONAL SELF

Building Block of Emotional Literacy

Understanding your psyche; your multidimensional,
authentic self, which is the inner design of every human being.

Core Competencies of Emotional Intelligence

Recognizing when you are centered in your conscious self and being
able to return to a state of equilibrium when under duress.

Practicing inner congruence. Centering in your conscious self, holding a
friendly, loving, and accepting attitude toward your subconscious self while
actively listening for the voice of your superconscious self (your intuition).

Working with and self-parenting any marginalized, wounded, reactive, or
disintegrated parts of your subconscious, moving them toward integration
and harmony with the rest of your psyche.

Being able to consciously create context and reframe situations
for personal empowerment, growth, and integration.

CHAPTER 3
THE PSYCHE

Overview

Part II of this volume examines the inner architecture of being human. Understanding your inner design gives you the keys to navigating life with greater ease and joy. This knowledge is designed to empower you to successfully undertake the necessary work of self-repair and self-development.

As was stated earlier, this material takes an ontological approach to understanding what it means to be human. (Remember that *ontological* means the study of the nature of being or consciousness.) A major concept and set of ontological distinctions that will explored in this section is that of the human psyche. Your psyche represents how three main types, or qualities, of consciousness are expressed through the vehicle of your physical body.

What Is the Psyche?

Psyche comes from the ancient Greek word for "life" or "breath." This meaning has evolved to denote the invisible animating essence that occupies the physical body. Traditionally, this has been called the soul or spirit, and is often referred to as Self with a capital *S*. It is the consciousness, or *being*, part of human *beings*.

Psychology is the modern-day scientific, or objective, study of the psyche. In many branches of twentieth-century psychology, the psyche is generally considered to be the same as the mind and does not include consciousness, or being. This is what is referred to as self with a small *s*. It involves studying how we think and behave. It is a more materialist, reductionist way of looking at what makes us human, which is primarily done through the lens of personality and identity. You could think of this as the *human* part of *human* beings.

Psychosynthesis and other forms of transpersonal psychology are a relatively recent evolution that integrates the spiritual (being) and mental and physical (thinking and doing) aspects of human experience. Transpersonal psychology is the only branch of psychology that addresses our ability to hold multiple fields of consciousness simultaneously.

We've integrated both these perspectives, that of the mind and that of consciousness, for a more holistic view of the psyche. Henceforth, whenever we use the word *self* in this material, we are referring to the inner being (Self), though for consistency and ease of reading we will only be using lowercase *s* (self). To avoid any unnecessary confusion, we will not be using the word *self* when we are referring to a person's identity or personality type.

To assist in inquiring into the nature of the psyche, we use a cognitive map called the three selves, which is a representation of how this convergence of consciousness and psychology plays out within us. The psyche is the inner design of being human and is a fundamental aspect of our shared humanity. Understanding the nature of the psyche allows for a deeper sense of our interconnection and provides us with a powerful, empathic place to stand while acknowledging and respecting our differences.

Our lived experiences are shaped to a great degree by gender, race, age, and culture. Part of the aim in exploring the nature of the psyche is to provide you with a tool or a context that is especially useful, even transformative, in the examination of these intersections of personal identity. This perspective is one that allows for deeper exploration and understanding of our differences while maintaining a sense of our interconnectedness: having a respect for, and appreciation of, our common humanity.

What Is Consciousness?

In order to understand the psyche, we must first define consciousness, which is a foundational concept that will be used time and again in this material. This is a vast subject: there are professors who spend their entire lives exploring this concept. Following is a brief distillation of the key distinctions about consciousness that are essential to know from the point of view of self-empowerment and personal evolution.

Consciousness is awareness. It is a state of being awake and present in the current moment while simultaneously being able to process and integrate information. An important aspect of consciousness is attention, which is focused awareness. Your attention—the ability to focus your awareness—shapes and constrains what occurs in your reality. If someone were to place an object in front of you, then that object would seem to appear and disappear as a function of where your attention was, even if you were continuing to look directly at that object.

An important aspect of consciousness is your experience of "I" or "I am." You have a place or space of being and awareness from which you observe and are cognizant of everything in your life. This space is your conscious self, the consciousness that is the space in which your reality occurs. Your relationship with consciousness and with your conscious self gets to the very heart of how you perceive your world and the limits of your perception.

How you're being determines what you're able to perceive, and it shapes and constrains every action you take. Until you understand how to be awake in life and be intentional about your ground of being—where you come from and how you approach life—you don't have access to your true core of power and agency.

Consciousness can also be thought of as your life force and vitality, the fuel or energy that animates your physical body. Without consciousness, you wouldn't be alive and sentient. Your being animates your body, not the other way around. The consciousness that infuses you with life is the same consciousness that infuses every living being. This consciousness is also called universal mind.

> "We are not human beings having a spiritual experience.
> We are spiritual beings having a human experience."
> —Pierre Teilhard de Chardin
> (scientist and philosopher)

From a spiritual or evolutionary point of view, becoming enlightened is a process of being more and more present to the consciousness within yourself and all living things. It is not about somehow changing or fixing yourself or needing to be different: it is about opening your inner eyes and awaking to your true nature as a conscious being. Consciousness is the basis of all creative activity and is sometimes referred to as the void. It is the boundlessness or nothingness from which we arise.

> "Among the great things which are to be found among us, the being
> of nothingness is the greatest." —Leonardo da Vinci

> "From consciousness your intent can modify future probability, it
> can modify what happens in the physical world, which means that
> consciousness is the fundamental thing, and that the physical world
> is a derivative of consciousness." —Thomas W. Campbell (physicist)

What Are Cognitive Maps?

One of the tools we will be using to illustrate certain areas of knowledge are called cognitive maps. Cognitive maps are tools for navigating your reality. They are mental models that are designed to give you insights into the nature of that reality. A cognitive map is not the truth or the reality itself. It is an illustration that points to a deeper truth, in the same way that a map of a city is not the actual city.

A high-quality cognitive map allows you to see something from a new perspective. It can give you a more expansive overview of the subject at hand than you previously had. We all look at life from a particular point of view, through a filter that is composed, at least partly, of our past experiences, attitudes, and beliefs. When we feel stuck, often the solution lies in being able to see the world, especially our inner world, from a more expansive point of view or a more elevated perspective.

There is frequently more than one illustration, interpretation, or way of looking at any specific aspect of life. In selecting the various cognitive maps used in this program, we've chosen the ones we've found to be the most useful for self-empowerment.

The Three Selves

Overview

The cognitive map we will be using to explore the psyche is that of the three selves, which illustrates the three main domains in which consciousness is expressed through human beings: the superconscious self, the conscious self, and the subconscious self. In more colloquial terms, you may have heard these referred to as the higher self, the centered self, and the lower self.

These three expressions of self, or qualities of consciousness, exist simultaneously, and together they compose the totality of the psyche. As mentioned earlier, this means that we are multidimensional beings and the understanding of how these parts all work together is referred to as multidimensional psychology.

The concept of the three selves is not new. Various interpretations have existed since at least the beginning of the twentieth century and probably much longer. For example, in his work *In Search of Being,* George Gurdjieff writes of three states of consciousness,[iii] which correspond to the three selves:

- Waking sleep, which is a state of being physically awake but still unconscious or operating on automatic, where the subconscious mind is running the show. This state relates to the subconscious self.

- Self-awareness, or self-remembering, which is a state of being present, awake, and mindful. It is remembering one's inner being by shifting into observer mode and using metacognition. This state relates to the conscious self.

- Objective consciousness, which is a contemplative state. This state relates to the superconscious self.

Psychosynthesis, founded in the early twentieth century by psychoanalyst Roberto Assagioli, is based in part on a variation of the three selves called *the egg of being*. The concept of the three selves also has its roots in Hawaiian spirituality and shamanism. More recently, spiritual teacher and social activist Gordon Davidson has written extensively on this concept in his book *Joyful Evolution*. He has been an important resource in defining the three selves, and we highly recommend his work to anyone who wishes to dive deeper into this topic.

The concept of the three selves is a powerful tool for self-mastery. Becoming more emotionally intelligent flows out of working with these three areas of your psyche. After years of inquiry, we have concluded that this cognitive map is the clearest, simplest, most holistic, and most empowering model that currently exists for understanding the inner design of human beings. Although we are not attached to this being the right or the only cognitive map of the psyche, we are confident that the three selves is a powerful tool for gaining self-mastery.

Characteristics of the Three Selves

- Each of the three selves is a living dynamic within you. These three selves are ever-evolving aspects of who you are. Each one embodies a specific quality of consciousness that has a unique type of intelligence. The three selves are distinct from one another; they operate in their own specific ways and have certain ways of working together. As a multidimensional being,[iv] you have these various qualities of consciousness operating simultaneously within, but your awareness of them at any given moment depends upon where your attention is focused.

- The three selves all exist in the present, in what is referred to as the timeless moment of now. You experience them when you are awake and being mindful. The content of the subconscious self is made up of programming from the past. The conscious self is able to reflect on the past and muse about the future. The superconscious self, although it can show up only in your experience of now, is oriented toward the future unfoldment of your personal evolution and who you are becoming. It is the conduit that allows you to intuit your soul's blueprint, or purpose, for your life.

- All three selves are equally important and exist in a co-creative partnership. The only way to gain access to all three selves is from your conscious self. When you are present and accounted for, centered in your conscious self, your psyche comes into alignment. From that place of awareness, you can actively listen for the intuitive voice of your superconscious self while also holding a loving attitude toward your subconscious self. We refer to this as positive inner congruence.

- The three selves are like nesting dolls, with the superconscious self as the largest, outer doll holding and enveloping the conscious self, which then enfolds the subconscious self. It would look like a very plump nesting doll, as research has shown that people tend to spend at least 95 percent of their lives operating from the subconscious and 5 percent of their lives, at best, in the conscious mind.[v]

- Even slightly increasing the amount of time you spend in your conscious self can have a hugely transformative impact on your life. Being able to embody your conscious self is one of the most important and fundamental premises of this program. As such, we will be covering several key aspects of the conscious self that can empower you to do this.

- As was stated in chapter 1, the three selves are often associated with specific energy centers in the body. We connect the conscious self with the heart, the subconscious self with the solar plexus, and the superconscious self with the crown, or top, of the head. Indeed, we use phrases that are congruent with this, such as, "I love you with all my heart" (the conscious self) and "I feel it in my gut" (the subconscious self).

- Most of the mischief and unworkability in life occurs when the subconscious self, rather than the conscious self, is holding sway over our responses and decisions. This is known as being in a state of unconscious waking sleep, as opposed to being awake and self-aware. Given this, we will be exploring in depth how the subconscious operates and how to work with it effectively in a later chapter.

- It is common to have an unconscious bias against the subconscious. Often it is seen as a somewhat wayward and dangerous place, certainly less worthy and important than the conscious and superconscious selves. A correlate can be seen in the way that many religions consider the body shameful and lower than spirit, which is exalted. But higher does not mean better and lower does not mean worse. Just as all four areas of human expression are equally essential and worthy and can be considered equally sacred (mind, body, emotions, and spirit), so too are all aspects of the psyche equally important and essential.

Because so many people are familiar with the term *higher self*, we occasionally use it in this material. Mostly though, we avoid using the terms *higher self* or *lower self*. This is not because they are inaccurate, but because we want to retrain our thinking away from unconscious biases and judgements. We do use the phrase *lower-self behaviors* later, to illustrate when we are being run by the negative ego. In this case, the word *lower* does refer to something that is dysfunctional and not optimal.

This is also why we don't refer to emotions as being positive or negative, or good or bad. These judgment-laden words can reinforce an avoidance of working with the more challenging emotions. Much to our detriment, by constantly thinking that they are negative or bad we have trained ourselves to repress and deny our more difficult emotions. By avoiding these emotions they tend to go unprocessed, which causes them to stick around, simmering just under the surface, which leads us to be unconsciously run by them. This is the opposite of what we really want.

Instead, we refer to emotions as being expansive or constrictive. Every true emotion, whether it is expansive or constrictive, has the potential for either positive *or* negative effects. For example, although we usually think of love as a positive thing it can go wrong and have negative impacts on us. Anger is often thought of as a bad thing but can be very positive and constructive, depending on how we work with it.

In the next several chapters we will dive more deeply into the distinct nature of each of the three selves. In doing so, we will be expanding upon the self-empowerment tools and practices that have been introduced in this chapter.

Summary of Self-Empowerment Tools and Practices

Strengthen your resilience by choosing to be in your centered, conscious self.

Hold a loving attitude toward your subconscious self.

Actively listen for the voice of your superconscious self and develop your intuition.

Create a sense of inner congruence by bringing your subconscious and superconscious selves into alignment with your conscious self.

CHAPTER 4
THE SUPERCONSCIOUS AND CONSCIOUS SELVES

The Superconscious Self

Key Attitudes: Oneness and inclusion.

Fundamental Drives: For union, expansion, revelation, and illumination.

Signature States: Stillness, nonattachment, and peace.

Energetic Center in the Body: The crown of the head.

Overview

The superconscious self is the place from which you have the broadest, most inclusive, and most expansive view of life. Your superconscious self tends to be oriented toward your future and who you are becoming. Having a relationship with your superconscious self is a critical component of experiencing joy and fulfillment in your life. It is where you locate your sense of purpose and mission, which is the energy that guides you in your unfoldment as a conscious being.

Being your most conscious, authentic self and living each moment as fully as possible, to the best of your ability, is the highest purpose you can give yourself. This creates the container, or space, within which every other purpose you have in life can exist.

A key aspect of being purposeful that gets overlooked is that it is fun. Every positive game you create has a purpose and a set of objectives to fulfill that are based on mutual benefit. Granting purpose to your everyday actions creates opportunities for having tremendous fun, being joyful, and experiencing satisfaction. With purposes that range from large to small, your superconscious self nudges you in the direction you are meant to go and allows you to imbue your life with meaning, and enjoyment.

The superconscious self is the composer of the symphony of your life.[vi] It is the place through which you gain access to your most refined, or highest, frequency of consciousness. It can also be thought of as the designer or the architect of your life and evolution.

Some other names for the superconscious self are *higher self, spark of the divine, pure consciousness, essence, presence, source, transcendental self, nonduality, objective consciousness, the rainbow bridge,* and *the muse.* For those on a spiritual path, the superconscious self can be thought of as the bridge to your spirit, your soul, the divine, universal consciousness, or God.

Your superconscious self communicates with you though vision, inspiration, and intuition, as well as through your sense of being called to be of service, to create art, to be a teacher, to master a skill, and so on. The voice of your superconscious self is clearest when you're actively receptive to it by practicing mindfulness or self-reflection, by being in silence or meditation, or by engaging in any other contemplative state.

The superconscious self is the place where you integrate all your life lessons. It is the origin of the urgings to be your best self and to make a difference in the world. It is also the source of your sense of integrity, your conscience, your reflective will (which has to do with manifesting your dreams and visions), and your ability to express unconditional love and acceptance. Ultimately, these urgings come from your spirit and your soul and are stepped down through your superconscious self.

Your sense of being drawn toward freedom and personal evolution ultimately comes from your soul. If you are reading this material, then you are receptive to this call. The nature of the soul is something that will be explored more fully in the final volume of this course.

The Gateway to Nonduality

Your superconscious self is what allows you to experience oneness and being interconnected, which is also called nonduality. The concept of nonduality derives from an ancient Sanskrit word *advaita*, meaning "not two," or "not separate." It refers to universal consciousness, which transcends the apparent differences between us, as the perceivers, and everything and everyone we perceive.

Nonduality is the idea that our inner being is a spark of consciousness, and that at the level of consciousness we are all one; there is no difference between us. Your consciousness is the same as mine, which is the same as your neighbor's, and so on. In other words, we may look different on the outside, but inside we are all the same.

As already mentioned, the superconscious self is the gateway to what has been called the soul, universal or divine consciousness, or spirit. Mystics and various wisdom traditions have long considered that it is from this higher level of consciousness that the energy that grants us existence emanates, and that when this consciousness meets physical matter, sentient life is created. The chakra centers are thought to function as electrical transformers that step this higher frequency down so that it can be integrated into the physical body through the nervous system.

Currently, the study of consciousness is no longer the exclusive realm of mystics. Scientists, especially those in the fields of quantum physics and epigenetics (the study of what affects gene expression), are also exploring the relationship between consciousness and matter.

As you practice being centered in your conscious self, you will naturally become more open to the higher frequencies of your superconscious self. These energies are experienced as an expansion of love, in all its various aspects, and mental illumination and intuition. This allows for a greater sense of unity and affiliation with all people, which includes respecting, embracing, and celebrating the beauty of our diversity.

Waking up to our nondualistic nature creates a powerful and empowering paradigm from which to address the many issues based on the fear of the other that plague our society. These are issues such as racism, xenophobia, sexism and misogyny, classism, egocentricity, and ethnocentricity. When differences are addressed from fear, separateness, and the narrow self-identification of the negative ego, more fear and separateness are generated. There is more objectification and demonizing of others, and less acknowledgment of our common underlying humanity, which leads to reduced understanding, empathy, and tolerance.

In the process of growing up, as we cultivate our inner emotionally mature adult, we are able to move from being egocentric and ethnocentric to being more universal in consciousness. By recognizing the underlying humanity and unity of all people and developing our ability to be authentically present with others, we can begin to lay the foundations of mutual respect and understanding. Recognizing and coming from our nondualistic nature is the ultimate respectful, compassionate, and inclusive approach to life.

The Conscious Self

Key Attitudes: You *and* me, responsibility, partnership, mutual respect, autonomy, harmlessness, and loving awareness.

Fundamental Drives: For growth and to become more present, aware, responsible, loving, and able to discern and integrate life lessons.

Signature States: Calm, steadfast, grounded, confident, relaxed, and in equilibrium.

Energetic Center in the Body: The heart.

Overview

You, the person reading these words, are a conscious self. You, the being who is listening to the thoughts in your head, are a conscious self. The conscious self is the place where your sense of autonomy and your agency is located. It is where you create meaning and context, where you interpret and integrate your experiences. The conscious self manifests in the present moment. It is your timeless sense of awareness that stays steady throughout your life.

A key to developing unshakable presence is to recognize your conscious self, the innate center of your awareness, as the place to stand and the ground of being from which to engage with all aspects of your life. This is an essential component of waking up. To function at a high level of fulfillment, you need to be operating from your conscious self on a consistent basis.

The conscious self is the conductor of the symphony that is your life. It can also be thought of as the director of your life, the arranger, the captain, the pilot, or the operator. When you are present in your conscious self by being in observer mode, you are in the driver's seat of your life. It is from your conscious self that you manage your life in functional ways, balancing your priorities and making responsible choices. Your conscious self is the CEO of the business of your life, with your superconscious self as the chair of the board and the parts of your subconscious self as the workers.

There are many other names and phrases for the conscious self. Some of these you might be familiar with, such as *inner being, presence, best self, centered self, ground of being, I am, awareness, authentic self, true self, essential self, the seat of autonomy, the conscious mind, the witness, the observer,* and *the listener.* As was mentioned earlier, George Gurdjieff referred to the conscious self as a state of self-awareness and self-remembering, which is also called metacognition.

It is from your conscious self that you make the choice to fully inhabit the present moment, to be awake to, and own, your experience of being alive. Given that your experience of your conscious self occurs in the present, the practice of mindfulness and meditation are both excellent ways to strengthen your connection with your inner being.

Your conscious self is the center of your sense of being, the central axis around which everything in your experience of being alive rotates. It is the place from which you can initiate healing and self-parenting. It is what is listening to the voices of your superconscious and subconscious selves, your negative ego and inner critic, and all your thoughts.

When you're centered in your conscious self, your three selves all show up in the present moment and come into a natural alignment. This gives you an inner congruence. You're able to receive the wisdom of your superconscious self while holding a loving space for your subconscious self to have its survival-based reactions to life. At the same time, you are able to be present to whatever reactivity is occurring in a way that keeps it from dominating your responses.

It is your conscious self that enables you to shift into observer mode. From this place of observation, you can take an internal step back from your automatic responses and behaviors to witness your thoughts, reactions, and emotions as they are occurring. In other words, your conscious self is the place from which you're able to practice metacognition by being self-aware and self-reflective.

The conscious self is your executive center, where you can locate your sense of personal power, synthesize content with context, and make choices about what you pay attention to. Some other components, or hallmarks, of the conscious self are *compassion, responsibility, respect, neutrality, appreciation, gratitude, an innate sense of optimism,* and *sufficiency.* This translates into having enough and being enough.

The more firmly you stand in the awareness of your conscious self, the more your present moves away from being run by your past survival strategies. Instead of your past determining how you show up in your present, your future—and your vision of who you are becoming—now predominate. Your future calls you forth much more than you are being driven by your past, and the entire backdrop of your life changes for the better.

Being Your Best Self: Manifesting the Qualities of Your Conscious Self

Overview

Everything about living your life above the line begins and ends with being present in your conscious self. This cannot be overemphasized. A certain set of key qualities, or aspects, of the conscious self are essential to understand and operate from if you want to be able to access your personal highest ground and consistently express your best self.

Understanding and coming from your conscious self is at the very heart of emotional intelligence. It is the most important takeaway from The Mastery of Integral Emotional Intelligence Program. It is essential to mastering the art of causing transformation on an everyday basis. A person who cultivates the ability to come from their conscious self—when that becomes their unshakable ground of being—will eventually be able to intuit everything laid out in this material. That said, the decades of research and practice that have gone into discerning these distinctions can save you a lot of time and effort and empower you to accelerate your evolution.

Because of its critical importance, we are going to delve more deeply into a set of ontological distinctions about the nature of the conscious self. All these aspects relate in various ways to the four elements of personal development that are required to create transformation on a sustainable basis: *waking up, growing up, clearing up,* and *showing up.* The qualities we will be exploring—being responsible, being respectful, being authentic, having integrity, and possessing the ability to create context—are essential to each of these four components. By internalizing these distinctions, you will be empowered to embody and come from your best self.

Being Responsible

Responsibility is reflected in all the attitudes and behaviors of the conscious self. To be responsible is to respond in the present by taking the role of being the creator of your own life. It is the source of your power and personal agency, and it is a both a place to stand and a way of being.

Responsibility starts with a declaration of willingness to hold the point of view, or attitude, that you are the cause, the source, or the creator of whatever occurs in your life. It is owning how you experience your life and your ability to author your response. It is also taking a stand to be the context, or container, in which the content of your life is happening; in other words, you are the space in which the content of your life exists, rather than you existing within its space.

Being responsible is the opposite of being in victim mode, which is in part a belief that your present is driven and determined by what happened in the past and you are powerless to affect the outcome. No matter what the cause, you feel at the effect of life. This leads to blaming and finding fault with others, increased negativity and hopelessness, and an avoidance of responsibility for the way things are. The fastest way out of being a victim is to find something about yourself or the situation that you can own and take responsibility for.

Responsibility is essential to personal power. Taking responsibility for something grants the power and personal agency to take action. It means looking for what isn't working and then striving to remedy it, thereby resolving the situation in as positive a way as possible. It means looking for whatever is missing and then providing it.

Responsibility allows for being complete and making peace with what has already happened, and for accepting and forgiving yourself and others. It means compassionately owning your mistakes, making corrections, learning the lessons, letting go, and moving on with greater self-mastery. There is not a lot of drama involved with being responsible.

Self-reliance is an aspect of responsibility. To be self-reliant is to take the initiative, rather than waiting for someone else to make things work for you. It can mean, for example, not stepping over or ignoring something that isn't working, simply because it isn't part of your job description to fix it. It can also mean supporting others in being self-reliant and owning up to their responsibility in a situation.

Responsibility is not about shouldering a burden or obligation, being at fault, taking the blame or the credit for something, or taking actions because you feel guilty or ashamed. It's not about trying to be in control or be right: it's about being empowered. It's a fundamental shift in approach that allows for greater access to personal power, authenticity, and the ability to discern life's lessons and gifts even when you are in a state of breakdown.

Autonomy and agency are often used interchangeably and have meanings that are closely tied to responsibility and personal power. Autonomy is self-rule, self-determination, independence, and freedom. Your ability to be autonomous and gain access to your personal power is determined by your skillfulness in returning to your conscious self and making choices and taking actions from there. It is the ability to be *at cause* in a situation, owning your reactions and freely authoring your responses.

> "The price of greatness is responsibility." —Winston Churchill

> "In the long run, we shape our lives, and we shape ourselves. The process never ends until we die. And the choices we make are ultimately our own responsibility." —Eleanor Roosevelt

> "We are made wise not by the recollection of our past, but by the responsibility for our future." —George Bernard Shaw

Acting from Love, Respect, and Compassion

Love is *the* defining feature of the conscious self. Loving awareness is at the very center of who you are as a conscious being. But what does love really mean? How do you express it? How do you get more of it? What does it look like to act in a loving way? Love is a vast and seemingly complex topic. Following are some key points for understanding love and how to embody it.

We all have unconscious and often conflicting biases about love. When we are operating below the line, in the grip of our fear-driven negative ego, we denigrate the importance of love and tell ourselves that love is for weaklings or is too painful and should be avoided. Or we are afraid we aren't going to get the love we long for, or that we will lose the love we currently have. In the face of our fears or pain, we become disconnected from our heart and lose the experience of love. We are often confused about what it looks like to be loving in our actions toward others, especially regarding how we manage our emotions and how we communicate.

Although love is an emotion, it is also an energy and an aspect, or quality, of consciousness. It is said that love is the essence of consciousness, and that consciousness is the essence of love. This is beautifully expressed in the following poem by Neal Rogin, from his book *Delightenment.*

> **"The source of the visible is invisible.**
>
> We come from the invisible spectrum of love,
> And manifest into the visible spectrum of light.

Light is love looked upon and seen.

Light is love slowed down enough to become visible.
The essence of all reality is love in motion.

The only thing faster than the speed of light
is the speed of love.

It is instantaneous.

Speed is infinite when something simply is.
Love is. There is no distance when love is.

Speed is a function of separation.
Separation is an illusion.
No separation, no time, no speed.

Love moves at the ultimate velocity.

Godspeed"

Love is hardwired into our very biology, and there are many ways that love manifests in our lives. These are some familiar ways that love is expressed:

- Appreciative love, as in, "I love my home."

- Romantic love, which can be expressed as, "I love you passionately."

- Relational love, such as, "I love my child."

- Intrinsic love, which is expressed as *joie de vivre*, as in, "I am in love with life."

  Intrinsic love is the inherent energy of love that is part of our consciousness. It is the natural wellspring of love that arises within us when we are not being fear-driven, which we experience as self-love, a loving acceptance of others, or a devotional or dedicated love of spirit. We also experience intrinsic love as reverence for life.

Like all genuine emotions, the expression of love has the potential for both positive and negative impacts. Love can either be liberating or possessive and oppressive; it can be magnanimous or needy. It very much depends on whether you are motivated from your heart or from some disintegrated part of your subconscious self. When love is expressed in manipulative, needy, possessive, controlling, or dominating ways, it becomes a distortion of genuine love. It is no longer love; it has devolved into abuse.

The purpose of much of the clearing up work you do to integrate the more reactive or disintegrated parts of your subconscious with the rest of your psyche is to expand your ability to experience love, both in the giving and receiving of it. In the next section we will address what is meant by integrating the more reactive parts of your subconscious. Sometimes, when this work is successful, it can viscerally feel like bands of constriction have loosened around your heart.

As you do this work of internal emancipation, you become better able to tune into the energy of love. You become a bigger and clearer channel for it. This love is infinite, and you experience more of it flowing within and through you as you free up your heart to become a better receiver for its frequency. As you become more skilled at tuning into the energy of love, your heart becomes a chamber in which, through your intent, you can amplify that love and send it back out into the world.

The ultimate expression of love is agape, or unconditional, love and acceptance. This kind of love is an aspirational state for each of us. When you tune into this transcendent love, you know that you are loved and have value simply because you exist. You are in touch with reverence for all life and have a sense of the sacred and an experience of oneness. You become universal, integrated, and cosmic-centric in terms of your ego identification, and you reach your most evolved state of growing up.

Although these moments are often considered to be mystical in nature, you don't need to be a mystic to have them. With sufficient practice and focused intent, anyone can have this experience. Even in small doses, when you direct this sort of love toward yourself, you can bring about profound healing from addiction, codependence, and other issues of self-worth. Feelings of gratitude often accompany this state, and cultivating gratitude and appreciation can help you tune into this experience.

As stated earlier, love and consciousness are intertwined: love is an aspect of consciousness, and consciousness is an aspect of love. This is not love in the romantic sense, but love as the powerfully beneficial force in any interaction or committed action. There is a grace, a lack of struggle, that is present when you imbue even the simplest of acts with love. Being conscious enhances your ability to love, and being loving enhances your ability to be conscious.

Being loving toward yourself can be expressed in the following ways:

- Being accepting of and nonjudgmental toward yourself.
- Using self-scrutiny and being honest about your reactivity and hidden agendas without blame, shame, or judgment.
- Having self-compassion and forgiving yourself for any mistakes you've made.
- Practicing self-advocacy and being in observer mode.
- Practicing self-care and being kind to your body.
- Trusting in your ability to handle whatever life brings.
- Refusing to get stuck in playing the victim role.
- Owning your reactions and authoring your responses.
- Processing and releasing challenging emotions.
- Respecting yourself and being responsible for meeting your authentic needs.
- Saying no to what makes you feel bad.
- Having fun and allowing yourself to experience pleasure,
- Being willing to be vulnerable, which allows for authenticity.

Being loving toward others is also expressed in a myriad of practical ways:

- Being respectful.
- Listening to another in such a way that the person feels known, and you both experience an increase in intimacy, enjoyment, and pleasure.
- Creating safety, emotionally or otherwise, and reducing the fear of loss.
- Being trustworthy and trusting.
- Being caring and generous.
- Being authentic and honest in a kind and responsible way.
- Being patient.
- Having healthy boundaries.
- Giving someone the benefit of the doubt.
- Being committed to another's growth and well-being.

- Supporting another in getting their needs met.

- Owning your reactions and authoring your responses.

- Expressing emotions responsibly, especially constrictive ones, such as anger.

Understanding that the conscious self is centered in the heart as loving awareness is an important key to living a fulfilled life. As mentioned earlier, the conscious self is the field in which you are aware of all four areas of human expression: your mental, physical, emotional, and spiritual bodies. It is from your conscious self that you actively respond to and author your relationship with all these aspects of being alive.

Being fulfilled in life is a function of self-love. The *only* channel, or frequency, of communication between these parts of yourself that results in fulfillment in any of them is love. For example, to be healthy and physically vital, you need to love your body and take pleasure in nurturing and moving it. This means treating your body with loving kindness, the focus of which is on creating sustainable health.

This requires a mature form of self-love, rather than a more adolescent expression where the focus is on treating yourself to the interim comfort of instant gratification. It means loving your body more, for example, than eating sugary or other addictive, ultraprocessed comfort foods that you know don't make you feel good in the long run.

To be emotionally fulfilled and joyful, you need to be able to lovingly embrace your challenging emotions so that they can be processed, released, and transmuted into something inspiring and uplifting. To be fulfilled intellectually, you need to love the world around you and be curious about it. All great acts of creativity and beauty are labors of love, including those that were born out of an experience of suffering.

Love is chemically hardwired into our biology and expresses itself as attraction. From an esoteric point of view, love is considered to be the great force of attraction that holds everything in manifest form. Biologically, the purpose of love is no less than creation and the continued existence of species. It is a powerful chemical force that compels living things to recreate and sustain themselves and it manifests in the chemicals that create pleasure in physical touch. Even when humans exercise their free will and choose not to procreate, there is still an intrinsic yearning for connection and union with others.

"From an evolutionary perspective, love can be viewed as a survival tool—a mechanism we have evolved to promote long-term relationships, mutual defense, and parental support of children, and to promote feelings of safety and security." —Jim Al-Khalili (physicist)

One of the main ways that love is expressed in action is by showing respect. We do this by appreciating someone or something, and regarding them in a reverential way. We hold them in esteem. Respect is the act of honoring a person by accepting them as they are, while also granting them the courtesy of seeing them as an autonomous, whole human being who has the power of agency, regardless of whether they are utilizing it.

Respect is a basic human right. Being respectful is acknowledging an individual's inherent strength and competence. It is being responsible for the impact that you make on another. It is holding in regard, and not violating, their boundaries. It is a commitment to honoring healthy boundaries, particularly ones that have to do with safety and security. Being respectful is being courteous, civil, and gracious

One of the most empowering things a parent can do is to be role model of respect and create an environment of mutual respect in their home. This includes self-respect and respecting others—and having the expectation of being treated with respect in return. Modeling respectful behavior grants a person the authority to request, and also to expect, to be treated with respect.

It is easy to be respectful of someone when they are operating from their best self. It is more challenging to be respectful when they are in a state of reactivity, disintegration, and dysfunction, or are otherwise behaving badly. Although you may not admire this mode of operating, you *can* honor that this person is making a choice to act in this way, even if it is an unconscious choice. You can honor that they have wounds, fears, and pain that are driving their behavior. You can honor that they will choose to grow beyond these behaviors when they are willing and able to do so.

Another main way that love gets expressed in action is through compassion. To be compassionate is to be *understanding, caring, sensitive, considerate, kind, tolerant, accepting, merciful, humane,* and *big-hearted.* Being compassionate means being able to see beyond someone's surface behavior to their deeper humanity. It is a way of engaging with others that is unbiased. It is being empathic, which is being open to understanding what is so about another person's experience, perspective, or truth.

"If you want others to be happy, practice compassion; if you want to be happy, practice compassion." —His Holiness the Dalai Lama

Compassion flows out of a curiosity and a desire to truly know and understand another. In a visceral way, compassion involves recreating within yourself some of what the other person is feeling, so that you can share in their experience in a direct way. This is also known as having empathy, and it allows you a window into their world. Understanding another person's reality is essential to having compassion for them. It is about curiosity and respect instead of pity.

"True compassion is not just an emotional response, but a firm commitment founded on reason. Therefore, a truly compassionate attitude toward others does not change, even if they behave negatively. Through universal altruism, you develop a feeling of responsibility for others: the wish to help them actively overcome their problems." —His Holiness the Dalai Lama

Consciously Creating Context

When you are awake and present, you can intentionally create an empowering context for the circumstances of your life, rather than feeling at the effect of, and disempowered by, them. Creating context for the content of your life is one of the most important functions of the conscious self—it is an expression of the conscious self in action. It is a powerful, transformative tool for granting meaning and purpose to what is occurring and for enhancing the quality of your life.

Understanding how to create context allows you to see new opportunities, lessons that can be integrated, and openings for action that were previously invisible to you. By understanding this critical function of the conscious self, you can accelerate your personal growth.

Context is the setting, the framework, or the container within which a statement, an idea, or the circumstances of an event can be fully understood and assessed. Context is often the beliefs or attitudes that allow us to discern and interpret the meaning of whatever content we are dealing with. Content can be held in a way that is either empowering or disempowering. For example, a breakdown can be contextualized as an opportunity for growth rather than as a discouraging failure. It can be contextualized as a learning opportunity instead of an excuse to give up.

The context you create for something and the attitude or approach you have toward it are always aligned. Therefore it is good to examine and change any attitudes you hold that are inconsistent with the context you want to create. For example, if you recontextualize a current breakdown as a learning opportunity and a step on the way to creating a breakthrough, then make sure you aren't holding on to an attitude of seeing yourself as a failure. A powerful attitude you could adopt is that true innovation *requires* failure *with* responsibility.

> "I haven't failed. I just found 10,000 ways that don't work."
> —Thomas Edison

Reframing, or creating a new context, is a technique for shifting your perception. The Quakers have an expression, *way opening*, which can occur when a difficult situation is reframed. For example, transforming conflict can be as straightforward as reframing a situation by creating a new context in which people attack mutual problems together, rather than seeing each other as the problem. This places all the stakeholders on the same side of the issue and allows for seeing new possibilities and shared needs and interests, rather than creating obstacles. This is an above-the-line, you-*and*-me, conscious self approach to dealing with conflict constructively.

An extremely empowering context you can adopt is a spiritualist attitude, or yogic approach, to life. It's said that you can't do anything bad to a yogi because they view everything that happens to them as an opportunity. Although not everything in life necessarily happens for the best, you can, through your awareness, strength of character, and ability to create context, have it *be* for the best—if not immediately, then in the long run.

This does not mean being naively optimistic or practicing what is sometimes referred to as conjectural optimism (also known as toxic positivity), which is a form of ignoring or denying the difficulties you are facing and trying to just smooth things over. Rather, by an honest and intentional engagement with these difficulties, you can discern a path forward that allows for increased knowledge and growth.

One of the most empowering skills that you can generate from your conscious self is the ability to create breakthroughs from breakdowns. This includes owning and working through any pain, loss, or upset inherent in that breakdown. A detailed guideline for turning breakdowns into breakthroughs appears in chapter 14 of this book.

There is a grace available when you discern the potential higher purpose and meaning of a situation. It is your choice whether to grant the situation that purpose and meaning. Even the most difficult of circumstances offers gifts in terms of opportunities for learning and growth. Even in death, which is considered to be one of the most challenging circumstances of all, there is the opportunity for peace and the cessation of physical pain. From a spiritual point of view, death is said to allow the soul to integrate all the lessons learned from that incarnation. Mystics have said that dying is like taking off a shoe that is too tight, and that there is a tremendous sense of freedom in the transition.

Challenges in life tend to fall into one or more of three categories: opportunities for learning and growth, opportunities for training and empowerment, or opportunities for building character. Often they are all three.

Being Authentic and Truthful

Living authentically has its basis in the conscious self. When your inner being is expressed, it has the following qualities, or characteristics, of being

a) *genuine, real, true, trustworthy, faithful,* and *honest;*

b) *reliable, dependable, conscientious, principled, ethical, appropriate,* and *mature;* and

c) *purposeful, responsible, at cause, autonomous, self-governing, self-determined,* and *emancipated.*

Fundamentally, authenticity is about honesty and transparency. It is the ability to perceive, own, and articulate your clearest or highest truth, and take actions and exhibit behaviors consistent with that truth. Appropriate, healthy interpersonal dynamics require that all individuals involved be honest and authentic about their feelings and needs. An important component of character, authenticity allows for the conscious creation of a future that is in alignment with your best self, your principles, and your values.

"Honesty is the first chapter in the book of wisdom."
—Thomas Jefferson

One of the biggest barriers to being authentic is fear, particularly fear of rejection or disapproval. Constantly looking outside ourselves for validation of our self-worth makes it virtually impossible to live an authentic life and experience true self-esteem. Another major barrier to being authentic is the avoidance of taking responsibility for our impact on others. Then, rather than being courageous enough to be honest and deal with the consequences, we dissemble and obscure what is really going on.

Authenticity requires cultivating your inner adult and having a firm commitment to making a positive impact and creating mutual benefit. Creating mutually beneficial outcomes *requires* being authentic. In other words, being honest about what is really true for you in a responsible and respectful way. A useful attitude to adopt is that when you speak your truth with kindness, it is ultimately to everyone's benefit.

Another empowering attitude is that there *are* solutions: there is always a way through a problem or challenge that is in everyone's best interests. If being authentic about something creates emotional disturbance, by being responsible for your impact you can then work to keep communication channels open. You can continue to do this until a way unfolds for everyone to feel better about the situation and how things are evolving.

Debating the nature and varieties of truth with all its nuances is something that could be done at great length. (All-night discussions by college philosophy majors come to mind.) The focus here, however, is on you being able to strengthen your sense of your personal truth for your own self-empowerment. Therefore, we will limit our discussion to understanding ultimate truth and relative, or personal, truth.

When people speak of "the truth," they are usually referring to one of these two categories: either ultimate truth (which is also called absolute or objective truth) or relative truth (which is also known as personal truth). Ultimate truth is about the laws that govern reality, such as the law of gravity. It includes things that are factual truths no matter what the circumstances, such as a square is never round. Science is the objective study of ultimate, or absolute, truth.

Both philosophy and psychology are the study of relative, or personal, truth. This sort of truth is the recognition and acknowledgment of what is occurring in your reality, to the best of your ability to observe and perceive it. Being able to discern what is true for you at any given moment is a function of your awareness, knowledge base, observational skills, and sense of discernment. Being able to discern your personal truth and own it is an essential component of acceptance: of yourself, of others, and of whatever situation you find yourself in. Growth isn't possible without acceptance of what is.

Relative truth also includes the understanding that there is no such thing as ultimate truth when it comes to people's experience. What people think is true for them is *always* subjective, and is influenced by many factors, including their preconceived notions and perceptions. As you have most likely experienced, people's interpretations and stories about an occurrence can differ greatly, depending upon their point of view. Usually, the best course of action is to be responsible for recognizing and speaking honestly about your personal truth to the best of your ability, while not negating another person's experience.

Discerning deeper truth requires practicing being awake in life and practicing self-reflection and self-scrutiny. Another aspect of personal truth is your ability to recognize and take ownership of your reactions, being honest about them while knowing that they are just reactions and are usually not your deeper truth. By delving deeper, beyond your reactivity, to see what is underneath, your truth has more resonance because it is more fully aligned with what is occurring in your reality.

Being Sourceful and Having Integrity

The source of something is the place from which it comes or emanates, such as the source of a river. As a human being, the source of your life is consciousness, or being. A phrase that is used in contemplative spirituality to describe this inner source is "the well of being."

When you are being sourceful, you are in touch with your inner being and are expressing the energy and qualities of your conscious self into the world. *Your inner being and your outer world expression become integrated and consistent.* When you are being sourceful it means that you are demonstrating self-mastery. This is an important concept to reflect upon, as it is one of the main points of these teachings.

Being sourceful is a form of personal expression that is aligned with your sense of your highest inner truth: you are expressing your best self in your relationships and in all the external circumstances of your life. This happens when you are in a place of inner alignment, or congruence. This means that you are present and fully seated in your conscious self, holding loving space for your subconscious self, and actively listening for your intuition, which is the voice of your superconscious self.

One way to think of enlightenment is that it is having an unshakable sense of self, of one's inner being. In today's world, very few people have the calling or the ability to go sit in a cave and meditate until they become enlightened. The challenge of modern society is to become grounded in your conscious self and then to express these qualities in your everyday life. There is a saying, "If you want to know how enlightened a person is, then look at how they treat their family and the people closest to them."

To be clear, the qualities of your conscious self being referred to are the ones that are covered in this chapter: creating context, having integrity, and being responsible, respectful, loving, compassionate, authentic, and honest. The goal is to be awake and heart-centered enough to be able to express these attributes in your daily interactions with others. The shorthand terms used to describe this way of operating in life are *being sourceful, living above the line* and *having self-mastery*.

Your integrity is your sense of being centered; it is who you really are as a conscious being and is your sense of feeling at home and happy within yourself. The state of having integrity is a specific combination of responsibility and honesty, where they both have become spontaneous and habitual. You are operating from a state of integrity when your first response to a situation is to default to your sense of responsibility for yourself, your reality, and what you have created, *and* to do so with honesty.

Being honest allows you to be in an appropriate dynamic (what is sometimes called being in "right" relationship) with whatever is actually occurring. Honesty and transparency are not for the faint of heart. They require real courage, strength of character, and a commitment to being authentic. When you come *from* responsibility and honesty, and these qualities are built into how you approach the world, then you are operating with integrity.

Several things can get in the way of being at home in our integrity. Playing at being a victim or martyr, with all the attendant payoffs, is a way to avoid taking responsibility for ourselves and our lives. Dishonesty is another way to undercut our integrity. Dishonesty is usually a fear-driven, negative ego response to the circumstances of life. It is another way of not being honest about our authentic needs so as to avoid having to be responsible for getting them fulfilled.

In his book *Radical Honesty*, Brad Blandin states that lying is a major source of human stress. We all tell lies and have many reasons for doing so. Some lies are small and seemingly innocuous—the little white lies we tell to smooth over social situations. Usually we justify these lies because we don't anticipate they will create bigger problems for us. At other times, the lies we tell become major sources of discomfort and shame.

Unfortunately, people often feel justified about lying when they have a hidden agenda, meaning that they are attempting to fulfill the defensive needs of their negative ego and will resort to using deception to manipulate others. When this happens, everyone involved loses in some capacity. Choosing to be honest is not about playing a morality game in which you get to be superior to others. Rather, it is about looking at the costs of dishonesty and inauthenticity and how they undermine your self-esteem. It takes being honest with yourself to admit that these costs even exist.

Mutual trust and emotional safety form the foundation of all healthy, loving relationships. Lying about things that are important to us and the people we relate to, betraying others, and manipulating by deception (also known as gaslighting) are forms of emotional abuse. This abuse destroys our connection with our integrity and our conscious self, and it traumatizes and alienates the people around us. It undermines the quality of our relationships and cancels our vote with others. Perhaps the real tragedy of this sort of dishonesty is that it automatically makes us defensive and adversarial, keeping us stuck in a state of unconsciousness losing dynamics.

"I'm not upset that you lied to me, I'm upset that from now on I can't believe you." —Friedrich Nietzsche

When we engage in deception, it sets up a vicious circle. We get caught up in living our lives in an unconscious, below-the-line state, acting out the defensive needs of our negative ego while we try to protect ourselves from discovery. Being dishonest can have substantial interim payoffs, like getting to avoid responsibility and vulnerability. Ultimately, though, the costs of maintaining a state of dishonesty are that we become inauthentic and live behind a false persona. We, and everyone around us, ends up losing and feeling dissatisfied and unfulfilled.

Perhaps the biggest cost of lying is that it leaves us feeling guilty, ashamed and unworthy inside, which only causes more feelings of being not OK. Only people who are totally shameless and are unwilling to confront their personal truth are oblivious to what maintaining deception is costing them. Integrity, honesty, responsibility, and our ability to trust ourselves are all essential to our sense of self-esteem.

"Lying kills people. The type of lying that is most deadly is withholding or keeping back information from someone we think would be affected by it. Psychological illness of the severest kind is a result

of this kind of lying. Psychological healing is possible only with the freedom that comes from not hiding anymore. Keeping secrets and hiding from other people is a trap."
—Brad Blandin, *Radical Honesty*

In summary, when you express your personal integrity, you are being sourceful. Your inner and outer worlds become congruent. You make choices and take actions that are from the heart, motivated by the desire for healthy relationship dynamics. Being sourceful and having integrity means owning your impact on others. You are continuously aligning and integrating your choices, words, and actions with a larger purpose or mission and with principles that are consistent with mutual benefit.

Summary of Self-Empowerment Tools and Practices

Recognize your conscious self as the center of your being, and cultivate and strengthen your connection to it through meditation and mindfulness practices.

Declare and hold an attitude of responsibility; refuse to give away your personal power by being a victim.

Be a role model of respect.

Practice the various forms of expressing love in action toward both yourself and others.

Love yourself enough to be self-accepting and self-advocating.

Love yourself enough to be loving and compassionate toward others.

Create context and reframe situations to grant positive purpose and meaning.

Take a yogic approach to life by embracing challenges as opportunities for learning and personal growth.

Take a stand for your integrity and authenticity and practice having your default in life be habitual responsibility and honesty.

CHAPTER 5
THE SUBCONSCIOUS SELF

Key Attitudes: You *or* me, adversarial, separateness, and caution (disintegrated), which can be transformed to you *and* me and enthusiasm (integrated).

Fundamental Drives: Survival; evolving to survive and thrive with healthy development of the subconscious self.

Signature States: Vacillates between being not OK and OK.

When the subconscious self is in a state of disintegration and being not OK, it is reactive and fear-driven, exhibiting drama, anxiety, nervousness, tension, an innate sense of pessimism and an attitude of scarcity. The more that love and acceptance are focused on the subconscious self, the more these emotional states heal, and the more integrated, calmer, joyful, and OK the subconscious self becomes.

Energetic Center in the Body: The solar plexus.

Overview

The purpose of the subconscious self is to ensure that you survive—and, ideally, thrive. It's the vast repository of your automatic processes, knowledge, and memories, as well as your learned behaviors and survival strategies. It contains the content of your personality, your personality type and drives, and everything that you identify with, including your racial and gender identities. Its responses and processes are based on lessons that you learned in the past.

The subconscious self is like the musicians in the orchestra who carry the flow of the music. It can also be thought of as the players, the crew, or the team members who carry out many of the processes that occur in your daily life. Some other names for the subconscious self are *the unconscious self, the lower self, the conditioned self, the unconscious mind,* and *the library of the past.*

George Gurdjieff referred to the quality of consciousness of the subconscious self as that of being in a state of waking sleep. Another way to think of waking sleep is that it is like being on autopilot. When you are not in your conscious self, awake and in observer mode, and your subconscious takes control of your thoughts and behaviors, you are operating in this state. Your eyes might be open, but you are not really present with whatever is happening.

Sometimes it is fine to be in a state of waking sleep, such as the times when you arrive home and realized you were on automatic and don't really remember the drive. At other times, it can harmful, for instance, if you were so distracted that you crashed the car. It can also be harmful if your subconscious is in charge and you automatically react, or overreact, to a situation and lash out at someone in a way that is hurtful.

There is a tremendous amount going on in your subconscious self at every moment. In terms of imagining the volume of everything your subconscious contains, try visualizing a gigantic warehouse that is as big as a football field. Then picture it being jam-packed with overflowing filing cabinets and piles of stuff everywhere. This is probably a profoundly insufficient analogy, but it points to the incredible amount of information your subconscious has stored and can recall instantaneously.

The subconscious self includes all your unconscious and unexamined attitudes, beliefs, and thought structures, as well as your sense of attachment and identity. Some other components include the ego and the negative ego, instinctual drives (the id), your enculturation and biases, habits, defense mechanisms, formulas for success and coping strategies, and compulsions. It includes your subpersonalities and archetypes, and what is referred to as your shadow.

Your shadow is simply a collection of the aspects of yourself that you haven't been ready to embrace and become conscious about yet. It includes the parts of you that traditionally have been considered areas of darkness, because they are lacking the light of your conscious awareness and are not yet fully integrated with the rest of your psyche. Your shadow also includes your unrealized positive attributes—the talents, gifts, and potential that you have not yet owned and are unaware of.

The subconscious self also includes your pain-body,[vii] which refers to a vicious and self-reinforcing cycle. Otherwise known as emotional baggage, the pain-body is the accumulation of old, unhealed wounds and bad feelings, and the negative thoughts and beliefs that are associated with them. We all go through life attempting to operate on top of the painful feelings these unexamined, unhelpful thoughts perpetuate. Our disempowering thoughts feed our bad feelings, our bad feelings then feed our negative, disempowering thoughts, and so on.

For example, if someone was abusive toward us when we were children, then we felt bad and told ourselves there must be something wrong with us for them to have treated us like that. Our bad thoughts about being unworthy then exacerbated the trauma, which escalated our negative thinking. Our negative thinking caused us to feel even more pain. And then we repeated this cycle, again and again.

We end up carrying all this pain around like a huge weight, often being in denial about it and unconsciously expending a lot of energy trying to hide it from others by adopting a tough persona. We ignore the pain, which has it go unprocessed, taking up a lot of space in our psyche and shaping how we show up in the present. This continues until we do the necessary mental, emotional, and spiritual work to heal ourselves. This includes processing our pain so that it can be released and examining our negative thoughts and attitudes and replacing them with ones that are more empowering.

The voices of your subconscious self are many and varied and make up the majority of the voices in your head. For example, each of your subpersonalities, such as your inner child and inner adolescent, has its own distinct voice. The loudest and most strident of these voices is usually that of your inner critic, which is also the voice of your negative ego. An important part of becoming emotionally intelligent is learning to differentiate between these voices and understanding how to work with them, so that you can heal and evolve these parts of yourself.

"Therefore it (your subconscious self) is alive within you, has its own consciousness and intentions, with its unique way of being, living, and attempting to fulfill its agenda. It has a great deal of power over the way you feel, think, and decide every day of your life. It has the capacity to initiate energies within you that you are often powerless to stop or control. We call them reactions, uncontrollable emotional and mental responses to people or situations."
—Gordon Davidson, *Joyful Evolution*

Moving from Disintegration to Integration

"Until you make the unconscious conscious, it will direct your life and you will call it fate." —Carl Jung

Specific parts of your subconscious self are either integrated seamlessly with the rest of your psyche or they aren't yet integrated, in which case they are referred to as being disintegrated. The path of self-mastery is one of continuously integrating more and more of the wounded, fear-driven, defensive, or otherwise dysfunctional parts of your subconscious self into harmonious alignment with the rest of your psyche.

The goal of working with the subconscious self is always to become more internally emancipated and free. Another way to say this is that the process of self-emancipation and individuation is one of intentionally moving more and more of the parts of the subconscious self that are in the disintegrated column into the integrated column. This is done through inner healing work and self-parenting.

Following is an explanation of what we mean by *disintegration* and *integration*:

A. *Disintegration:* To resume the musical analogy, everything the orchestra of the subconscious self knows was learned in the past. In the meantime, its musicians are doing the best they can to play something appropriate to the present moment. But not infrequently, what is being played is out of tune with what is occurring.

   Often a reactive pattern that was created in the past is being replayed and is not appropriate to the present situation. When this happens, you experience a state of disintegration and feel not OK, moving away from a sense of your calm, centered self. You move from being in equilibrium to a state of disequilibrium or reactivity.

B. *Integration:* For integration to occur, the musicians need the maturity of the conductor, the conscious self, to step in to create context and provide clear, workable direction. The conscious self assumes management of the situation, including illuminating any misconceptions or negative thinking, correcting unhelpful patterns, and initiating healing any wounds from the past. Often integration involves the inner adult (the conscious self) reparenting the wayward, out-of-tune part of the subconscious self.

   Based on the content it receives, the conscious self makes choices that are in harmony with what is presently occurring, and the subconscious self can relax and do its job of providing the necessary information to the conscious self about how to navigate life. When the relationship between these two selves is in an appropriate balance and partnership, the natural state of the subconscious self is one of equilibrium, happiness, and enthusiasm, with perhaps some relief that the inner adult has shown up. In other words, there is a state of integration.

The following analogy may be helpful in terms of understanding the difference between integration and disintegration. When your body is healthy and whole, it seems to recede into the background and goes about its business of supporting you in living your life. When your subconscious is integrated and whole, it also seems to disappear, receding into the background and supporting you as needed.

Having a part of your subconscious in a state of disintegration, however, is a lot like having a physical injury. You might have a relatively minor injury, such as a sliver in your finger, but suddenly that finger feels huge and is taking up an enormous amount of your attention. Similarly, when you have a wound that you are carrying in some part of your subconscious, even if it is relatively minor, it can seem to take up a lot of real estate in your psyche.

A trigger is created and gets reactivated every time something occurs that reminds your subconscious self of its old wound. In colloquial terms, this is known as having your buttons pushed. Just like your finger needs to heal so that it is no longer a source of pain, parts of your subconscious need to heal so that they become integrated and are no longer a source of reactivity. In healing the fear, or pain, or whatever else is stored in your psyche around your old wounds, your reactivity dissipates and is replaced with a sense of equanimity.

The primary intention of the subconscious self is to help you be safe and secure, live a long and healthy life, and prosper. All your positive experiences are stored there. The gifts of your subpersonalities, such as the playfulness and creativity of your inner child, are there and waiting for expression. All the skills you have acquired to create art, music, and whatever else you love are there. All your knowledge and life experiences live in your subconscious self as subpersonalities or archetypes, ready to be called upon whenever desired or needed.

When you combine the loving awareness of your conscious self with the experiential knowledge of your subconscious self, joy is a natural outcome. Being present in the conscious self while holding a loving, friendly attitude toward your subconscious self is an important key to your happiness and well-being.

> "Nothing in life is to be feared, it is only to be understood.
> Now is the time to understand more, so that we may fear less."
> —Marie Curie

It is not necessary to approach this part of yourself with fear or dislike. Although many parts of your subconscious are survival-oriented and driven by fear, you, as a conscious self, don't need to be. Rather, you can recognize that your subconscious self is doing the best it can in any situation, given your history, and is anxiously hoping that you will show up in your conscious self and give it guidance.

This is *especially true* when you feel stressed and are caught up in lower-self dysfunctional behavior patterns. Rather than judging yourself harshly when you've reacted badly to something, you can have compassion for the fact that your subconscious self means well but can be quite misguided and inappropriate to the current situation. This is because everything that it knows was learned in the past. A more empowering context is that your reactivity and any perceived failings point the way forward for healing and integration. They show you where you need to do some inner clearing-up work.

Subpersonalities, such as your inner child and adolescent, are a major aspect of your subconscious self. Given that you are almost always in one subpersonality role or another, a simple rule of thumb is that when you are feeling happy, OK, and in a state of equilibrium, chances are that this specific subpersonality is healthy and fully integrated with the rest of your psyche. When you are feeling unhappy, not OK, and in a state of disequilibrium, then that subpersonality is holding some sort of wound or pain from an unmet need you had in the past. This subpersonality is not integrated and therefore needs some loving attention and self-parenting from your conscious self. How to identify which specific subpersonality role you are in and how to self-parent will be covered in more depth in a later chapter.

The pain and discomfort are a clue that you need to put on your detective hat and get to work diagnosing the dynamics of the issue. You might never discover the exact cause of your wound, and fortunately you don't need to in order to heal. If you *can* discover the origin of your wound that can be illuminating, but you don't always need to get to the source to heal and gain freedom from its impact on your psyche.

You can process your wound, however it is currently showing up in your experience, by taking an integral, or multi-pronged, approach that incorporates various perspectives. Following are some examples of practices you could employ:

- By understanding the dynamics and emotions surrounding your wound to the best of your ability, you can then reexperience them (physically, emotionally, and mentally), with the intent to let them go.

- In meditation, you can imagine giving your pain to your higher self and soul, or to one of the elements, such as the earth, fire, or water.

- You can be self-loving by practicing forgiveness.

- You can put your fears under the microscope and examine them closely, revealing their insignificance and you discover that they are just a paper tiger. Or if you discover there are legitimate concerns, you can then take steps to address them.

You know when you have been successful at healing whatever was out of alignment when the discomfort disappears and your subconscious goes back to working seamlessly, receding into the background again. Then your subconscious is doing its job of being a vehicle for the expression of your best self into the world.

Your subconscious is incredibly sensitive, and one of the ways it protects you is by being hypervigilant. It is instantly receptive to very subtle differences in energy and emotional tones. It is also very sensitive to your attitudes toward yourself, whether you're being kind and loving or filled with self-loathing. Another rule of thumb is that the kinder you are toward yourself, the more your conscious self is in charge. Conversely, the more self-loathing and self-denigrating you are, the more your negative ego, the voice of your inner critic, is in charge.

Parts of the Subconscious Self

What Are Subpersonalities?

Subpersonalities are specific personas you take on that are like little parts of your overall personality. Each of these personas, or archetypal characters, has a life of its own; it is a living part of yourself and has a dynamic sense of its own intentions and agendas and its own thoughts and feelings. In all probability, many of your subpersonalities function in an integrated manner, but it is also likely that some are not integrated and need the help of your conscious self to evolve.

When you were growing up, you developed complex coping mechanisms for dealing with difficult, usually recurring, circumstances in your life. These coping strategies formed into a persona—a role or a mask—that you then presented to the world whenever you were in a similar situation or experienced stress. This is when you get triggered and have an automatic reaction to a situation that reminds your subconscious of something uncomfortable or painful that happened in the past. Whatever the role or persona was that got created will then come storming up to the surface (usually in a defensive stance) to take charge—for better or worse.

When you adopt a subpersonality, it is as though you assume a costume for whatever play is currently onstage. This persona influences your facial expressions, your body posture, the tone and volume of your voice, what you think and say, your emotional reactions, and how you feel physically.

"When you identify with a particular wound it creates an emotional blueprint within your emotional body referred to as a subpersonality. Without realizing, you begin to build your whole identity and life around this blueprint, thus believing it is who you really are. Your subpersonality is not the real YOU, it is part of you, but it is not you.

> "To make this distinction is crucial. You need to realize that a
> subpersonality suffering from a lack of self-esteem or low
> self-worth is only a part of you, an extension of your emotional body.
> Rather than identifying yourself as 'I am insecure' you need to state,
> 'A part of me is insecure.' This kind of discernment is truly
> empowering. It removes this insecure subpersonality
> from the position of power and puts you in the driver's seat."
> —Natasha Dern, *Subpersonalities: Who's Calling the Shots?*

Common Types of Subpersonalities

Following are descriptions of four main types of subpersonalities.[viii] The subpersonalities we will be working with most extensively in this program are stage-of-life characters and lower-self characters. These are not all the various types of subpersonalities, but they are the ones most useful to understand for our purposes.

Stage-of-Life Characters

These subpersonalities are related to the various developmental stages you move through as you grow up. Depending on how old you are, you will have some combination of an inner child, inner adolescent, inner young adult, and inner mature adult. You also have a future self, which is the personification of who you are becoming. Each of these parts has unique gifts that enhance the quality of your experience.

These stage-of-life characters are typically where you have stored any unhealed wounds you experienced while growing up. These wounds often occurred when you had needs that didn't get met or were violated in some way, and shame got attached to that character. When a stage-of-life character feels damaged, it needs love and self-parenting in order to evolve, that is, in order to become happier and more fully integrated with the rest of your psyche.

For example, whenever you start acting in a way that reminds you of when you were an adolescent, you most likely *are* in the grip of your inner adolescent. The same goes for the people around you. Needless to say, it is usually much easier to see this in others than it is to see it in ourselves. When a stage-of-life character takes over, it is often because you have some developmental needs that didn't get met during that time of your life. This caused a wound that keeps getting triggered in present time.

To get your inner adolescent to stop trying to run the show in a dysfunctional, immature manner, you will need to reflect on whatever needs you had that didn't get met during that time of your life. Then you can do the self-parenting and inner healing work to integrate that subpersonality with the rest of your psyche. Your relationship with your inner adolescent will be strengthened, and you will be enabled to draw upon the gifts of that part, such as its curiosity about life, courage to take risks, and playful nature.

Composite Characters

One of the primary ways that your subconscious self stores information is not by topic, but rather as a cluster of knowledge that is associated with a subpersonality. For example, your subconscious doesn't file a recipe for a mojito in an "Awesome Drinks for Summer" folder; it files it under the character called your inner barkeeper. When you have friends over for cocktails, your inner barkeeper kicks into gear, helping you out with all the knowledge and experience you have already accumulated about mixing drinks. The same is true for being a nurse, a musician, an artist, an accountant, a parent, or a teacher—any and all roles you have in life.

Filing content in your subconscious in this manner is the most efficient way of accessing what you need to know in the present, when you have taken on a particular role for a certain amount of time. Some of these roles or subpersonalities will be much stronger and more fully developed than others, and their makeup will be unique to you.

The more these roles are fully integrated—happy, healthy, in partnership with, and being directed by, the conscious self—the smoother your experience will be of accessing the knowledge stored there. For example, if you are a professional counselor, coach, or therapist, when you are in your conscious self, present, awake, and counseling someone, you don't need to try to consciously remember everything you have ever learned about being a counselor at every single moment. This would be an overwhelming way to have to live life.

Instead, your subconscious mind, working through your counselor subpersonality, will offer up the necessary information to the conscious self if and when it is needed. If your counselor subpersonality is fully integrated, then chances are you will experience a great deal of satisfaction and happiness, even joy, when you are embodying this role.

To take this integration analogy a step further, when you really love a part of yourself, such as your inner teacher, and you imbue it with purpose and value, you create the possibility for a very fulfilling life. This could be a purpose of being of service to others, or a goal to be the most inspiring teacher you can be, and so on.

In addition to being fulfilling, giving purposeful goals to these parts of yourself can also be a great deal of fun. For example, you might give your inner gardener the goal of discovering the most fragrant roses or visiting as many famous gardens as possible. Then every time you encounter a highly perfumed rose or visit a renowned garden, you have an enhanced experience of fulfillment, inspiration, joy, and fun in the process.

Inner Reflections of Intimate Relationships

Your subconscious is working 24-7 to assist you in being safe and secure. One way it does this is by closely observing the best ways in which to relate to the people you are intimate with. Your subconscious then uses these past observations to create an inner reflection of these individuals to help you figure out how to relate to them in the present. This might include all the little things they like, ways of interacting with them in the past that have worked or didn't work, and so on. This reflection is like a living, breathing hologram of a person who is, or was, important in your life.

Foremost of these are your inner mother and inner father, or any other significant caretaker or authority figure from your childhood. These are the people most critical to you in terms of who you formed attachments with when you were very small. When dealing with issues such as healing and releasing any shame or repressed anger that occurred in your relationship with these individuals while growing up, it is powerful to have a dialogue with these subpersonalities to complete the past and help both them and you evolve. This is especially true when that individual is no longer alive to interact with.

Part of the disorientation and grief that is experienced when you end an intimate relationship, whether intentionally or through them passing away, is due to that person taking up so much space in your psyche as an inner reflection subpersonality. Losing that person can feel like the pain of having a phantom limb: there is an ache inside where they are no longer integrated into your reality, and you need to find ways to make peace with the subpersonality still residing within you.

Lower-Self Characters

When you're caught up in behaviors that are not constructive and are, in fact, interfering with or damaging your relationships, you're acting out a lower-self subpersonality. These are the most disintegrated parts of yourself, with the victim persona being the most common form of these lower-self characters.

These subpersonalities are a constellation of specific and predictable feelings, thoughts, and actions. Their reactions are instinctual, unthinking, and automatic. Their energy is very distinct from the energy of your conscious self. They manifest when you feel a combination of stress, emotional reaction, and helplessness; they don't generally appear when you're calm and relaxed. Lower-self characters tend to inhabit the roles and dynamics of the drama triangle and are usually fear-driven.

These lower-self characters are usually the ones that wreak the greatest havoc in your life and can be the most challenging to work with. They often carry some sort of constrictive emotion, such as fear, pain, anger, or shame. It is helpful to remember that these parts of yourself want to have you survive and thrive. They are trying to be helpful, but they just don't have the maturity to know how to go about it in a healthy, workable way.

Of all the subpersonality types, these lower-self characters require the most self-acceptance, self-parenting, and loving attention from your conscious self to become integrated with the rest of your psyche. After recognition, the next step is always acceptance, because it is impossible to heal anything that you cannot embrace and own. The chapter on getting free of your negative ego will go more deeply into these characters and how to best heal and integrate them.

What Are Archetypes?

Archetypes are collective representations of subpersonalities that all people share to varying degrees. Archetypes are external personifications of parts of your collective subconscious: the martyr, the queen, the king, the sage, the warrior, the angel of mercy, and so on. Just as with working with subpersonalities, the value of working with archetypes is as a tool to help you bring aspects of your subconscious self to your awareness so that you can work constructively with these parts.

"Archetypes are everywhere. Our life and this world we live in are governed by countless archetypal patterns of power that influence each of us. In turn, we act on those influences in our daily life through every single choice we make, right down to the clothing we wear to the person we fall in—or out—of love with, to the addictions we have, to our success—or failure—in our choice of business deals. Every choice we make is connected to an archetypal pattern. Every relationship we have is magnetized through our archetypes.

"We are attracted to people because we share harmonious archetypal patterns. A Princess seeks out a Knight. A Warrior often looks for a Damsel. Addicts look for Addicts and always find them. Rescuers need a Dependent Child or Victim seeking assistance. Both mistake their mutual dependency for 'love'—a classic archetypal relationship."
—Caroline Myss, *Sacred Contracts*

Inner Feminine and Masculine Aspects

We are all familiar with the concept of yin and yang, which is a representation of feminine and masculine energy. No matter what your gender identification is, you have some combination of both feminine and masculine energies within. Therefore it is worth taking a few minutes to inquire into what the relationship is between these energies and your psyche.

Feminine and masculine energies are not confined to the subconscious self. They color and affect all the parts of your psyche and your expression in the world. These energies are part of your meta-container, the qualities of consciousness that hold all the various parts of you. There is a yogic saying that the consciousness of spirit is singular and when it meets the human psyche and physical matter it becomes dual, both feminine and masculine, which is an interesting and poetic image. These energies are universal and are part of who you are as a conscious being, beyond anything to do with your gender identity.

Another way to think of these energies is that they are like opposite ends of a battery, one end holding a negative, or receptive (feminine), charge and the other a positive, or assertive (masculine), charge. In this case, *negative* and *positive* are neutral terms and simply refer to the direction of energy flow. This magnetic polarity controls the direction of the energy current and is essential for keeping the energy moving. Simply put, you give and receive energy, and both forms of energy are intrinsic to being alive.

We all have a softer, more receptive side and a more forthright, assertive side. You need the strengths of both these qualities of energy to thrive. *Everyone* needs a healthy balance and expression of both their feminine side and their masculine side to experience well-being. One is not better than the other; they are both essential.

What is important to note regarding the subconscious self is that everyone has enculturated and internalized ideas, ideals, and biases about what being masculine and being feminine mean. Many traits traditionally seen as either masculine or feminine receive this label as a function of prevailing cultural norms, meaning that these labels are mostly based on a patriarchal view of the world.

Seeing masculine energy as superior to feminine energy is a type of fear-based, negative ego-driven, unconscious losing game and dynamic that is global. Within the construct of patriarchy, *everyone* (male, female, and nonbinary) ends up paying an enormous cost in terms of the lost potential for mutual benefit.

Chauvinism can be considered an equal opportunity employer, in that rigidity and narrow-mindedness about gender roles can affect, and you could say infect, people of every gender-identification. All our unexamined beliefs and assumptions about gender identity, the degree to which our self-worth is tied to our sense of gender, and so on, reside in our subconscious self as a foundational element of our self-identification.

Part of the path of emancipation is becoming familiar with your internalized concepts and biases regarding femininity and masculinity. By bringing these biases up to the surface, you can choose to upgrade them. You can drop the old, constrictive beliefs and outdated ways of operating and become more skillful at calling upon these energies in constructive ways, as and when they are needed. There is a lot of fun, creativity, and fulfillment to be had while playing with the polarities of these two energies.

What Are Personality Types?

The subconscious self also includes your personality type or characteristics. As human beings, there are some universally common ways in which we construct our defenses and our coping strategies and in which we approach life. The study of personality types is the work of decoding these common dynamics.

You may be familiar with some common personality typing tools, such as the Enneagram or the Myers-Briggs Type Indicator. From a metaphysical point of view, astrology can also be seen as a personality typing tool. Less widely known than astrology is a system in esoteric philosophy called the seven rays. These seven rays are the main qualities of energy that influence everything in manifest form, including our personalities.

Personality typing is not meant to define you, or put you in a specific, predetermined box. The main value of understanding your personality type, and whatever defensive patterns might be associated with it, is that this understanding can bring greater awareness of your unconscious drives. This enables you to be more at choice about how you respond to people and circumstances. Often your personality type will give you clues about where you tend to automatically default to when you are stressed. It can also give you clues about how to best go about becoming more integrated and functional.

Your personality is made up of both the characteristics you were born with, referred to as your nature, and the ones you developed in response to your environment—how you were nurtured. It is not a case of nature *or* nurture; it is both together. The characteristics you were born with are often referred to as your innate temperament. Being a child is always an incredibly vulnerable time, in which one is often in a state of disequilibrium and totally dependent upon the goodwill of others.

Although childhood can be a joyous experience, it can also sometimes be frightening, traumatic, and painful. From infancy, all human beings establish certain habitual patterns of response to their environment so that they can survive and feel more stable. By the time you became a young child, these habitual patterns of response had turned into a personality type. These habitual patterns are made up of defensive strategies that get used in almost every situation, regardless of whether or not that strategy still works. Many people spend their whole lives unconsciously gathering evidence about why their childhood defense strategies are still essential to their emotional or physical security.

You can work in an emotionally intelligent way with your personality type by bringing awareness to these unconscious, self-protective, and reactive responses. Once you are awake to the protective purpose of these habitual patterns, you can relax the hold of your personality type's automatic reactions and choose responses that are self-advocating and more beneficial to yourself and others.

The Enneagram: A Personality Typing Tool

Although there are many personality typing tools, the one we find the most useful and work with the most is the Enneagram. The roots of the Enneagram are ancient and can be traced all the way back to Pythagoras. It was reintroduced and expanded upon early in the twentieth century by George Gurdjieff.

The Enneagram is a cognitive map you can use for understanding the underlying unconscious motivations that drive your behavior and that of others. Identifying your Enneagram type and learning how to work with it is something that is highly recommended as a tool for empowering your personal growth and becoming more emotionally intelligent.

Part of the value of the Enneagram system is that not only is it a tool for recognizing and bringing up to consciousness your unconscious drives, but it also points to the path of self-actualization and integration for your personality type. Fully understanding how to use the Enneagram as a tool for self-emancipation is a larger topic than will be covered here, and there are many excellent resources and teachers available on this subject. For our purposes, we want to illustrate some basic principles of how this system works and how it might potentially be useful for you.

Each of the nine Enneagram personality types is driven by a particular compulsion that is obsessively used to try to survive the difficulty and vulnerability of being human. In the Enneagram system, each type has a particular wound attached to it. This wound greatly impedes the ability to navigate life in an integrated and functional way. These wounds get created in childhood and could be viewed as areas of arrested development (the concept of which will be covered later in the chapter on ego development).

There is a theory in esoteric philosophy that we can be born already carrying a wound, especially if it is something we didn't heal in a previous lifetime. We have a soul contract in this incarnation to learn to heal whatever this woundedness is about. This relates to the concept of choosing our parents so that we will grow up in a dynamic that is conducive to us fully exploring and learning how to heal ourselves.

Discovering how to go about this healing becomes one of our major life lessons. The theory is that we give ourselves these challenges so that we have sufficient grist for the mill, that is, the kind of challenges that enable us to grow and become more evolved. This is an attitude of, "Obstacles do not block the path; they are the path."

At the end of the day, it may not really matter what the origin of your woundedness is. What's important is that we all seem to have areas where we have unprocessed, repressed pain and are unconsciously and compulsively using survival strategies that aren't in our best interests.

When you work with healing your wounds and their attendant compulsions and defensive patterns, you can rise into the more evolved, integrated version of your personality type. You are empowered in your ability to create and experience extraordinary well-being.

Following is a display of each of the nine Enneagram types and the primary wound attached to each one. Each type has a primary personality drive, which is listed with the number of the personality. You will see that there are several names associated with each type, which have been coined by various Enneagram teachers. We have included more than one name for each type to give a bit more of a feel for what each type is about.

The Nine Enneagram Types and Their Original Wound		
Type & Drive	**Name**	**Wound**
1 To reform	The Perfectionist, the Reformer, the Righteous Judge	Issues around trusting others, especially around being disapproved of, or found fault with. "I don't get the approval I need."
2 To be loved	The Giver, the Helper, the Fairy Godparent	Issues with trusting myself to get my own needs met. Focused on meeting the needs of others and getting their approval. Abandoning my authentic self.
3 To achieve	The Achiever, the Performer, the Producer	Issues with loving myself and others. My self-worth is tied to accomplishment. "I am what I do."
4 To be special	The Romantic, the Tragic Artist, the Individualist	Loss of hope or faith in others to love me and make me feel special. "There must be something wrong with me." "Something is missing from my life."

5 To think and understand	The Observer, the Thinker, the Sage	Loss of hope or faith in myself to succeed at handling the intensity and pressures of life. Issues with being overwhelmed and lacking energy.
6 To be safe	The Questioner, the Loyal Skeptic, the Guardian	Loss of trust in myself and others. Anxious about my abilities. Cautious and self-protecting. "Others can't be counted on." "Life isn't safe."
7 To discover	The Adventurer, the Epicure, the Hedonist	Insecure and suspicious of others' ability to be loving. Issues with feeling free to love. Defended against the pain of being hurt by loving others.
8 To be self-reliant	The Challenger, the Protector, the Boss or Leader	Issues with power and needing to be in control of the situation and other people. Fear of being messed with. Substituting strength and power for self-love.
9 To seek peace	The Peacekeeper, the Mediator, the Ghost	Issues with going for harmony at a cost to myself. Loss of faith in my and others' ability to handle conflict well. Coping by being passive, self-effacing, conflict avoidant, and resigned.

Often when people first start looking at the various personality types of the Enneagram, they resonate or identify with more than one role. The easiest way to get started and discover your specific type is to complete one of the questionnaires that are available online, such as the one from The Enneagram Institute,[ix] which is called the Riso-Hudson Enneagram Type Indicator (RHETI), or the Stanford Enneagram Discovery Inventory,[x] which was created by David Daniels. There are many excellent books on the Enneagram, some of which are listed at the back of this volume in the recommended reading section. *Discovering Your Personality Type,* by Don Richard Riso and Russ Hudson is a good introduction to the Enneagram and includes a personality typing questionnaire.

Universal Personality Traits That Cause Disintegration

There are a handful of constrictive personality traits that we all share to some degree. They are the most familiar of all the limitations to our personal growth. No one gets a full pass on these. If you are a human being, then you have at least one of these personality traits and most likely two or more. They are all fundamental obstacles that, unless addressed, keep you locked into lower-self behavior patterns.

Conversely, when you own and work with your version of these traits, they can become a pathway to integration and emancipation. In his poem, "The Faces at Braga," David Whyte says:

"When we fight with our failing
we ignore the entrance to the shrine itself
and wrestle with the guardian, fierce figure on the side of good."

These seven personality traits are: *arrogance, self-deprecation, impatience, martyrdom, greed, self-destruction, and stubbornness.*[xi] Because of the pervasiveness of these traits, and because they are the main personality stumbling blocks that we need to overcome, they are called chief features. These traits are all closely tied to the fear-driven, defensive needs of the negative ego, which we will be covering in detail in a later chapter.

> "In modern times, we call the seven dragons by more scientific names: dysfunctions, psychopathologies, defense mechanisms, addictions, abnormal and aberrant behaviors, neuroses, and antisocial behaviors. They are the dragons behind every obstacle to human potential. They are the dragons that masquerade as power, brilliance, modesty, strength, colorfulness, sacrifice and fortitude."
> —José Stevens, *Transforming Your Dragons*

The default with each of these chief features is to express them in negative, disempowering, below-the-line ways. When you bring the awareness of your conscious self to these disintegrated, subconscious aspects, you can integrate and transmute them into more positive, empowering, above-the-line characteristics and ways of operating.

For example, arrogance that is expressed as self-importance and superiority can fade away as you consciously work with that energy to evolve it into something much more positive, such as self-respect. In the following diagram, there are examples of how each chief features is automatically expressed in a disintegrated way, and what it can be transformed into when you work to integrated it.

Chief Feature	Automatic Below the Line (Unconscious)	Transformed Above the Line (Conscious)
Arrogance	Superiority, conceit, hubris, self-importance	Pride, a positive perspective on accomplishments, self-regard, self-respect
Self-deprecation	Self-abasement, degradation, humiliation	Humility, modesty, humbleness, lack of vanity, vulnerability
Impatience	Intolerance, irritability, annoyance, exasperation, frustration, being judgmental, lashing out at others	Daring, acceptance, spontaneity, boldness, bravery, self-contained, grounded
Martyrdom	Persecuting, victimizing, constantly suffering, self-sacrificing to be better than or to get love, resentment, self-pity	Selflessness, sacrifice for a greater cause, altruistic, compassionate, noble, magnanimous
Greed	Insatiable, constant dissatisfaction, gluttony, covetousness, self-indulgence, scarcity, never enough	Seeking fulfillment, passion, enthusiasm, zest for living, manifesting abundance and gratitude
Self-destruction	Self-sabotaging, masochistic, self-harming, out of control	Altruistic, sacrificing for a greater cause, generosity
Stubbornness	Inflexible, obstinate, willful, uncooperative, immovable, rigid	Determined, purposeful, unwavering, dedicated, resolute, intentional, fortitude, persistence

One of the ways you can work with these chief features is to discern for yourself what the underlying fear is that is driving this trait in yourself. Following are some of the common ways that fear drives these chief features, but the specific formulation of your chief feature, or features, will be unique to you.

Examples of how specific fears can drive a chief feature:

- Greed is usually driven by a fear of scarcity, of not getting enough.

- Impatience can be driven by the fear of missing out.

- Self-deprecation is usually the fear of inadequacy, of not being good enough, and a lack of self-trust.

- Stubbornness is often driven by a fear of change or of being dominated.

- Self-destruction can be driven by feelings of hopelessness and unworthiness. Sometimes it can be driven by a fear of lack of control or is a response to overwhelming pain and shame.

- Martyrdom can be driven by a fear of responsibility or a fear of being unlovable.

- Arrogance can be driven by insecurity and a fear of unworthiness. It may look like confidence but can be an overcompensation.

These personality traits start showing up in childhood. To some degree they may be a function of your temperament (nature), but to a very large degree they get formed by your response to your environment (nurture). When you were very small, you inherited and internalized your parents' chief features and made them yours. Or, in the process of rebelling against them, you developed a different chief feature. Either way, they became part of your conditioned way of operating.

Something that parents of teens often find destabilizing is that adolescents tend to cycle through most, if not all, of these chief features. They try them on for size until they settle on a primary one, and perhaps one or two secondary ones, as they head into young adulthood.

For example, most teenagers, even the seemingly well-adjusted ones, briefly flirt with the chief feature of self-destruction, which can manifest in myriad of ways. This can be a very dangerous time, given the fact that the conscious decision-making center of the brain doesn't fully develop until the mid-twenties and teens are flooded with hormones, making emotional responses much more extreme.

The goal in calling attention to these challenging personality traits is to empower you in recognizing, owning, and working constructively with whatever combination of chief features you have, so that you can become more emancipated. As you mature and gain more self-mastery, you may find that once you have transformed your main chief feature, then your secondary one, or ones, seem even more noticeable, which can inspire you to work on getting free of them as well.

When an individual doesn't take on leading a self-examined life and becoming internally emancipated, by the time they reach middle age their chief feature will have become solidified. This leads to an inflexibility or brittleness in attitudes and behaviors that make them difficult to be around. This is the source of several negative stereotypes of older individuals, such as being a disapproving, crotchety old man, or a lonely or bitter old lady.

Going into detail about identifying and getting free of these chief features is more material than is practical to cover here, but more information can be found in José Stevens's book *Transforming Your Dragons.*

Summary of Self-Empowerment Tools and Practices

Recognize when you have a wounded, or disintegrated, subpersonality, and work toward healing and integrating that part.

Bring unconscious biases about feminine and masculine energy and gender identification up to your awareness, and then let them go.

Discern when and in what situations it would be beneficial to call forth and express more of your inner feminine or masculine energy.

Use a personality tool, such as the Enneagram, to identify your unconscious personality drives, and then work to relax their hold on you.

Identify and integrate your chief feature or features.

CHAPTER 6
CONNECTING WITH YOUR SUPERCONSCIOUS AND CONSCIOUS SELVES

Overview

Once you understand the nature of your three selves, you can begin to look at how you can strengthen your connection and relationship with each of these parts of yourself. In addition to integrating these parts of your psyche in ways that are more beneficial to you and the people around you, it is also important to understand how these components can work together in positive, synergistic ways.

The key thing to keep reminding yourself—the main mantra in this material—is that your conscious self is your center. It is the place where each of us feels most at home in our own skin, so to speak.

As has been said several times already, when you are intentionally embodying your conscious self, you are in a state of inner congruence: your three selves come into alignment. By holding an attitude of loving acceptance toward yourself, you are more able to hear the voice of your superconscious self and to work effectively to heal any disintegrated parts of your subconscious self. You have the possibility of operating in life in a way that is sourceful: where your behaviors and actions are congruent with the qualities of your conscious and superconscious selves.

Here is a review of some key points about the conscious self that were covered previously:

- Your conscious self enables you to shift into observer mode. When in this mode, you are able to take an internal step back from your automatic responses and behaviors and witness your thoughts, feelings, reactions, and emotions instead of unconsciously and reactively acting them out.

- It is from the conscious self that you make the choice to fully inhabit the present moment, to be awake and responsible.

- A key to developing a sense of unshakable presence is to recognize the conscious self, your innate sense of awareness, as the place to stand and the ground of being from which to come into all aspects of your life. Everything in life occurs within the space of your conscious awareness.

- Functioning at a high level of fulfillment in life requires operating from your conscious self and expressing the qualities of that part of yourself, such as respect and responsibility, on a consistent basis. When you do this, your inner being is congruent with your outer expression and you are being sourceful.

- Your conscious self is the center of your being. When you are awake and present, it is the central axis around which everything else in your life rotates and is oriented toward. Your conscious self is the central place from which you can observe and engage with all four areas of human expression (mind, body, emotions, and spirit).

A summary of some of the key points about each of the three selves is included in the following two diagrams. These diagrams are not meant to be a complete representation of everything that the three selves encompass, but rather to give a concise, overall sense of their main qualities. They can also be downloaded from The Highest Ground Institute's website.

Overview of the Three Selves

Crown Center

- The Composer
- Creates the Symphony
- Purpose / Mission / Vision
- Life-Learning / Karma

Key Attitudes: Oneness & Inclusion
Fundamental Drives: Expansion, Union, Illumination
Signature State: Stillness, Nonattachment

Superconscious Self

Heart Center

- The Conductor
- Synthesizing Center of Context & Content
- The Witness / The Observer
- Where We Make Choices From, Including the Choice to be Present in the Moment
- Where We Manage Our Lives, Balance Our Priorities, Actively Receptive to the Superconscious Self

Key Attitudes: You and Me, Respect, Loving Kindness
Fundamental Drives: To Become More Present
Signature State: Steadfastness, Calmness

Conscious Self

Solar Plexus Center

- The Orchestra / The Players
- Subpersonalities
- Feminine & Masculine Aspects
- The Ego & Negative Ego Aspect
- Lower Self & Lower Self Behaviors
- The Library of Our Past
- Automatic Processes

Moving from Disintegrated to Integrated:

Key Attitudes: You or Me to You and Me
Fundamental Drives: Surviving to Thriving
Signature States: Reactive to Equilibrium

Subconscious Self

Aspects of the Three Selves

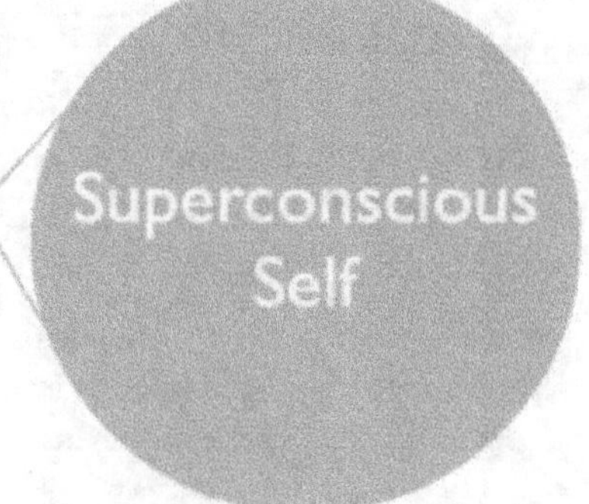

We Are One

- Essence, Presence
- Intuition, Integrity
- Will, Conscience
- Purpose, Vision, Calling
- Unconditional Love & Acceptance
- Benevolence, Service
- Muse

I'm OK, You're OK

- In the Present, Loving Awareness
- Responsibility, Respect, Nonadversarial
- Authentic Self, I Am
- Self-Actualization, Personal Power, Being at Choice, At Cause
- Creating Context, Purpose & Meaning, Responsibility
- Conscious Creation of Future States
- Equilibrium, Detachment, Neutrality, Sufficiency
- Synthesis & Insight, Wisdom & Understanding
- Love & Self-Acceptance, Passion & Commitment
- Forgiveness & Healing, Compassion, Empathy, Gratitude

Disintegrated Aspects -
I'm Not OK, You're Not OK

- Reactive and Fear / Shame / Anger Driven
- Victim / Rescuer / Persecutor
- Egocentric, Self-Defensive, Adversarial
- Life Happening To Me, Not Caused By Me
- Negative Rumination of Past & Future
- Wounds, Trauma, Pain Body
- Inner Critic / Negative Ego
- Harmful Habits, Beliefs, Patterns
- Contracted / Constrictive / Blocked Body, Mind, Emotions
- Suppressed, Repressed, Shadow
- Addictive / Compulsive
- Scarcity

Strengthening Your Connection
with Your Superconscious Self

Being Contemplative

One of the most effective ways of strengthening your connection with, and receptivity to, your superconscious self is by practicing being contemplative. In Western culture, being contemplative is usually thought of as being deep in thought.

There is another definition of being contemplative that applies here, which is quieting the mind sufficiently so that you can do both of the following at the same time:

a) Be lovingly present, fully grounded in the here-and-now, with what is occurring in your conscious reality. This is presence with a small *p*.

b) Be actively and lovingly receptive to the voice of intuition and the urgings of your superconscious self and your soul or spirit. This is known as Presence with a capital *P*.

Mystics regard contemplation in its purest form as gifts of moments of agape.[xii] This is when you experience flashes of unconditional, transcendent love and are present to your interconnection with the consciousness in all living things.

Being contemplative is a two-step process. Being mindful is about being present, whereas being contemplative begins with mindfulness and then incorporates actively listening for the voice of your superconscious self, which is also the conduit for your soul and spirit. This is the voice of your inner guidance, or intuition, and is qualitatively different from the other voices in your head.

You cannot be contemplative without being present in your conscious self, and practicing being contemplative also helps strengthen your connection with your conscious self. More about mindfulness is covered in the next section on the conscious self.

Contemplation begins in your calm, centered, conscious self. From the place of being the witness or observer, you can incorporate contemplative practices to help you develop your capacity for quieting the mind while in the midst of everyday distractions and chaos. Being contemplative is supportive in taking a heart-centered, loving, and compassionate approach to life. Contemplative practices have many benefits, including reducing stress, enhancing creativity, and granting a greater sense of purpose and meaning.

There are many different forms of contemplative practices, which appeal to different temperaments and to changing preferences. Some are done in silence, and some, such as participating in a drum circle, are done out loud. Some involve stillness and some involve movement. Some are solitary and some can be done in community. What all these practices have in common is that they are various ways of quieting the mind while being present and maintaining a loving, open receptivity to what is occurring both externally and internally.

The challenge is to find the practices that suit you and then find ways to incorporate them into your everyday life. It could be turning off all your devices for a period of time, taking a regular walk in nature, or having a meditation practice. It could be doing yoga or painting. The key is not so much the practice but how you approach it. With all the busyness of twenty-first-century life, carving out moments of inner quietness to be receptive to your higher impulses has never been more important.

The Center for Contemplative Mind in Society has created an illustration, The Tree of Contemplative Practices,[xiii] which gives examples of practices from many traditions. This illustration can be downloaded for free from their website.

Strengthening Your Connection with Your Conscious Self

Beyond Identity: Remembering Who You Really Are

A powerful way of centering yourself in who you are as a conscious self, rather than reactively operating from your subconscious self, is a practice that is called disidentification. When you get overly identified with the content of your life it narrows your sense and perception of who you are as a conscious being. Conversely, whatever content you can disidentify from gives you access to more of your personal power and agency.[xiv]

Your identity consists of everything you know about yourself. This includes your physical attributes, your gender identification, your race, how you were brought up, your history, your beliefs, and your values. It also includes your accomplishments, your personality type, the stories you tell about yourself, what others say about you, and so on. From your understanding of the three selves, you can extrapolate that how you've defined your identity is primarily a function of the content of your subconscious, especially your subpersonalities and personality traits.

It is a common mistake to think that the content of your life, your identity, is who you really are. Having an identity is not a bad thing: in fact, it's essential to feeling alive and having a rich and pleasurable experience of life. At the same time, it can limit you and obscure who you really are as a conscious being. In other words, you *have* an identity but you are *not* your identity.

Practicing disidentification creates the opportunity to recognize who you are: the self or the consciousness that is the space in which all the content of your life and reality occurs. At your essence, you're the point, or space, of awareness called "I am," the being that listens to all your various parts and chooses your way forward.

The following guidelines and meditation for practicing disidentification have been adapted from Will Parfitt, *The Elements of Psychosynthesis.* This in turn was influenced by the earlier work of Roberto Assagioli, who is the founder of Psychosynthesis.

> "We are dominated by everything with which our self becomes identified. We can dominate and control everything from which we disidentify ourselves." —Roberto Assagioli

Practicing Disidentification

- **Behavior Disidentification:** *"I have behaviors, but I am not my behaviors."* Keep disidentifying who you really are from your behaviors. For example, just because you might get annoyed or complain at times and act like an irritable jerk doesn't mean you *are* an irritable jerk. Your behaviors tend to be primarily a product of your subconscious self, which are driven by your emotions and needs. You *have* behaviors, but you are more than the sum of your behaviors.

- **Story Disidentification:** *"I have my story, but I am not my story."* Keep disidentifying who you really are from your story. Recognize that you have a story, or several stories, but you're more than your stories. You are a conscious self in the present moment, not a compilation of stories that are rooted in the past. Who you are is the space in which all your stories occur.

- **Body Disidentification:** *"I have a body, but I am not my body."* Keep disidentifying who you really are from your body. Remember that you have a body, which is a wonderful vehicle through which your consciousness expresses itself, but you are more than your body. This applies to your gender and race as well. Whatever degree of masculine or feminine energy you embody is just another filter through which your consciousness is expressed.

- **Mind and Thought Disidentification:** *"I have a mind and thoughts, but I am not my mind or my thoughts."* Keep disidentifying who you really are from your thoughts. You have a mind, but you're more than your mind—that collection of thoughts, attitudes, beliefs, and memories. Who you really are is the observer, or witness, and using your will you can direct your thoughts, make sense of them, and choose how to use them. Who you are is the awareness that is listening to your thoughts.

- **Emotional Disidentification:** *"I have emotions, but I am not my emotions."* Keep disidentifying who you really are from your emotions. Your emotions are like water in the ocean: constantly flowing and ever changing. Who you are is the steady, calm space in which your emotions occur. You are the awareness that holds and makes sense of your emotions. You have emotions, but you are more than your emotions.

- **Disidentification Toward Others:** *"Others are more than their behaviors, story, appearance, attitudes, or feelings."* Just as you can practice disidentification toward yourself, you can practice it toward others to remember who they really are. This leads to a greater sense of compassion, both for them and for yourself. When you relate to another person as a conscious being, not just to the content of their identity or their behaviors, your relationships undergo a qualitative shift for the better. In stressful circumstances it can be particularly challenging, as well as extremely helpful, to remember that a person *has* their behaviors: their behaviors are not who they are.

Disidentification Meditation

The purpose of this meditation is to assist you in connecting more powerfully with your conscious self, which is beyond all your identification with and attachment to the content of your life.

Part of this meditation is done with eyes closed and part with eyes open if it is necessary for you to follow the affirmations. You will find it helpful to have a copy of these affirmations to glance at as you are doing this meditation.

1. Sit in a comfortable position for meditating. Close your eyes and take a few slow, deep breaths. Focus on relaxing and letting go of any tensions from the day. Practice breathing slowly until you feel yourself drop into a meditative state. It can be helpful to sound a tone, such as *om*, a few times as you exhale.

Once you are in a meditative state, imagine a glowing ball of light in the center of your chest, radiating light like a sun. When that is established, do the following:

- As you *inhale,* imagine a pillar of light moving upward from your heart center and out the top of your head toward the sky.

- As you *exhale,* imagine that energy looping back down through your head and heart and out the bottoms of your feet into the earth.

- As you *inhale,* imagine that energy looping back up through your feet to your heart and out the top of your head.

- *Exhale and inhale* a few more times until you feel that the flow is looping smoothly, and then once again center the glowing ball of light in your heart.

2. Say the following affirmations to yourself, preferably out loud:

- I have a body, but I am not my body.

- I have a physical appearance, but I am not my physical appearance.

- I have a gender, but I am more than my gender.

- My body is the vehicle through which my consciousness is expressed.

- My body has physical sensations, but I am more than my sensations.

- My body may be constantly changing states in terms of well-being, but who I am as a being is constant.

- I am grateful for the vehicle of my body, which allows me to experience life, but it is only a vehicle.

- I honor my body and take care of it, but it is not my true self.

- I have a body and sensations, but I am not my body or sensations.

Take a few moments to breathe with your eyes closed, imagining the glowing ball of light in your heart.

3. Say the following affirmations to yourself:

- I have emotions, but I am not my emotions.

- My emotions are like water, always flowing and changing. My emotions and feelings are transient, but who I am as a being is constant.

- I experience expansive emotions, such as joy, but I am more than my joy.

- I experience contracted emotions, such as fear, but I am not my fear.

- I am learning to work constructively and positively with all my emotions, but I am more than my emotions.

- I have feelings and emotions, but I am not my feelings or emotions.

Take a few moments to breathe with your eyes closed, imagining the glowing ball of light in your heart.

4. Say the following affirmations to yourself:

- I have a mind, but I am not my mind.

- I have thoughts, but I am more than my thoughts.

- I am the being who is listening to my thoughts.

- I have a choice about what thoughts I am going to empower.

- I am the stillness beyond all the noise going on in my head.

- I am grateful for my mind and all the knowledge it has about my inner and outer worlds.

- I have a mind and thoughts, but I am not my mind or my thoughts.

Take a few moments to breathe with your eyes closed, imagining the glowing ball of light in your heart.

5. Say the following affirmations clearly and slowly to yourself:

- I recognize that who I am is the witness to, the observer of, all that is occurring in my reality.

- I consciously use my will to author my responses to that reality.

- I recognize that I am a conscious self.

- I recognize that I am a spark of consciousness.

- I am loving awareness.

- I am a conscious self.

Take a few moments to breathe with your eyes closed, imagining the glowing ball of light in your heart. When you are ready, open your eyes.

Cultivating Mindfulness and
Being in Observer Mode

A fundamental skill needed for being emotionally intelligent is developing your ability to move from a state of waking sleep, unconsciously and automatically driven by your subconscious self, to a state of being awake and in observer mode in your conscious self. An effective way to do this is by practicing mindfulness, which is a state of active, open attention to the present. Mindfulness is a way of being, not just a technique, although there are many practices that assist in cultivating it.

Various terms to describe mindfulness are *awareness, attention, focus, presence, being present,* and *being awake.* Mindfulness is an attentive awareness of the reality of things, without judgment, in the present moment. Spiritual teacher Jon Kabat-Zinn defines mindfulness as paying attention in a particular way: "On purpose, in the present moment and nonjudgmentally" and "doing it as though your life depends upon it," because it does. Being present isn't about arriving somewhere else: it is about revealing what is already here, right now.

One important quality of the conscious self that hasn't been mentioned yet is that of neutrality. Being in observer mode is about being present to what is, rather than being caught up in judgmental, negative thoughts about what is occurring and wishing it were different. It is a grounded, steady, open, accepting, nondefensive stance toward life. Only by being fully present in a nonjudgmental way can you practice discernment while listening for the voice of your intuition. This allows for a more accurate and empowering reading of what is occurring in your reality. It enables you to make positive choices about your responses, which leads to more positive outcomes.

Being centered in the conscious self is a choice to be mindful on purpose. Unless you cultivate the ability to hold yourself steady in your conscious self by being mindful and practicing metacognition, you will forever be at the effect of your emotional reactions and disempowering negative thoughts. These thoughts have a tendency to be all over the place, causing worry about the future, which is known as *catastrophizing*, and decision-making that is reactive and based on the past.

It can be hard to distinguish between your thoughts and what your authentic experience is. Like most people, you probably have had plenty of training and practice in thinking. But unless you have been intentional about pursuing your spiritual growth, you probably haven't received very much training or practice in present-moment awareness. Remember that spirituality is about who you are as a conscious being and how you are showing up in the present.

When you are not being mindful, you are in a state of waking sleep, hindered in your ability to experience your body or emotions and unable to fully own your reactions. Being in a state of waking sleep means you are being unobservant and missing a lot of what is occurring. It severely hampers you in terms of being at choice about how you might respond to your reality, because you aren't fully present to it.

Being present grants you the possibility of embracing your experience of your mind, body, emotions, and spirit, and maintaining a healthy relationship between your inner and outer worlds. The present moment is the only place where it is possible to "experience your experience." People who are spiritually aware know that you must show up and be present to experience "Presence." You can never be any closer to God or spirit than you already are in this moment. Remember that there is no place to go: there is only waking up.

Resonance Breathing Technique

The resonance breathing technique is a powerful somatic exercise for calming the mind and body to enhance the experience of being present in the moment. In the spiritual realm, breath is the primary symbol of your life force (called prana in Eastern traditions) and the way in which you breathe can help you regulate that life force.

In addition to breathing oxygen in and carbon dioxide out, breathing has a very large influence on the state of your autonomic nervous system. It is good to pay attention to this because the autonomic nervous system, as its name implies, is responsible for automatically governing all the subconscious aspects of your mind and body. Autonomic function underlies virtually every aspect of your health and well-being.

Your autonomic nervous system consists of two principal branches. The sympathetic branch is responsible for activating or accelerating and the parasympathetic branch is responsible for deactivating or decelerating. They work much like a gas pedal and a brake in a car.

As it turns out, the rate of breathing strongly influences sympathetic function. More rapid, shallow breathing results in a stronger sympathetic, or accelerating, effect. Depth of breathing strongly influences parasympathetic function and for this reason slower, deeper breaths result in a stronger decelerating effect. Consequently, there is a breathing frequency and depth at which both the sympathetic and parasympathetic effects are equal, thus facilitating autonomic nervous system balance.

Interestingly, this is also the moment when heart and lung functions are in exact harmony and the cardiopulmonary system is operating at peak effectiveness and efficiency. Resonance breathing, which is also sometimes known as coherent breathing, facilitates autonomic system balance and cardiopulmonary resonance.

The practice of resonance breathing is very simple. It requires that you breathe at a specific rhythm and at a comfortable depth. This rhythm is one breath per about 12 seconds for a total of five breaths a minute. This is about three times slower than typical adult breathing, and for this reason resonance breathing might seem a little foreign or awkward at first.

You can do this exercise on your own with your eyes closed, taking relaxed, comfortably deep breaths while you count to six on the inhale and six on the exhale. Try to do it for at least 5 minutes. Even better, there is a free app for resonance breathing available that is simply called "The Breathing App." It was developed by Eddie Stern and Deepak Chopra and allows you to set the length of your breathing with different tones. Stern's description of resonance breathing was very useful in creating the preceding explanation of why and how this process works. The app has a timer, so you can choose the length of your resonance breathing session. This is also a very powerful exercise to do in a group.

Summary of Self-Empowerment Tools and Practices

Be contemplative and listen for the voice of your intuition.

Disidentify from your emotions, thoughts, feelings,
and behaviors to remember who you really are.

Cultivate mindfulness to strengthen your connection with your conscious self
and your ability to be in observer mode.

Use breathing techniques to lower stress, become present and
regain equilibrium.

CHAPTER 7
INTEGRATING YOUR
SUBCONSCIOUS SELF

Overview

Working effectively with the three selves requires adopting a loving attitude toward all the parts of who you are. This attitude is expressed as self-love, self-respect, self-advocacy, self-acceptance, and self-trust. It sounds simple, but as humans we tend to be masters at unconsciously putting ourselves down or feeling unworthy, making this one of the things we struggle with the most. We are unable to heal the parts of ourselves that we are not willing to accept. An attitude of self-love is critical for successfully working with your subconscious self.

Imagine that you have an internal emotional scale with angst, sadness, and depression on one end and peace, happiness, and joy on the other. Then imagine that you have an emotional setpoint on this scale.[xv] This is your emotional default position, or how you generally feel when you're calm, centered, and in equilibrium. You can raise this default emotional setpoint by working with and healing any disintegrated parts of your subconscious. As your subconscious becomes more integrated, you expand your experience of equilibrium, peace, and happiness. Your internal emotional setpoint will rise, and you will naturally feel more joyful over time.

Self-Parenting

An important job of the conscious self is to hold the subconscious self in a loving space and provide guidance, much like a parent would with their child. This looks like being in your calm, mature conscious self and adopting a kinder, more loving attitude toward your reactive, rambunctious subconscious self. This is known as self-parenting and is an important skill in working effectively with your subconscious self.

To untangle, heal, and integrate dysfunctional parts, the subconscious self *needs* the awareness and maturity of the conscious self to make sense of what is going on and to give guidance as to what to do about it. Self-parenting is when you become, in effect, your own coach or mentor in order to heal and repair the damage caused by feeling wounded at earlier stages of your life. It is reminding yourself, "I'm OK," "I am competent and able," "I can discover my underlying genuine needs and fulfill them," and "I am a whole and complete human being."

Self-parenting can only be done from the conscious self, looking compassionately at the reactions, patterns, and wounds of the subconscious self to discover any unmet needs you may have and then determine how to meet them. It involves being an advocate for yourself in the present. Respecting yourself and having healthy boundaries about being respected in current-time situations can help to heal the pain of not being respected in the past. Often we will keep repeating a dysfunctional dynamic until we discover ways of healing and shifting it, that is, until we feel that we have finally mastered the dynamic and gained our freedom.

Often the best way to self-parent your subconscious is to meet it where it's at. This means being in a meditative state, which more closely matches the dreamlike quality of the subconscious. One way to do this is by working with your inner child through meditation, imagination, and internal conversations to provide in current time those things that were missing earlier in your life.

How would you treat yourself if you were a child that you loved and whose needs and desires you respected? Using your imagination, you can advocate for your inner child and give them the guidance, care, compassion, and environment that was missing when you were a child. Being kind to yourself, rather than self-punishing, is a hallmark of self-parenting and self-advocacy.

Taking on the above-the-line role of being a coach to yourself is a form of self-parenting. For example, whenever you're feeling anxious about something, you can coach yourself to stop and reflect more deeply on what your fear is about. Remind yourself to breathe or do any other mindfulness practices that work for you. Reassure yourself that you're not going to die, be shamed, or be punished if you fail or make a mistake. Remind yourself that you are grown up and are competent, willing, and able to handle whatever happens. Coach yourself back off whatever ledge you were on and into a calmer, more centered state.

If you want to parent yourself through your anxiety and create greater freedom from feeling nervous, then you could meditate on what part of yourself is so panicked—such as your inner child, who got humiliated in front of the class—and let that part know that they can relax. Let them know that you, as a mature conscious self, can handle this. Then imagine yourself stepping in and handling the situation.

In addition to facilitating the healing of old wounds and releasing the pain of unmet needs, the practice of self-parenting can replace negative parenting patterns you absorbed as a child. Doing this sort of self-parenting, coaching, and inner child work can raise your inner emotional setpoint to a more joyful, less reactive place.

Recognizing Messages from Your Subconscious Self

Getting past your fears about your subconscious self helps you to hear, sort out, and respond to the messages it is trying to send you. Due to a lack of understanding, people often have an adversarial, fear-driven relationship with their subconscious self. A major assumption that is made is that it's like Pandora's box: a dark and scary place that should never be opened. In and of itself, the subconscious is not dangerous. What is dangerous is ignoring it and what it is trying to tell you. Unfortunately, you might do this automatically if you're unconsciously afraid of what you'll find there if you look too closely.

It is easy to be worried that these seemingly damaged or dysfunctional and disintegrated parts of your subconscious are secretly who you really. A lot of unconscious effort can go into actively denying them and their messages, which ends up with you feeling bad and possibly questioning your sanity. In actuality, the voices of your subconscious self often point to parts of your psyche that need attention and healing.

The following is an approach to working with the voices in your head that can foster a sense of feeling grounded and sane:

1. Listen to the voices in your head, especially the more strident ones, *without* acting out what they are saying.

2. Tune into the energy of each voice and see if you can discern what part of your subconscious it belongs to.

3. Recognize that these voices are often distorted, reactive, or hurt parts of your subconscious, which are desperately trying to tell you about something that needs attention.

4. Listen more deeply, beyond the actual words these voices are saying, to see if you can discern the underlying, unfulfilled needs from which they arise.

You will have to use your discernment to figure out what part is speaking to you and get beyond or underneath the words to examine and understand *why* they are saying what they are saying. Then you can gain the necessary insight into how to best work with this part. It requires being in observer or witness mode to sort through and distinguishing between the various voices in your head. For example, the voice of intuition is different from the voice of the inner critic, the voice of the inner child is different from that of the muse, and so on.

There is a qualitative difference between the energy of the voices coming from your conscious or superconscious selves and those of your negative ego. These voices of the lower-self aspect of your subconscious, which is often referred to as your monkey mind, are more punitive, limiting, reactive, and defensive. The voices of the conscious or superconscious self are more accepting, respectful, and calmer. They are also more thoughtful, positive, expansive, and hopeful.

Practicing Forgiveness

Healing and integrating the disintegrated aspects of your subconscious self requires that you understand and practice self-forgiveness. Forgiveness is the opposite of punishment or retribution. Forgiving someone means you have granted them a pardon for a past mistake or failure and have absolved them of the harm they have done to you or someone else. Implicit in the act of forgiveness is the assumption that you have intentionally ceased directing negative thoughts toward yourself or the person who has wronged you.

Forgiveness is an extremely powerful tool for getting free of the past, releasing built-up constrictive emotions, and healing old wounds. It is an intentional and voluntary process of changing your feelings and attitudes regarding an offense that has occurred. Forgiveness is a conscious intention to let go of any fear-driven, defensive needs of the negative ego that might be activated: the desire for revenge or retribution, the need to control or to look better than, the impulse to be right and have others be wrong, wanting to be superior to, and so on. In other words, you have ceased blaming others or yourself, and they (and you) are now pardoned.

When someone wrongs you, they are directing negative energy at you. This negative energy usually originates from their negative ego and a sense of being wounded that they are unconsciously trying to compensate for or off-load onto you. Forgiveness is a way for you to release that negative energy, rather than absorbing it permanently. It is a purposeful way to get free of negative thoughts that are self-blaming or blaming toward others, as well as any emotions that are attached to feeling like a victim, such as self-pity or self-loathing. As a result, the constrictive feelings you have been harboring, such as resentment, pain, hatred, or anger, can be processed and begin to recede.

There is a common misunderstanding that we need to forgive for the sake of the person who has wronged us. We feel conflicted and resist forgiving because we don't want them to reap the benefit of our largesse, and yet we judge ourselves as petty and terrible if we don't. However, forgiveness benefits the forgiver as much or more than it benefits the one who is being forgiven. This is because carrying around repressed feelings of hurt, anger, hatred, and resentment are toxic to your mind, body, heart, and soul. Although these emotions are legitimate responses to having your needs disregarded and your boundaries violated, if they are left unprocessed they can stagnant.

Forgiveness is something that you do first and foremost for yourself. In other words, do it for your sake, not theirs. Do it because you refuse to continue being psychically bonded with the perpetrator. Refuse to allow them to continue to take up valuable space in your psyche, and refuse to stay stuck in the past, constantly reliving old, painful experiences and feeling not OK inside. Will they receive benefit from your forgiveness? Yes, certainly. Do they deserve it? Maybe. Maybe not. But that is incidental to the benefit that you give yourself.

Another reason to practice forgiveness is that you don't want to stay stuck in self-pity and feeling like a victim. Demand of yourself that you take back your power. Own any part that you may have played in the transgression and make amends if necessary. Refuse to accept any shame they have tried to cause or off-load onto you. Using your imagination, give it back to them. That is their shame, not yours. Whatever they did may have been denigrating, but you can refuse to let it be a commentary on who you are or your self-worth. It is much more about them than it is about you.

Humans have a basic need for self-acceptance and for acceptance by others, and this requires being forgiving toward yourself, forgiving others, and being forgiven. Forgiveness is an essential component of growth, and it requires that you learn how to acknowledge your missteps and inadvertent offenses, experience remorse about them, and make amends. Being able to forgive yourself for any past mistakes or perceived failures is essential to your growth and to healing any old wounds you might be carrying in your subconscious.

Feeling genuine remorse empowers you to learn from your mistakes and failures and strive to be and act in ways that are more consistent with your best self.

Remorse is an uncomfortable but empowering emotion. It is directly connected to your conscience, which is an aspect of your superconscious self. It is one of the emotions that is most closely connected to your sense of self.

The purpose of remorse is to nudge you toward more fully expressing your best self through your thoughts and actions. By allowing yourself to experience remorse, you can discover your motivation to make amends. In the process, you will discover that you are forgivable and that it is okay to make mistakes and to fail sometimes.

Guilt and remorse are two emotions that often get confused; the distinction between them gets collapsed. For the purpose of self-empowerment, it is useful to draw a clear demarcation between them. Guilt is more of a negative mindset than a real emotion. We mostly use guilt to punish ourselves and others, to manipulate people into doing what we want by guilt-tripping them, and to avoid having to take responsibility by dramatizing how terrible we feel about what we did. In other words, guilt has us operate below the line.

Genuine remorse, on the other hand, has us be more of our authentic selves and operate above the line. A useful self-empowerment guideline to follow is to allow yourself to fully experience remorse while refusing to indulge in guilt. Remorse works; guilt doesn't.

A successful forgiveness process usually requires that you forgive yourself first before you grant forgiveness to anyone else. Take responsibility for the situation in any way you can. Forgive yourself and stop beating yourself up for any part that you played in that situation. Accept that whatever happened is now part of your life story, and see how you can integrate the experience and use it to strengthen your sense of self and your resilience. Integrate any life lessons you can take from what has occurred.

Forgiving another person is not the same as condoning, forgetting, or excusing the transgression. This would require failing to notice, or being in denial about, the offensiveness of the behavior. Having your boundaries violated can be painful, even traumatizing. You will need to recognize and own your pain in order to process and heal it and move on.

It can be helpful to remember to disidentify the transgressor from their hurtful behavior. Remind yourself that they have an inner being, even if they aren't acting like it, and that their behavior is not who they really are. Dig deeper to see if you can imagine and understand what sort of woundedness they may have that is driving their defensive losing behaviors. What pain might they be carrying around, most likely unconsciously, that would motive them to act so reprehensibly? Chances are they are unconsciously attempting to off-load some of their pain and shame by lashing out and hurting others.

Often perpetrators have been abused in some way. The parent we haven't forgiven might have been acting out unresolved pain from their childhood, and it ended up getting all over us. According to the National Association of Adult Survivors of Child Abuse, fully 50 percent of all children in the United States have experienced some form of abuse.[xvi] Many suffer from toxic stress and will continue to when they become adults. This does not excuse anyone's behavior or absolve them from responsibility, but it can be helpful to understand the dynamic that is driving abusers to act out in inappropriate ways. This is summed up by the expression, "Hurt people will hurt people."

Asking, "What happened to them?" can be more empowering than thinking, "How dare they act this way!" A helpful way to gain access your compassion is to imagine how awful it must feel like to be in their shoes. How terrible, how not OK, would you have to feel inside to treat others that badly? It might even be possible for you to feel some gratitude that you aren't in their shoes. Bottom line: you may not be able to forgive someone for *what* they did, but you may be able to forgive them for *why* they did it.

> "When another person makes you suffer, it is because he suffers deeply within himself, and his suffering is spilling over. He does not need punishment; he needs help. That's the message he is sending."
> —Thich Nhat Hanh

Centering Breath Technique

This is a quick breathing exercise for recentering and creating calm while in the midst of intensity. It is especially helpful as first aid, when you are feeling in disequilibrium or are in a state of reactivation, having a flare-up of thoughts, emotions, or physical sensations from the past, and are in the grasp of a lower-self subpersonality.

Do this breathing technique with your eyes closed, if possible, but you can keep your eyes open if the circumstances require it. This was adapted from an exercise by Ilene Val-Essen, from her book on conscious parenting called *Bring Out the Best in Your Child and Your Self.*

Once you have practiced this a few times, you can use it anywhere, even when you are in the middle of a conversation. You can adapt this exercise in any way that works for you. The important thing is to develop a practice of deep breathing that you can easily default to whenever a strong emotion or reaction threatens to knock you off-balance and has you tensing up.

As with resonance breathing, try to inhale and exhale slowly to a count of six. If that seems too difficult, then make an adjustment so that you are taking comfortable, deep breaths.

1. Take a deep slow breath, filling your diaphragm with air. As you inhale, imagine a ball of energy made up of golden-yellow light in your solar plexus. Exhale slowly.

2. As you breathe in again, imagine raising that ball of energy up to your heart, where it joins and swirls with a beautiful shade of green light. Exhale.

3. Breathing in again, imagine raising that yellow-and-green swirling ball of energy up to the top half of your head, where it joins with violet light. Exhale.

4. As you inhale, imagine the energies combining.

5. As you exhale, imagine sending this calm, loving energy from your brow out into the room. Or you can send this energy out through your throat if you need help in calming your speaking.

6. Repeat as required.

Inner Child Meditation

The most effective way to approach working with any of your stage-of-life subpersonalities is in a meditative state. When you are in a meditative state, you are much closer in vibration to your subconscious self. In other words, you are meeting your subconscious in the dreamlike state where it exists, rather than trying to shout at it from your conscious self.

Following is an outline of a version of how to do an inner child meditation, which will give you a sense of how to do this on your own. This meditation can be adapted to any of the other stage-of-life subpersonalities. For example, by simply changing a few words you can easily use this outline to work with your inner adolescent. This meditation has been adapted from one developed by Gordon Davidson, the author of *Joyful Evolution*.

When doing any sort of meditative work with your subpersonalities, remember that it is *essential* to maintain a loving, nonjudgmental attitude, with everything about you and every part of you fully accepted.

There are several benefits to be gained from working with your inner child. By using your imagination to provide your inner child with what was missing in your childhood, you allow your subconscious self to experience having these needs fulfilled in current time. This can be profoundly healing. In fact, it can be so effortlessly healing as to be startling.

Another benefit of connecting with your inner child is that it can help you to open to your experience of self-love and self-compassion. And finally, your inner child is a font of playfulness, creativity, curiosity, and joy. When your inner child is happy, these qualities will expand in your life. When your inner child is joyful because it's needs are being met and you are sending love toward it, your emotional setpoint raises and you naturally feel happier and more joyful as you go about your daily life.

In this meditation, two things will happen:

1. You are going to create a point of love and light in your heart center.

2. While holding that loving space, you will connect with your inner child to see what you can learn about them. You will be getting to know your inner child and creating a more real relationship with them.

1. Prepare to meditate:

- Take a few moments to prepare to meditate by slowing down and calming down. This includes finding a comfortable seated position, perhaps imagining a cord pulling up from the top of your spine, up and out the top of your head to align your spine. Or you can do this meditation laying down.

- Closing your eyes and take a few slow, comfortably deep breaths. Imagine your body relaxing and your emotions and your thoughts calming. Do this for a few moments until you feel yourself start to slip into a meditative state. An easy way to slip into a meditative state is by starting with 5 minutes of resonance breathing.

- Then, if it feels right, dedicate this meditation to your higher self, your soul, or some other higher power.

2. Focus on your heart and open your heart center:

- Imagine feeling a radiant sun of light and love centered in your heart. Feel that love and that warmth flowing within.

- Feel that love rising upward through yourself, through your superconscious self and up to your soul, that great being above you, which is radiating its love and its light and its purpose to you all the time. Just be—loving and appreciating what your soul is contributing to you.

- And now invite your soul and your superconscious self to bring some of their love to you, to radiate that love into your heart. Feel the love of your soul and your superconscious self blending with that love you have as the conscious self, the love that is already there in your heart. Imagine the love blending, harmonizing, and strengthening there.

- Allow that united love to flow toward your subconscious self in your solar plexus center. Radiate that love from your soul, your superconscious self, and your heart to your subconscious—loving and appreciating and thanking it for all that it is doing to help you and support you.

- Invite your subconscious to bring its love into your heart. See if you can feel an increase of love in your heart.

- Now feel the love of all four—your conscious self, your superconscious self, your soul, and your subconscious, all loving and appreciating one another, blending, and synergizing their energies in your heart.

- Recalling your intention to have a loving, co-creative relationship with your subconscious, radiate your love once again to your subconscious, in its own world in your solar plexus center.

- Let your subconscious know that wonderful things that are now possible, as you begin to work together to fulfill your soul's intention.

- Open a beautiful, neutral, and loving space that you are holding for your subconscious in your solar plexus, letting it know that any part of it is welcome—that everything will be loved and accepted, and everything is allowed.

3. Approach your inner child lovingly and respectfully:

- Imagine who you were when you were three to five years old. Imagine this living being within you. If they appear to be older or younger, then that is fine: just go with whatever occurs for you. If it helps, then you can remember a picture of yourself at that age, but keep in mind that you are connecting to a living being, not just a static picture.

- Once you have an image of them in your mind, approach your inner child with great sensitivity and respect. See if you can experience fully loving your inner child. If it helps, then you can imagine that this is your very own child. How would you feel about this little person if they were yours?

- In fact, they are your child: they belong fully and completely to you. When they aren't connected to you, to your conscious self, they are an orphan—lost and adrift. See if you can open your heart to your compassion for this being, and see if you can imagine your conscious self as the true parent of this child.

- How does your inner child appear to you? What is their condition? What are they wearing? What is their emotional state?

- You can invite your inner child to come sit with you, perhaps on your knee. If they are willing, then you might want to embrace your inner child. Just hold them and rest together in the love that you are radiating toward them. Allow yourself to feel the unconditional love that they have for you. Allow yourself to feel the relief and the comfort of the love that you have for one another, if that is so for you.

- Take some time to appreciate the innate qualities of this unique child: what are the qualities they possess? Recognize their bravery, their innocence, their curiosity, their playfulness, and their creativity. Really be present to the truth of their innate worthiness, their beauty, and the gift that they are to you and to the world.

4. Dialogue with your inner child:

- Offer them your support and your love. Whatever state your inner child appears to be in, whether they are happy or unhappy, invite them to say what they need from you. What would your inner child like that would truly be beneficial and helpful? Wait and see how they respond.

- See if you can provide whatever your inner child is asking of you. Use your imagination to give them what they need. In other words, what were you missing at that time in your life that you can now give yourself?

- If you want, you can ask your inner child if they like the environment where they are or if they would like something to change. You can invite your inner child to share with you how they would like things to be in their environment. What would make them feel happy? And then using your imagination, provide the kind of environment they would love to be in.

- You can engage with your inner child in any way that they might invite you to engage with them. Do they want to play in some way? Do they want to show you something or take you somewhere?

- If they have questions about your relationship with them, such as why they haven't heard from you before, then you can explain that to your inner child if you like. Take a few minutes now to be with them and see what unfolds.

- Whenever you feel ready, you can ask your inner child if there is a gift or anything they would like to show you or give you—anything that might be helpful in your journey and for your unfoldment. Just allow them to respond. You can simply go with whatever unfolds.

- And now dialogue with your inner child about your gift, and see what you can learn or understand about it.

5. Close your meditation:

- When you feel ready, let your inner child know that this is the beginning of a relationship that you would like to continue, if that is true for you. Share your love for and appreciation of your inner child. Thank them for being willing to connect with you.

- Whenever you feel ready, say goodbye to your inner child for the moment. You're not really leaving, but your focus is moving away. And if you would like to stay with your inner child somewhat longer, then that's fine too. Whenever you are ready, open your eyes.

Summary of Self-Empowerment Tools and Practices

Use self-parenting to heal and integrate the disintegrated aspects of your subconscious self.

Identify and manage the various voices in your head and don't buy into the voice of your inner critic.

Practice forgiveness to heal wounds and get free of your past.

Experience remorse and end guilt.

Use meditation to work with your stage-of-life subpersonalities, such as your inner child and inner adolescent.

PART III

CULTIVATING YOUR INNER ADULT

Building Blocks of Emotional Literacy

Understanding needs and how they drive behavior.

Understanding the nature of the ego and the negative ego, and what happens when developmental needs don't get met.

Core Competencies of Emotional Intelligence

Being able to successfully identify unmet authentic needs and address their fulfillment in constructive ways.

Being able to recognize the difference between functional and dysfunctional needs: the genuine, legitimate needs of your psyche versus the defensive needs of your negative ego.

Being able to recognize when you are in the grip of your negative ego and being able to relax its hold when you are.

Being able to work successfully with your subconscious self to identify and heal areas of arrested development, dismantle defense mechanisms, and integrate lower-self behaviors.

CHAPTER 8
RECOGNIZING
AUTHENTIC NEEDS

Understanding Needs

Needs motivate us. They drive everything in our lives—our thoughts, emotions, and behaviors—but we're mostly oblivious to them. If you want to know what is motivating you or others in a situation, then you need to find out what everyone's underlying needs are. Understanding needs is an essential element of being able to deal constructively with conflict.

> "Human needs theorists argue that one of the primary causes of protracted or intractable conflict is people's unyielding drive to meet their unmet needs on the individual, group, and societal level."
> —Sandra Marker, *Unmet Human Needs*

Human survival depends upon getting any number of essential needs met. These include not only the physical basics of food, water, clothing, and shelter, but also include many nonphysical things needed for healthy human growth and development. These are needs in all four areas of human expression: mental, physical, emotional, and spiritual.

There are many opinions as to what constitutes fundamental human needs. For the purposes of this material, the following list of needs has been extended beyond those needs essential to basic survival to include needs essential for attaining and maintaining exceptional well-being. These authentic needs include, but are not limited to, the following:

1. *Physiological survival*: Clean air, clean water, nourishing food, shelter, clothing, and safety from predators or disease.

2. *Security:* Emotional security, which includes loyalty, commitment, trust, and kindness. Freedom from the threat of physical, emotional, or psychological harm, including protection from abuse or violence of any kind, and peace of mind.

3. *Love and connection:* Partnership, honesty, support, mutual benefit, belonging, affiliation, peer acceptance, friendship, and family or intimate ties.

4. *Self-esteem:* Feeling respected, being self-respecting and self-advocating, feeling validated by and valuable to others. Having worth, being seen as deserving, getting acknowledged for your work or contribution, making a difference.

5. *Freedom and autonomy:* Being free of domination or unwanted obligations. Having enough psychic space, possessing the ability to make choices, experiencing acceptance of your uniqueness.

6. *Inner peace and spiritual connection:* Presence, inspiration, meaning, truth, selflessness, and self-transcendence. Experiencing unity and purpose, serving a cause that is larger than yourself.

Sometimes needs and interests are terms that can be used interchangeably, especially if you are concerned with what is in everyone's best interests or mutual benefit. Finding out what someone's interests are in a situation can often help to reveal their needs.

Understanding and listening for people's deeper needs is necessary for resolving and transforming conflict. This is a lesson from conflict resolution practitioners, who have learned to understand and apply needs theory. Conflict is a normal part of life; it can have either constructive or destructive effects, depending upon how you approach it. Engaging with conflict from a perspective of human needs gives you a profoundly transformative tool with which to navigate challenging circumstances in your personal life.

Needs are deeper than wants. Needs are specific things you must have to thrive, such as food, safety, love, respect, and freedom. In contrast, our wants are an expression of our desire nature, and our want lists can seem endless. Often, wants are driven by an unconscious sense of scarcity and can never really be fulfilled. Whenever there is discord, addressing the authentic needs of individuals first, rather than trying to fulfill everyone's wants, will help tremendously in cutting through the drama of a situation.

Needs are the basis of human rights; associated with every human right is a fundamental human need. When your needs have been disrespected, you will most likely feel that your boundaries have been violated, and possibly your very sense of self. Abuse in any area of life is a gross violation of boundaries and fundamental needs, especially the needs for physical and emotional safety and security, peace of mind, and validation of self-worth.

Unacknowledged needs can wreak havoc with your life. You can pierce through a lot of chaos, confusion, anger, and disagreement to get to the heart of an issue by focusing on the needs you and others have. Identifying the authentic, legitimate needs of everyone involved in a situation can illuminate the way forward, turning a difficult, conflicted, or otherwise dysfunctional situation into a more compassionate and mutually satisfying one.

There is another type of needs that people often confuse with authentic needs. These are the defensive needs of the negative ego, such as being right, controlling others, being better than, looking good, having more than, and so on. These needs are usually driven by fear and a desire for self-protection that is unhelpful, irrational, and out of sync with what is occurring. They are synonymous with lower-self payoffs and instant gratification, and they are usually profoundly adversarial in nature.

These defensive needs are often referred to as having a hidden agenda, and attempting to get them met is often done by some form of manipulation. When people try to get their defensive needs met, they often end up acting in selfish, oppositional, denigrating, and hurtful ways. These defensive needs of the negative ego and their interim payoffs are covered in detail in chapter 10. For now, suffice it to say that in terms of creating healthy, mutually beneficial outcomes, the defensive needs of the negative ego are not the needs to validate or give energy to.

The Needs of the Psyche

Another way to look at authentic needs is through the lens of the three selves. Each of the three selves has specific, genuine needs that are unique to that self. These needs are holistic in nature and include the genuine needs of all four areas of human expression (mind, body, emotions, and spirit). Having these holistic needs met creates the possibility for the full actualization of being human. Self-actualization is the attainment of your full potential and capabilities while also reaching emotional and spiritual maturity. It is what occurs when your legitimate needs in all four areas are consistently met over an extended period.

All the needs of the three selves exist simultaneously, all the time. You have a built-in sensing ability that allows you to instantly feel when you have needs that aren't being met in any of the four areas of human expression, even if you might not be able to clearly articulate what they are. When your needs for physical survival are not being met, they will tend to displace a lot of other needs in terms of where you put your attention. If you have studied Maslow's hierarchy of needs, then you will be familiar with this concept.

Happiness is a function of having the needs of your three selves met. Joy is a function of having these needs met in ways that are consistent with the qualities of your conscious self. Joy is the innate resonance, or vibratory field, of your conscious and superconscious selves. The experience of joy and its related emotions, such as inspiration, passion, gratefulness, and excitement, is part of your internal navigation system, which can help guide you on your purpose line of unfoldment and self-actualization.

The greatest needs of your three selves are to be loved, to be loving, and to experience connection and unity. These needs imbue your life with meaning and purpose. When you navigate through life getting your needs met while expressing the qualities of your conscious self—respect, responsibility, compassion, integrity, and authenticity—you have greater access to the innate joy of your inner being. Your experience of joy expands when you are being sourceful and are operating in ways that are consistent with fulfilling your purpose as a conscious being. This is when your fundamental needs are met in ways that are based on mutual respect and benefit and you are embodying loving kindness in action.

Other ways of infusing your life with joy include creating win-win dynamics and infinite, positive, and expanding games with the people around you while revealing more of your authentic self and radiating loving awareness. Attempting to get your needs met by control, domination, or by any other negative ego mode of operating will not bring you joy. You might experience a lot of energy and excitement, but you will not experience profound joy.

> "Happiness is a how, not a what. A talent, not an object."
> —Hermann Hesse

Looking at your authentic needs through the lens of the three selves can give you a greater sense of what each self is all about and how to work with each one effectively. This is particularly useful in understanding how arrested emotional and ego development happens and what to do about it. More about this will be covered in the next chapter.

Getting these genuine needs met in childhood is essential for healthy ego development. Unmet needs are always a source of pain, and often they are a source of toxic shame. When you have needs that haven't been met and there is arrested ego development, you will need to heal the wounds this created in your psyche by utilizing techniques such as inner child work.

One of the hallmarks of becoming an adult is taking full responsibility for recognizing and meeting your authentic needs. We all know what it is like to be around people who are needy. They are busy avoiding responsibility for meeting their own needs and dramatizing their bad feelings about not having them met. Instead of taking responsibility for meeting their needs, they expect everyone around them to be responsible for making them feel better inside. You feel like you are losing when you interact with them because you can never give them enough love, attention, acknowledgment, or material things to fill the empty void they have within.

Each of us also knows what it feels like whenever we slide into being needy and expect others to fill the empty void, or lack, within us. The way out of this trap is to first look within yourself to see how you can meet your own needs. For example, if you feel that love is lacking in your life, then a good place to start in getting that need met is with self-love, rather than expecting or demanding more from the people around you. There are many ways that you could go about doing this.

You could, for example, work on recognizing and releasing any fears that you have about love, such as the fear of abandonment, so that you can more fully experience the love that is already present. You could become less judgmental and more accepting. You could strengthen your relationship with your conscious self and rest in the boundless love that your soul and spirit have for you. You could adopt the attitudes of "I am completely (100 percent) responsible for the quality of my relationships," and "If I want more love in my life, then I will be more loving." And you could be self-generating by putting the effort into finding ways to express being more loving toward others, such as being of service and creating moments of genuine encounter and connection.

The following diagram shows some of the most important, legitimates needs of each of the three selves. Internalizing the understanding of these needs will empower you to recognize when you have authentic needs that are not being met and to clearly identify what these needs are. This is particularly useful when you are in disequilibrium or conflict. When you know what your unmet needs are, you can own them and make assertive requests about getting them met. These requests are not just ones that you make of others: they can also be requests that you make of yourself.

Remember that no one is trained from an early age to recognize their needs and that this is a universal area of weakness. In fact, your upbringing has most likely been working against you. For example, women have been enculturated to be caretakers and put their own needs last or deny them completely, while men have been taught to deny their emotional needs to avoid being seen as weak.

It will take practice to become accomplished at recognizing your own real needs and the legitimate needs of others. You may find it helpful to download and display this diagram so that you can refer to it frequently as you are learning to distinguish genuine needs.

Needs of the Three Selves

Ultimate Need: For Union or Oneness

- **Truth**, revelation of life's mysteries
- **Beauty**, reverence, gratitude
- **Harmony**, calmness, peace, silence
- **Expansion**, growth, illumination
- **Interconnection**, unity, inclusivity

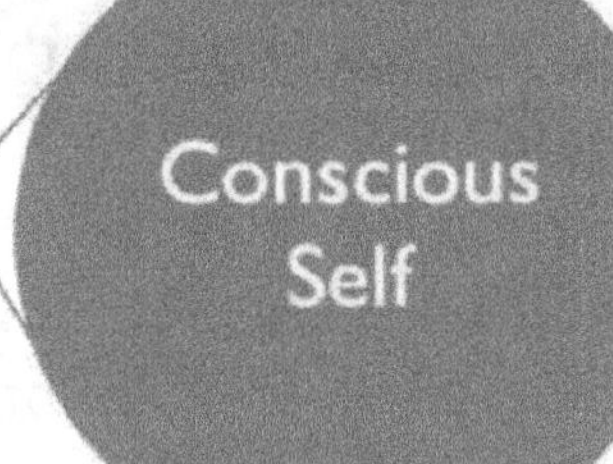

Ultimate Need: To Be Loving and Respectful

- **Integrity**, self-worth, value, integration, fulfillment
- **Self-awareness**, self-reflection, to be present to experience
- **Self-respect**, mutual respect, dignity, partnership, co-creation
- **Vocation**, purpose, contribution, achievement
- **Congruency**, loving dynamic with superconscious and subconscious selves (self-advocacy, self-parenting, self-care)
- **Alignment**, spiritual awareness, inspiration, context, meaning

Ultimate Need: To Be Loved and Respected

- **A non-toxic environment**, sustenance, shelter, healthy physical growth, warmth, rest, movement
- **Security and safety**, physical, emotional, financial peace of mind
- **Protection**, safety from harm and abuse
- **Structure**, order, consistency, stability
- **Connection**, kindness, affection, loving touch, closeness, healthy attachment
- **Respect**, be treated with consideration
- **Understanding**, be heard, known, trusted
- **Stimulation**, opportunities to grow, learn and discover

Working with Needs Constructively

An important emotional intelligence skill is taking a needs-based approach to understanding people's motivations when dealing with disagreement. Turning around a problematic situation is almost always about identifying the genuine needs of the individuals involved and then discerning how these needs can best be met.

There are two main options you have when facing a stressful situation or breakdown:

1. The most common, knee-jerk reaction to dealing with conflict is to ignore the underlying, unacknowledged needs and get caught up in and engaged with the surface drama. This aggressive approach tends to escalate whatever the problem is. Another knee-jerk reaction is to take a more passive approach. This also involves ignoring the underlying, unacknowledged needs while trying to smooth things over and pretend that everything feels OK, when in fact it feels very much not OK. This is referred to as stepping over what isn't working.

2. The second option is that you can step back and look a bit deeper to identify what the legitimate needs of each person are that are driving the situation, so that you can figure out how to meet these needs. This may require having a conversation, when things have calmed down sufficiently, about everyone's needs and then problem-solving together about how to best meet them. This healthy, or functional, approach requires being in observer mode and using self-reflection and assertive communication.

A key to dealing with conflict constructively is being able to recognize that there are legitimate needs involved and then identifying what they are. Following are some useful questions you could ask yourself or the other person:

- What would it take for me, or for you, to feel better about whatever is occurring?

- What needs do I have that aren't being met in this current situation?

- Are these authentic needs or are they defensive needs of my negative ego? Do I have a hidden agenda that I need to acknowledge?

- Is there something that you need from me that you aren't getting?

- Is this need something that I can fulfill for myself? In other words, how can I take care of myself so that I feel good about myself and the situation and not wait for others to take care of me?

- Is there a request I could make that would be mutually beneficial?

- Is there some way that I can model the fulfillment of this need in how I am being? For example, being respectful while requesting respect, being a good listener when requesting to be heard, and so on.

Once you have a sense of what the legitimate needs are, you can address and problem-solve what it would take to have these needs met. This requires being responsible for taking the necessary actions for meeting both your own needs and the needs of others, and for making assertive, nonblaming statements and requests as necessary.

"People often feel shame or guilt when they slip into lower-self behavior. While it's true that this behavior is ineffective and can be harmful, it helps to see it in context. If we look beneath everything else—the feelings of fear, helplessness, and stress—we discover the true root of our behavior: a legitimate need. It might be the need for peace and order or the need to feel in control or simply the need to take care of practical matters. There's nothing bad about having a legitimate need; we just have to find a more effective way to meet it."
—Ilene Val-Essen, *The Quality Parenting Program*

Examples of Dysfunctional versus Functional Approaches

The following are some examples of taking a dysfunctional versus a functional approach to dealing with underlying needs. You may or may not relate to these specific examples, but the intent is for you to gain more insight into how you tend to approach any area of conflict in your life, and what you might do instead that would be more beneficial.

1. A man is in what he thought was a committed relationship, but his partner is acting as if they might leave him to be with someone else, causing him to be upset and fearful. There are a couple of directions in which he could choose to go.

   a) He lets his fear drive his behavior. He becomes suspicious, turns passive-aggressive, and starts making snide comments. He gets angry and picks fights over inconsequential things. Or he takes a more passive approach, avoiding asking for an honest discussion for fear of making things worse. He withdraws, which only drives his partner further away. This increases his feelings of helplessness and upset.

b) He takes the time to get centered and calm, and lets his partner know that he needs to have an open and honest conversation about where they stand and what their feelings are for him. He asks if they have any needs that are not being met. He requests some reassurance as to what they're committed to in the relationship. He asserts what his needs are.

If he doesn't speak up, then the discomfort between them will likely increase. There will probably be all sorts of miscommunications because they are not discussing what they really need in order to thrive together. Unless he speaks up, he will not give his partner a forum in which they might reveal that they are feeling neglected, or lacking in fun and excitement in their life, or whatever else it is that they might need.

By both partners being honest about their needs and making assertive requests about getting them met, they can determine how to be in an appropriate, healthy dynamic with each other. Perhaps they can resolve how things are between them or perhaps not. Either way, honest, openhearted communication about what they each need is the best and kindest way to negotiate moving forward, whether it ends up with them being together or apart.

2. Every time a female manager brings up an idea or responds to a question from her boss, he interrupts and talks over her. She feels publicly shamed by his treatment of her when this happens in front of her team.

a) When she doesn't say what she needs in terms of being respected and being heard because what she says has worth, this treatment continues. It undermines her authority with her direct reports, causes a breakdown in teamwork, and results in lost productivity. She ends up intensely disliking her boss and his management style. This lowers office morale and contributes to an unpleasant, even toxic, workplace.

b) She gets coaching from one of their peers about how to approach her boss in a respectful and an assertive way. She expresses to her boss that she feels there is a communication breakdown that is having negative consequences in their workplace. She affirms her commitment to the success of the team and to treating her boss with respect and requests that he do the same for her, including not interrupting when she is speaking. This leads to creating some workable agreements between them about interacting with each other in a more respectful way.

3. A college student returns home with her first semester's grades in her hand. Her B average is not good enough for her mother, who launches into a tirade about all that she and her husband have done for her and how her daughter isn't taking full advantage of the opportunities she has been given. In this situation the mother is being a persecutor and is playing a losing game at her daughter. If the daughter allows herself to stay stuck in feeling victimized by her mother, then she will get caught up in this losing game.

a) The young woman swallows her anger at being so disregarded and put down by her parent. She ends up either doubting her inherent worth or rebelling in righteous wrath and indignation by dropping out of college. She rejects her mother and disrespects her going forward. This puts her right onto the drama triangle, entangled in playing losing games with her mother.

b) The daughter draws upon her calm, centered self and sits down with her mother when they are both feeling more in equilibrium. She lets her mother know how hard she is working in college, and how much she appreciates her support. She lets her know how hurtful it is to her to have her hard work be so discounted. She tells her mother how much she loves her and how essential mutual respect is in determining whether they are able to spend family time together.

Setting Healthy Boundaries

Boundaries allow you to separate who you are, and what you think and feel, from the thoughts and feelings of others. They also allow you to make clear demarcations in terms of your needs about how you are being treated. Healthy boundaries are always aligned with your higher principles and help strengthen your character. They are essential for maintaining your personal integrity and well-being, and for having respectful, loving relationships.

Maintaining healthy boundaries is an expression of responsibility, self-love, self-respect, and self-care. Taking a stand for your self-worth and saying no to something that makes you feel bad is an act of self-love. It is difficult to be a victim or a martyr while simultaneously having good boundaries.

Healthy personal boundaries are the physical, emotional, mental, or psychological limits you establish to protect yourself (and others) from being negated, dominated, judged, manipulated, abused, used, or violated. They can also be boundaries that you set with yourself to discourage self-harming or self-sabotaging behaviors, and to encourage healthy behaviors that are consistent with self-love. Setting healthy boundaries is a topic that will come up several times in this material and is an important skill to develop with regard to meeting your authentic needs.

Boundaries are generally thought of as limits that you need to set with others, but perhaps the most important boundaries are ones that you set with yourself. When you set inner boundaries that are consistent with your higher principles, these boundaries become the guardrails for your behavior and the field of play in which you allow yourself to operate.

If you are committed to being respectful and modeling mutual respect, then you will need to set any number of boundaries with yourself about how you communicate and interact with others. Giving others the benefit of the doubt before jumping to conclusions about their motives, not allowing yourself to make others wrong, and not using disrespectful language: these are all examples of inner boundaries. When you are willing to set boundaries with yourself and abide by them, it gives you tremendous authority to request, and to expect, having healthy boundaries in your relationships with others.

Sometimes it may seem that your own needs are in conflict with one another. For example, you may need to balance your need for closeness and intimacy with your need for autonomy, which can lead to confusion about where to draw the line. At other times, it is crystal clear about what is a hard stop or a deal breaker in terms of where your boundary is.

Although we often don't realize it, we each have a highly refined (if unconscious) radar for knowing when we have a need that isn't being met. We feel not OK inside and experience disequilibrium. Recognizing when you are feeling not OK, when you have needs that aren't being met, and then being assertive about setting and maintaining good boundaries are skills that need to be cultivated. Although you may be someone who finds it easy to set healthy boundaries, many people don't even realize they need to until they feel negatively impacted or violated in some way, oftentimes repeatedly.

Just as we weren't taught how to recognize authentic needs, we have not been taught to understand boundaries. When you are learning to set healthy boundaries, it can feel awkward and as though you are sometimes missing the mark. It is a helpful practice to allow that to be okay with you. As with any skill worth developing, it requires practice, patience, and persistence.

One way to look at your integrity is that it is a condition of being unified and sound, a state of being whole and undivided. When your needs are getting met, you have the possibility of experiencing being whole and standing in your integrity as a human being. At these times you are in a state of stasis, meaning you feel OK and are in a period of calmness, peace, and equilibrium. It is easy to extrapolate that having the interests and needs of the individuals in a society met, and their boundaries respected, can help to bring about peace, calmness, and equilibrium on a societal level.

The principle of mutual respect, which includes self-respect, requires that you speak up about what doesn't work for you and doesn't feel OK. For example, you might feel not OK when you are experiencing an invasion of your personal space, or are being harangued, overridden, gossiped about, or left out of communications or plans.

When you feel uncomfortable in a situation, it will serve you to first check in with your conscious self and inquire as to what the legitimate need is that is not being met or is being disrespected and messed with. This helps you to discern what your healthy boundaries might be in this situation. You can then make assertive requests for your needs to be respected and met, and for certain boundaries to be honored. Assertive requests include respect for both parties, and they replace complaining, having emotional blow-ups, or making the other person wrong.

Boundaries with other people often need to be negotiated, and these boundaries can be flexible and change over time as people and situations evolve. This is especially true for people you want to maintain close and trusting relationships with.

When boundaries are created arbitrarily from a place of reactivity, they can easily become punishing. Setting unilateral, unacknowledged boundaries without making assertive requests and negotiating agreements can seem controlling and be confusing and hurtful to the people you are close to. Establishing healthy boundaries requires being responsible for the impact those boundaries will make on others and being respectful of their feelings and values, as well as your own.

If you discover that your needs aren't going to be met or your boundaries honored, then at least you have a clearer understanding of the field of play. You can make the necessary adjustments in terms of how you want to engage. You can reorient your relationship to this person, including distancing yourself from them if that is necessary for your well-being.

Mutual respect means that you also pay attention to when other people's boundaries are being trampled upon. When you overstep another person's boundaries, however unintentionally, then making amends is the respectful thing to do. You can do this by genuinely apologizing and offering understanding or empathy for their discomfort. You can affirm your respect for them and have them clarify their needs so you can be more respectful in the future. You both have the right to have your legitimate needs and boundaries respected.

Summary of Self-Empowerment Tools and Practices

Recognize and advocate for your authentic needs, and make assertive requests about getting them met.

Identify and address the deeper legitimate needs that are driving a conflict or upset.

Set healthy boundaries and show respect for other people's boundaries.

CHAPTER 9
EGO DEVELOPMENT

Overview

In this chapter and the next, we will be delving more deeply into understanding the subconscious self and exploring an important component of it, the subconscious mind and how it operates. We will be focusing on the nature of the ego, the stages of ego development, and what happens when there is arrested ego development. We will be drawing a clear contrast between how the healthy ego and the negative ego operate, as this can illuminate the underlying causes of negativity and dysfunction when they occur.

What Is the Subconscious Mind?

The subconscious mind is a huge repository and a recording device for all the information, learning, stimuli, and responses of your life. This function is habitual and, once programmed, plays the same information and responses again and again. The subconscious mind includes everything you have ever learned and all your memories. Following is a quick review of subpersonalities, particularly the composite and lower-self ones, as these are important aspects of understanding how the subconscious mind and the ego operate.

As was covered earlier, the subconscious mind stores much of this information in composite subpersonalities. You can think of these composite subpersonalities as roles or personas. For example, everything you might know about gardening is stored in your inner gardener: where to put specific plants based on their needs for soil and light, how to use a rake, when to water, and so on. This subpersonality arises only when you are in gardening mode. Then that role emerges with all its stored knowledge to assist you.

Inhabiting a composite subpersonality is similar to being an actor who adopts a role in a play. The difference is that we don't need to study for the role, we take on its mantle unconsciously and effortlessly. Like a character in a play, a subpersonality role has certain beliefs, attitudes, body postures, and emotional states that go along with it. When a subpersonality is integrated, it seamlessly gives up to the conscious self any information that is needed to navigate the current situation.

Often these experiences get stored as behavior programs and they shape 95 percent or more of our experiences.[xvii] Following are some examples of these behavior programs:

- Learned abilities, including thought processes and muscle memory.

- Positive and negative proclivities and patterns, and good and bad habits and routines.

- Ingrained preferences.

- Pet peeves, buttons, and triggers that cause irrational reactions.

- Addictions, compulsions, and obsessions.

One of the brilliant aspects of the subconscious mind is that it remembers everything you've ever learned how to do. Every time you drive a car or ride a bike, you can thank your subconscious mind that you don't have to learn how to do it all over again. You *want* the subconscious mind to be running the show a lot of the time because you would never be able to master all the vast number of life's details without it. When your subconscious is working well, it is invisible and is operating in the background of your life.

However, it is essential to become awake to those times when we're letting our subconscious run the show when it shouldn't be. Usually this occurs when we are under stress and a wounded part of our subconscious tries to take over. This is a lower-self personality, and it is being run by our negative ego. Lower-self characters are reactive and defensive, and are usually fueled by old and unresolved feelings of fear, pain, anger, shame, and guilt. When this occurs, we need to wake up and make choices from our conscious self instead of from our negative thoughts or emotional reactions.

> "Since subconscious programs operate without the necessity of observation and control by the conscious mind, we are completely unaware that our subconscious minds are making our everyday decisions. Our lives are essentially a printout of our subconscious programs, behaviors that were fundamentally acquired from others (our parents, family, and community) before we were six years old. As psychologists recognize, a majority of these developmental programs are limiting and disempowering."
> —Bruce Lipton, *The Biology of Belief*

What Is the Ego?

Overview

Your ego is the content-processing capacity of your subconscious mind. It helps you make sense of life and all its minutiae. If you didn't have an ego, then you wouldn't be able to process and differentiate between the thousands of pieces of information coming at you at any given moment.[xviii] The ego processes and differentiates everything in your life so that you can navigate and survive. When you look out at the world, you don't have to think, "That is a chair. That is the color blue. That is a person. That is grass." These are things that you just know. Your ego is a marvelous creation, and it is your ally.

There is a very big difference between the healthy ego and the negative ego, which is what we will be exploring in this chapter and the next. The purpose of your healthy, or mature, ego is to deliver up the necessary information to your conscious self; the job of your conscious self is to provide the context and purpose for that information and make intelligent choices about what to do with it. The negative ego is what happens when people are in a state of waking sleep, when there is no one present, awake, and at home to make these executive decisions.

The ego has gotten a bad name and is blamed as the source of many people's difficulties and downfalls. For those seeking spiritual growth, there is often talk about killing off the ego and getting rid of it altogether. There is also a form of denial that is known as the spiritual bypass, where you try to transcend your ego. When someone is said to have a big ego, it's a derogatory remark, often meaning that they're overconfident, too ambitious, domineering, or arrogant. What is really going on is that they don't have healthy ego development. They are operating below the line in an unconscious way, and their negative ego is running the show.

When a person's ego has developed in a healthy manner, they will embody any number of positive qualities, including a stable sense of self-awareness and self-worth and a healthy degree of assertiveness, self-confidence, and self-motivation. People with a healthy ego tend to have the ability to set and achieve their goals. They are resilient and have the desire and competence to overcome difficulties and excel in their endeavors. This is because having a healthy ego goes hand in hand with a strong connection to one's authentic self, which allows for a positive sense of self-esteem and self-worth.

When you're present in your conscious self and your ego is functioning in a healthy manner, your ego seems to disappear. The healthy ego becomes invisible because it's just doing its rightful, productive job. When, however, you have unresolved wounds and trauma from the past and you have disconnected from your sense of authentic self, your ego has a hard time functioning in a healthy, invisible manner.

When you are carrying unprocessed fear or pain that you are repressing, this creates the conditions in which your negative ego gets engaged. It can take over your experience of being alive and leave you feeling upset and reactive. Being caught in the grasp of your negative ego is to your psyche what the inflammatory response is to your body when that response becomes chronic. It can have toxic, even fatal, consequences. As you will see when we get to the chapter on unconscious losing games and dynamics, your negative ego is also what is driving the roles of the drama triangle in your life.

Stages of Healthy Ego Development

Just as human beings evolve physically, mentally, and emotionally throughout the developmental stages of life, so too does the ego. Developmental stages are the commonly agreed upon phases of growing up. We will be focusing on the childhood categories of infant, young child, older child, and adolescent. In addition to these, there are the more mature developmental stages of young adult, adult, and elder.

In each developmental stage there are predominant needs that must be fulfilled for healthy ego development to occur. The healthy ego gets formed when the needs of your subconscious self are met on a consistent basis as you're growing up. These needs were covered in the previous chapter under the needs of the subconscious self, and include being loved and respected, feeling safe and secure, and so on.

It's essential to your well-being and your sense of fulfillment that you have a strong, healthy, well-functioning, and mature ego. But don't panic if, as a child, you had needs that didn't get met. You are not alone: virtually no one escaped childhood completely unscathed. There is no such thing as a perfect parent, and even if you were fortunate enough to have loving, well-intentioned parents, it is pretty much impossible for any parent to be able to fulfill every single one of their child's needs at every moment of their lives.

Everyone is served by learning, at some point in their development, to reparent themselves in order to heal any wounds they have from unmet needs in childhood. Whatever unmet needs you have can become the grist for the mill—the raw material for you to work with—that is necessary for your personal growth and development. You don't need to feel like a victim of your life and upbringing. By owning and accepting whatever has occurred and adopting the attitude that there is value you can create from whatever you have experienced, you can take back your power and agency.

Remember that it *is* possible to do the inner work of clearing up old wounds and defense structures and integrating these parts of your psyche. Everyone must learn, to some degree, to become their own healer if they want to be internally emancipated and have a mature, healthy ego. This process of healing begins with strengthening your connection with your conscious self and holding a loving and accepting attitude toward your subconscious.

From ages two to six the predominant brainwave in children is theta, which is the same brain wave as deep meditation or hypnosis. During this period, children have what can be described as a spongelike brain. This theta brain wave state of early childhood allows the subconscious mind to be in maximum absorption mode. During this time, very little energy is given to maintaining filters of discernment or evaluation.

Everything that occurred in early childhood, all the impressions, reactions, opinions, and emotions, went into our brains as fact and truth. When we were young, we learned literally *everything* the adults and older children around us said and did. And we learned all of it as the truth about reality, the way that things really are and need to be, regardless of how dysfunctional the dynamics were. This is what is known as imprinting or conditioning.

Perhaps one reason for this lack of filters is that for children to survive and avoid constantly putting themselves in mortal danger, they need to absorb a vast amount of information very quickly. For whatever reason, during this period there's a great potential for things to go awry, especially when parental or other authority figures make negative comments or are abusive in any way. All this gets embedded in our psyche as self-perpetuating facts or truths about the world, who we are, and our worthiness.

"Given the precision of this behavior-recording system, imagine the consequences of having your parents say you are a 'stupid child,' you 'do not deserve things,' will 'never amount to anything,' 'never should have been born,' or are a 'sickly, weak' person. When unthinking or uncaring parents pass on those messages to their young children, they are no doubt oblivious to the fact that such comments are downloaded into the subconscious memory as absolute 'facts' just as surely as bits and bytes are downloaded to the hard drive of your desktop computer.

"During early development, the child's consciousness has not yet evolved enough to critically assess that those parental pronouncements were only verbal barbs and not necessarily true characterizations of 'self.' Once programmed into the subconscious mind, however, these verbal abuses become defined as 'truths' that unconsciously shape the behavior and potential of the child through life." —Bruce Lipton, *The Biology of Belief*

The following chart illustrates the main developmental stages in children. The predominant brain waves for each developmental stage[xix] are also included. This helps to illuminate why the imprinting, conditioning, or programming of your subconscious mind was so powerful when you were very young.

Developmental Stage	Healthy Ego Development	Predominant Brain Wave
Infant (preverbal, birth to age 2)	Am I getting enough? (Safety, security and survival, love, and respect)	Delta (sleep)
Younger child (2 to 6 years)	Same as above	Theta (meditation, hypnosis)
Older child (6 to 12 years)	Same as above	Alpha (calm consciousness)
Adolescent (13 to 19 years)	Am I good enough? (Belonging, sense of value, affiliation, and image of self)	Beta (active, focused consciousness) and gamma (intense focus and concentration during peak performance)

What Is Arrested Development?

When the phrase *arrested development* is used in this material, we are referring to a combination of psychological and emotional factors that can hold a person back from acting in an emotionally mature way. Even though the term *arrested development* is currently not widely used in psychology, this concept can be a very useful tool for self-empowerment. For example, when you recognize some area of your life in which arrested development is displayed, it can help you to discover what needs to be healed in yourself to be more functional, healthy, and happy.

Arrested development happens when a person's developmental needs as a child, adolescent, or even young adult don't get met, and the formation of a healthy subconscious self and ego get inhibited. This leads to the creation of unconscious coping mechanisms, defensive structures, and survival strategies that may initially work but eventually become self-limiting and even self-destructive. These unconscious dynamics are the basis of many of the losing games that are played in life. They also cause a person's connection to their authentic self, their inner being, to be undermined and weakened, resulting in a lack of self-worth and low self-esteem.

As we age, we often react in old, familiar ways to situations that unconsciously remind us of painful experiences in the past, making our responses out of tune with what is occurring in the present. Usually, these earlier times were painful because we had needs that didn't get met. Our subconscious carries the memory of this pain and the defense and coping mechanisms we put together to deal with it back then. When this happens, we feel triggered. Our reactivity seems to take us over, and it pulls us away from being fully present. It is as though we are involuntarily acting out an automatic, unconscious script. We get thrown into autopilot. There is very little possibility for creativity or true spontaneity unless our original, authentic needs are somehow acknowledged and met.

Whenever someone you are interacting with suddenly regresses and starts acting much younger than their biological age, it is a sign that arrested development is present in some form. This person is unconsciously reacting out of a wound that originally occurred when their developmental needs didn't get met. They have slipped into a state of unconscious waking sleep, are not fully present, and are disconnected from their inner adult, their conscious self. The reactivity of this old, unresolved pain causes them to retaliate, creating more pain. This cycle continues until the pain is somehow processed and the original wound is healed.

This same dynamic applies to each of us. When we start to think, feel, and act like we did when we were six, that is a clue we had an important need, or needs, that didn't get met then. Whenever our emotional or psychological development becomes arrested at a particular stage of life due to consistent wounding, we will need to use self-parenting to work with our inner child to heal that wound and clear its defensive residue. That said, the fastest way to consistently short-circuit a descent into the reactivity of arrested development is a commitment to self-advocacy, which means practicing being in observer mode and returning to your conscious self.

It is difficult to act like a responsible adult and make healthy choices when we are stuck in acting out reactive patterns from the past. Often people who grew up in an environment that was dysfunctional in some way are convinced it didn't have any impact on them, even when they have recurring patterns of unworkability in their lives and relationships. This is a common form of denial and points to the need to use self-acceptance and self-inquiry to look deeper. A key to success is remembering that we don't need to adopt a victim attitude about the past, which would be unhelpful and antithetical to healing. Instead, we can look for opportunities for inner emancipation.

Common Wounds of Developmental Stages

Following are some examples of common wounds at the various stages of development. In addition to the three childhood developmental stages, we are also including common wounds for the young adult and adult stages. There are many wounds that can occur at any of these stages, and bringing family dynamics to light can play a huge role in determining the cause of these wounds. These examples are meant to assist you in understanding and reflecting on what specific unmet needs you might have had while growing up.

Infancy through Toddlerhood

A primary wound that occurs during this time comes from being inadequately loved by parents, caregivers, or family members. This is especially traumatic if it is accompanied by feelings of being unsafe. One of the most common effects of arrested development during this stage is that children mistakenly accept the dysfunctional behavior, commentary, and emotional responses of their parents as normal. They begin to believe that these are acceptable ways to express love.

Unfortunately, yesterday's victims often become tomorrow's perpetrators. Many people who were victims of a physically abusive parent's anger, unless they have done the necessary healing work, can become abusers of their own children. If being yelled at and punished for their every misstep was how they were raised, then they may well have automatic, unconscious urges to treat their child and anyone else with whom they have an intimate relationship the same way. When they were children in the sponge-brain state, they internalized that this was a normal and acceptable way to express themselves.

Childhood

A common wound during childhood occurs when a parental figure is being derisive, negating, or punishing, or is psychologically attacking a child's sense of self by negatively comparing them with other children. A child whose parents are not supportive will get caught in these dynamics, and part of the child's subconscious becomes trapped at this stage of development, much like a fly that is caught in resin becomes amber.

A secondary wound can occur when other influential family members or caregivers don't advocate on the child's behalf by insisting that amends be made when harm is caused. They don't insist that parenting styles be changed to respect, validate, and rebuild the child's sense of self-worth. If this advocacy is not done and the child feels emotionally abandoned, then this leaves an indelible imprint of "I'm not getting enough of what I need to thrive," and the shame of "I must not be lovable or worthy of support."

The child's experience that all support has to be earned and that all love is conditional leads them to develop a well-fortified defense structure of suspicion, cynicism, hostility, and wary mistrust. The people that the child should have been able to count on for loving support have proven to be untrustworthy. This leaves the child floundering in a state of insecurity and uncertainty, feeling unworthy or less than others, not OK, and somehow wrong.

Adolescence

These wounds all hinge upon the degree of respect from, and acceptance and inclusion by, the adolescent's peer group. Arrested development at this stage is usually caused by wounds from peer disapproval, such as feeling excluded from a peer group or rejected by desired friends or the objects of adolescent passions. Any repetitive public shaming or embarrassment caused by teachers or coaches in front of contemporaries can leave deep scars. Disrespectful treatment by family members just compounds these wounds of feeling unworthy and not good enough to be accepted, liked, included, or befriended.

The prefrontal lobe, which is the center of conscious thought, reflection, and decision-making, is not fully developed until the mid-twenties. This can lead to a lot of black-and-white thinking and lack of impulse control in teens. Adolescents are in danger of crashing and burning very dramatically, especially because they are old enough and physically mature enough to be very capable of inflicting permanent damage on themselves or their perceived tormentors. This can have tragic results, as has been demonstrated by school shootings and the rate of teen suicides. The wounds of this stage of development can be lethal or permanently disabling to a person's sense of validity.

Young Adulthood

Failure, rejection, and embarrassment are major issues for young adults and provide ample opportunities for wounding. This can keep a person stuck in certain types of defense strategies that are typical for someone who is not yet a fully mature adult. One example of young adult pain is called failure to launch: a person struggling unsuccessfully with the transition into adulthood and being fully responsible for their own viability.

Sometimes an adolescent will experience a big success that they can't fully integrate, causing them to overidentify with that success. If they can't repeat or sustain that success as a young adult, then they might feel like a loser or a failure as they get older. Or a teenager might became obsessively fixated on a romantic interest and experience unrequited love. They might then feel inadequate to having an intimate love relationship as they mature into adulthood. Or they may be afraid of being hurt again and become love and intimacy avoidant.

Adulthood

A key thing to note in the following examples is that when we carry arrested development forward into adulthood, we are completely unconscious of it, and the hold of these dynamics is extremely powerful in shaping and driving our actions. These unconscious behavior patterns have devastating impacts on us, and on our relationships as adults.

The following two examples are of cisgender, heterosexual people, but there are corresponding dynamics in other gender orientations.

1. *What might it look like when an adult male has arrested development that began in his teen years?* Imagine that this person had an entangled relationship with an emotionally needy mother while growing up. She expected him to make her feel better inside, and constantly withheld her approval so that she could manipulate him into doing what she wanted. He felt abandoned by her emotionally and forced into being the adult in the relationship, which is known as *parentalizing* or *parentification*. This leads to him feeling resentful and getting stuck acting like a rebellious adolescent in his later love relationships.

Projecting his image of his mother onto his partner, this man gets caught up in being adversarial, dishonest, and punishing. Unless he does the necessary healing work, he will spend the rest of his life unconsciously trying to get back at his mother by mistreating his partner or whomever the current source of feminine energy is in his life.

Although he craves it, he is afraid of love and intimacy because his relationship with his mother was smothering. He might even go so far as to maintain a secret life, endlessly seducing women to win their approval and stroke his negative ego, in an unconscious attempt to fill the void inside caused by the lack of feminine approval growing up.

2. *What might childhood arrested development look like in an adult female?* Abandoned by her father after her parents' divorce when she was little, this woman has difficulty creating healthy intimate relationships with men. She unconsciously feels like she is undeserving of having a steady, nurturing male presence in her life. She experiences a sense of emptiness and feels hopeless and desperate about finding the love she yearns for.

This woman gets caught up in patterns of seeking love in all the wrong places. She becomes clinging and needy, hoping to find someone to fill the void within, which is caused by the lack of security and validation that the steady, nurturing, masculine adult presence a father would ideally have provided. She might act like she's a princess who needs to be rescued by a knight in shining armor or have other unrealistic expectations of an intimate partner.

Summary of Self-Empowerment Tools and Practices

Be able to recognize arrested development in yourself and others.

Use self-reflection and self-inquiry to identify any areas of wounding you are carrying from earlier developmental stages, when you had needs that weren't met.

Use self-reflection and self-inquiry to identify how any arrested development from these unmet needs might be adversely affecting your life now, and what sort of healing work you might need to do.

CHAPTER 10
GETTING FREE OF YOUR NEGATIVE EGO

What Is the Negative Ego?

Overview

The function of the negative ego is to try to ensure our survival by operating our internal navigational system when we're in a state of waking sleep. As previously mentioned, it is similar to the autopilot function in an airplane. When there's no one home, when we're operating from our subconscious self and are not in our conscious self—present, awake, and in the driver's seat—our ego becomes a negative ego. This is because it is being forced to make decisions for which it lacks the right type of awareness, intelligence, or discernment. When this happens, our behaviors become reactive, adversarial, survival-oriented, and fear-driven.

The bad news is that we all have a negative ego. This is another one of those parts of life where nobody gets a pass. But the good news is that it is entirely possible to relax the hold of your negative ego and create lasting value for yourself in the process. By using self-reflection as you read through the following material, you can empower yourself to recognize the specific and unique ways in which your negative ego works. It then becomes possible to disidentify from your negative ego and relax its hold. You *have* a negative ego, but you *are not* your negative ego.

The negative ego is labeled negative for good reasons. *Negativity* in this sense means denial or negation, disapproval, feeling bad, and feeling not OK. It also means denigration, disconnection, separation and isolation, failure, distrust, and disintegration. Remember, the voice of your negative ego is also called the voice of the inner critic, that voice in your head that is punishing and that puts you and others down. Your negative ego is the repository for all your negative thoughts, beliefs, and attitudes. These include the overly self-protective ones that generate bad feelings and cause disconnection from other people.

Your negative ego has its own energy, which is very distinct from the calm energy of your conscious self. When you slide into your negative ego, there is usually a visceral feeling in your body and a reactive, not OK emotional state that goes with it. The negative ego holds an attitude of pessimism, which is the tendency to automatically default to seeing the worst aspects of what is occurring and having a lack of hope about the future.

Whenever you catch yourself generating negativity and being adversarial, it is a sign that your negative ego is engaged, and you have a wound or some pain that you haven't yet healed and are unconsciously trying to avoid. It is worth considering the possibility that the vast majority of negativity in our daily lives may be caused by energy that we are generating from within, from our negative ego, rather than by what is being directed at us externally.

A common dynamic of fear is that when we are unconsciously fear-driven, we tend to manifest the very thing we are afraid of. Often it is our fear of negativity that has us default into being defensive, which creates and attracts more negativity. A basic rule of thumb is that the less you generate negativity, the less it will manifest around you. It *is* possible to end negativity in your personal life, and committing to doing so is one of the most empowering, beneficial stances you can possibly take.

Formation of the Negative Ego

The formation of the negative ego, which is also known as the false persona or false self, began when we were infants. When we were very young children with spongelike brains, we weren't equipped to observe or examine our own thoughts or those of the authority figures around us. We saw fear-driven grown-ups acting out the defensive needs of their negative egos, and we learned to emulate that way of operating. Being run by the negative ego is often something we absorbed from our parents or other authority figures and bought into because of our survival fears.

We unconsciously adopted the defense mechanisms that our negative ego either came up with or copied from others to protect us from the scary things in life. The wounds that occurred when we were growing up and did not get our developmental needs met created fertile ground for our negative ego to get engaged. Perhaps the most positive thing we can say about our negative ego is that we did manage to survive childhood.

When we were children, if our legitimate needs didn't get met on a consistent basis, then our connection to our conscious self got undermined and weakened.

Although it isn't possible to damage the conscious self or soul, it is possible to damage the mechanism by which we connect to our sense of self. Fortunately, this connection can be rebuilt and strengthened. In shamanic traditions this process of reconnection to our sense of self is referred to as soul retrieval and is critical to any healing journey.

Here is a description of how this disconnection typically happens and how the negative ego takes over. As children, when painful situations became too much to bear, we disconnected from our hearts and our sense of self so that we could cope with all the overwhelming, stressful feelings we couldn't process. We experienced toxic shame and began to feel not OK inside on a chronic basis, experiencing a loss of self-esteem and buying into the lie that we were not worthy. This trance of unworthiness displaced our natural sense of self: our sense of joy, wonder, confidence, and aliveness.

Eventually, because we felt helpless and didn't have the ability to process and heal these wounds, or the awareness to keep bringing ourselves back to our conscious self, we withdrew and gave away our agency to direct our lives to our ego. In the void this disconnection created, our ego became a negative ego when it started desperately trying to steer our lives and make decisions for which it isn't equipped. Trying to protect us from harm, our negative ego became very strident, telling us what it thought the right things to do were so that we could win in life.

Characteristics of the Negative Ego

When your negative ego is being allowed to run your life, it causes suffering for you and for the people around you. The negative ego is the part of you that thinks it's okay for relationship dynamics to be played in an "I win, you lose" format. Any win-lose game is always a lose-lose, or zero-sum, game, because if you win at someone else's expense, then you lose all or part of your relationship with them. This ends up being costly and painful. Win-win, or mutual benefit, is the only kind of interaction in which you can truly win without negative consequences.

A common experience reported by people who have had a near-death experience is one of going through a review of their lives, where the emphasis is on how they have treated other people. Repeatedly, this seems to be the most important thing: not what they accomplished but how well they treated others. This points to the true significance of our relationships and the severity of the costs to us when we let our negative ego run the show and generate losing games and dynamics with the people we care about.

The negative ego tends to be overly dramatic, treating most choices or circumstances as if they were a matter of life and death, which is very rarely the case. This life-and-death urgency is a fabrication to ensure its continued existence and power over us. In our fear-driven world, the negative ego is working overtime, setting up defensive strategies and amassing an unseemly amount of power over people's lives.

Another dynamic that can cause the negative ego to get engaged is deception. When we lie or overwise misrepresent ourselves, we create a gap between what is real and what we are pretending occurred, which creates an internal dissonance. This causes us to become defensive. We try to uphold and defend our version of the facts, while knowing full well that it is a fabrication. We become fearful of being found out. We have abdicated responsibility for getting our genuine needs met in an honest and forthright way. Whenever we are being defensive, self-protective, and trying to look good or be right, we are firmly in the grip of our negative ego.

Deception forces us into an adversarial stance, into what is referred to as *being in a state of perpetration*. There are a lot of feelings of being not OK that go along with this state. It pitches us onto the drama triangle, where our version of reality must win over what is true. We start playing losing games with others, using manipulation and gaslighting to keep them from discovering what is real. Usually these dynamics will escalate until, as so often happens, the truth eventually comes out. This causes feelings of betrayal, which can have a devastating impact on our relationships.

Another thing to keep in mind about the negative ego is that it never totally goes away. It is a mechanism that is always in the background, waiting to arise and hijack your reality. Like a missile defense system, your negative ego is hypervigilant about your survival. It can flare up and start sending off rockets when you are least prepared to handle it: when you are feeling stressed or vulnerable, when you feel as though you are failing in some way, or when you have been criticized or are being critical of yourself. Negative ego generated panic attacks can occur in the middle of the night when there is negativity or stress in your life that you have internalized.

The negative ego might not be very discerning or intelligent—it is subconscious, not conscious, after all—but it is relentlessly single-minded in its strategies and drive to win no matter what and avoid ever losing. It has an investment in having you win at these games because losing looks like death to it. While attempting to defend itself at all costs, your negative ego adopts a stance that is profoundly adversarial to your conscious self and your life. Left to its own devices, because it is so profoundly adversarial and fear-driven, your negative ego will ultimately come to see you and your conscious self as one of the enemies it needs to win against.

For all its dysfunction, your negative ego is trying in a convoluted way to protect you and help you survive. Ironically, however, because the negative ego has such a distorted sense of self-preservation, if you leave it in charge, then it will eventually kill off the quality of your relationships and your life. When the influence of the negative ego becomes extreme, it can cause people to become self-destructive, suicidal, homicidal, violent, or otherwise temporarily unhinged and out of touch with any positive sense of reality.

If you have seen *2001: A Space Odyssey,* then you can see echoes of this behavior in how the computer named HAL operates, ultimately killing off all the crew of the spaceship in a disastrous attempt to save itself. This dynamic also occurs in nature when an organism, instead of being in a symbiotic relationship with its host, destroys it and unwittingly kills itself in the process.

This dynamic is something that we each experience on a micro (or personal) level, but it is also something that we are collectively manifesting on a macro (or societal) level. As a whole, we are a level-zero (or zero-sum) civilization, meaning that our predominant expression is adversarial and below the line. Many of us are mesmerized, in a trance of arrogance and entitlement, thinking that we need to get the fear-driven defensive needs of our negative egos met (to be in control, to dominate, to be right, to get more, to be better than, and to avoid responsibility), and are playing this out in our relationships at a societal level and with the environment. We are certainly not operating in a conscious, symbiotic, co-creative relationship with our host, the earth.

We have come to a crisis point, in which having a sufficient number of people who are heart-centered, operating above the line, and have a fundamental attitude of you *and* me, is critical to our ability to survive and thrive. In other words, we must evolve to the next level of civilization, in which the predominant approach to each other and our planet is heart-centered, respectful, co-creative, and nonadversarial.

> "It is difficult for modern man to conceive of a time when there will be no racial, national or separative religious consciousness present in human thinking. It was equally difficult for prehistoric man to conceive of a time when there would be national thinking, and this is a good thing for us to bear in mind."
> — Alice A. Bailey, *Education in the New Age*

Your negative ego traffics in power trips, guilt trips, pride, prejudice, and all manner of habitual defense mechanisms. These are at the expense of not only your conscious self, but also of your relationships with others and your joy and satisfaction in life. Perhaps the least helpful thing you can try to do, however, is to kill off your negative ego by taking an adversarial stance toward it. All healing is an expression of love and acceptance, and we need to own and embrace even this most disintegrated aspect of ourselves so that we can begin to work with it productively to relax its hold over us.

It is incredibly important that you learn how to recognize, observe, and objectify the voice and dynamics of your negative ego and disidentify yourself from it. You *can* choose to relinquish (give up, or surrender) your negativity and refuse to participate in generating a negative conversation about yourself, others, or whatever situation you find yourself in.

The following excerpt from the poem "The Power of Not Now" by Neal Rogin, from his book *Delightenment,* speaks to the nature of the negative ego.

"Why is your ego self, your Me, so fearful of Now,
of the actual present moment?

It seems its three operating rules are

1) Not here.
2) Not now.
3) Not me.

So the avoidance of being present in time or in space, and
the absolute refusal to be in any way responsible for
anything that happens, is its primary function.

If not now, when? The ego says, 'Later.'
If not here, where? 'Over there.'
If not you, who? 'That guy.'

Your ego must at all cost not let the present moment
come to consciousness, because it does not exist Here
and cannot exist Now. It can only exist, or appear to exist,
in the lie of later, over there, with that guy."

Defensive Needs of the Negative Ego

Just as each of the three selves has its authentic needs, the negative ego also has its own specific type of needs. These are referred to as the defensive needs of the negative ego. These defensive needs are toxic and are always fear-driven in some way. Unfortunately, people often confuse genuine needs with defensive ones. They put tremendous amounts of energy into getting the defensive needs of their negative ego met, at the expense of the quality of their lives and relationships.

At their core, these defensive needs are about establishing an adversarial stance toward life and other people to ensure that you are protected. Usually, this is to a degree that is unnecessary and self-sabotaging. Although your negative ego tells you that these defensive needs are necessary to your survival, the cost of fulfilling them is greater and greater dysfunction, pain, and disconnection. The process of taking back your life from the hold of your negative ego is one of disarmament, in which you lay down your weapons for wounding yourself and others and shift from being adversarial to nonadversarial.

The ultimate defensive need of the negative ego is to ensure its survival at any cost, no matter how much pain it is causing us or the people we interact with. The more these defensive needs are fulfilled, the more the negative ego is reinforced. It is extraordinarily easy to fall into a codependent relationship with one's negative ego. What being codependent means in this case is having a relationship that enables you to maintain destructive, irresponsible, adversarial, and addictive behavior patterns at any cost, because you feel enlivened by the interim payoffs you are getting from them.

In terms of the payoffs these defensive needs generate, there is a lot of juice, or intensity, in the negative energy that gets created by acting them out. This is often an inflated sense of self-righteous excitement, aliveness, or entitlement. Payoffs are always about instant gratification, rather than long-term benefits. It is easy to mistake these payoffs for winning, but they eventually end up costing you and everyone around you in one way or another. In actuality, these costs occur most often in the realm of your connection with others, whether intimate love relationships, family, friendships, or partnerships at work.

The two main ways that these defensive needs get acted out is by being either passive or aggressive. A lot of this has to do with personality types and traits, but often people will either fall into the aggressive, "mighty-me" camp, or the passive, "mini-me" camp. People who default to being aggressive will often come across as bullies or persecutors, while people who default to being passive will seem to disappear or withdraw, stonewalling and otherwise avoiding communication.

Some people have mastered being passive-aggressive, which is a type of losing strategy that has them actively avoiding responsibility for getting their legitimate needs met. Instead, they lash out, expecting others to fulfill their needs, and blaming and punishing them when they don't. This is very much a combination of a victim and a persecutor game.

Remember that when you are acting out any of these defensive needs, it is a sign that you have unhealed wounds and are disconnected to some degree from your sense of self, your worthiness, and your self-esteem. To feel better inside, you will need to disidentify from these defense structures and return to your conscious self. As challenging as it may be to remember this about yourself, it can be even more difficult to remember this about others when they are being adversarial toward you.

Following is a list of some of the most common defensive needs of the negative ego. All these defensive needs are fundamentally tied to a lack of self-esteem. They are all about building up a person's false persona whenever and wherever they might have disconnected from their sense of their authentic, conscious self. These defensive needs are all manipulative and fear-driven in some way. This is not a definitive list, and you may recognize other defensive needs in yourself or in people that you know.

- *To be right.* To win and avoid losing, to blame and to have others lose or be wrong. This can manifest as self-justification or self-righteousness.
- *To be better than or superior to.* To prove worthiness over others, needing to make others seem inferior in order to make oneself feel superior. This can manifest as arrogance, cynicism, condescension, denigration, patronizing, or shaming others.
- *To be in control.* To dominate, to exert influence, to manipulate (often by deception), to bully and avoid domination, or to use force to make oneself feel or look stronger than others.
- *To avoid hurt or pain.* To be self-protective and avoid pain or conflict. This can manifest as denial, resistance, or hostility. This can also manifest as being passive or stonewalling.

- *To get attention.* To be willing to engage in drama or to get negative attention in an attempt to prove worthiness. Also can manifest as revenge dramas against someone who has withdrawn their attention.

- *To avoid responsibility and be codependent.* To remain childlike, to be a victim, or to not be responsible for oneself. To be self-important by being indispensable to another so that the other isn't responsible and remains a needy victim.

- *To get more, to have more than, or to be the most.* To prove self-worth by going for outer form rather than inner substance. This can manifest as a scarcity mentality, jealousy, competition, or greed.

- *To get approval.* To validate self-worth by pleasing others in a compulsive way. Needing to look good, be the best, or be perfect to be accepted, sometimes resulting in an attitude of "I'll show you" when not feeling approved of. This can manifest as being a martyr by compulsively putting other's needs first and ignoring one's own needs.

When we are caught up in our negative egos, we're trying to control and assert power over others or the situation to get our defensive needs fulfilled. Often there is a lot of adversarial emotional energy involved, which can get expressed quite dramatically, even violently. We might have a lot of repressed emotion about how unfair life is, a sense of desperation about it ever working out, or a drive to constantly be perfect to win against others. The behavior patterns associated with these defensive needs are called lower-self behaviors. A hallmark of these behaviors is a lack of respect, both of self and of others, and a lack of personal responsibility.

Acting out reactive, lower-self behaviors in a loud, emphatic, and angry way is often confused with being authentic and having personal power. In Western culture, this is especially true when it is a male doing the yelling. This sort of behavior by men is viewed much more favorably than the same behavior by women.

When a male is shouting and being self-righteous, often he is thought of as just being authentic and expressing himself: it's who he really is. Being forceful and domineering is mistaken for autonomy and agency. What is really happening is that he is expressing his habitual, reactive negative ego, as opposed to being true to his heart-centered, conscious self.

Often, when someone is indulging in lower-self behavior, it is unconsciously appealing to others, because it grants permission and agreement for them to behave badly as well. You can see this dynamic played out in national politics. Shameless, lower-self behaviors by political leaders appeals to and reinforces their followers' lower-self behaviors and the payoffs they get from them. It validates their negative ego drives and encourages them to try to win over others by acting out their very worst selves.

By holding a loving attitude toward yourself and practicing being in observer mode, and by being the conductor of your life while you reparent yourself with self-love, you can relax the hold of your negative ego and let your healthy ego do the job it was meant to do.

Negative Ego Reactions versus Conscious Self Responses

Following are examples of two challenging situations, which illustrate the difference between dysfunctional reactions from the negative ego and functional responses from the conscious self.

Being Unfairly Criticized or Unjustly Accused	
Negative Ego Reactions	**Conscious Self Responses**
Feel defensive and angry at being put in the "I am not OK" spot.	Understand the other person's frame of reference. Acknowledge that not all people see things in the same way. Use assertive language to make requests about my needs and boundaries.
Feel afraid that no one will believe my innocence or that my reasons for doing what I did were valid.	Take back my power by being assertive, and inquiring whether the other party would like to hear the facts of the situation.
Counterattack by blaming the criticizer for being an uninformed idiot who jumps to conclusions.	Have some compassion and curiosity about why this person is reacting the way they are. Find out what's really going on with them.
Question the stability and validity of my relationship with the criticizer or accuser.	Get more connected with them by appreciating my relationship with them. Put in some strong boundaries regarding respectful interactions.

Leave the scene in a huff, seething with righteous resentment, and fuming for the rest of the day as I replay the scene in my head again and again.	Take time out to regroup. Find something to respect or appreciate about what they said, while turning down the volume on my negative inner voice.

Receiving a Sullen or Openly Hostile Response	
Negative Ego Reactions	**Conscious Self Responses**
Get angry at the other person, and try to convince them that I am right.	Reflect to them the validity of their reaction, given the difficulty of the situation. Use assertive language to express how I feel and how they have affected me.
Feel anxious or worried that I will never get through to them in a way that works for both of us.	Use reflective listening to get through to them. Use a series of inquiries or guesses about what is really going on and what their deeper needs might be that aren't getting met.
Criticize them to someone else, such as their parent, another supervisor, a friend, or colleague.	Enlist the aid of someone who has a closer relationship with them or who has more wisdom or skill in handling their reactions than I do.
Defend my strategies by calling their abilities into question.	Make an offer to them of what I perceive might be their preference in how to be treated. Make a request about how I would like to be treated.
Give up on them and just let them do whatever they are going to do while I go lick my wounds.	Ask them what would feel good to them, right now, in this situation, and share what would feel good to me.

Negative Ego Subpersonalities

As we have covered previously, there is a whole category of subpersonalities called lower-self characters. These are the subpersonalities that are related to the negative ego. They are the personas that you unconsciously adopt whenever you slip into trying to get a defensive need of your negative ego met. As such, they are the most important ones to work with to relax the hold of your negative ego.

To review, your lower-self subpersonalities take over primarily when you feel stressed and are experiencing any of the following fears:

- You're not good enough or you will somehow lose out.

- Your authority will be threatened, and your control will be lost.

- You're going to feel pain that you can't handle.

- You'll be ignored or your perception will be refuted.

- You'll be left out or have no useful purpose.

- You won't get your physical needs met.

- You'll be denied acceptance or approval by others.

Whenever you feel your survival is threatened, the chances are good that a lower-self subpersonality is ready to rise up. This will be whichever subpersonality your subconscious thinks most closely matches the situation and can protect you the best.

The scared part within tries to help you survive by being either aggressive or passive. This part of you will want to either get big to deal with the situation or get small and withdraw. This subpersonality is certain that you can't handle the situation without its help because at some point in the past, most likely when you were very young, you weren't able to deal very well with something similar.

When you're stressed and a lower-self subpersonality takes over, its sole purpose is to try to reduce your anxiety. Usually, though, because it is based in the past, the way it goes about this isn't very effective or appropriate to the present moment. It only succeeds in generating more anxiety and bad feelings between you and whomever you are interacting with. Whenever a lower-self subpersonality is engaged, there are a lot of not OK feelings going around.

At the end of this chapter, there is a section on how to work with these lower-self characters to relax their hold on you. This involves applying observational skills, intention, love, acceptance, humor, and self-parenting to help your lower-self subpersonalities mature and become more integrated.

Relaxing the Hold of Your Negative Ego

How to Tell If Your Negative Ego Is in Charge

We are either coming from our conscious self, awake and owning our reactions, authoring our responses, and operating above the line, or there is a good possibility that we are being driven by the disintegrated parts of our subconscious self. This has us be in a state of waking sleep, operating below the line, with our negative ego in charge. As soon as we start unconsciously acting out our reactions, we allow our negative ego to show up and run the show.

Following are some questions to help you figure out where and when your negative ego might be taking charge. If any of these dynamics are going on in your life, then you can be certain that your negative ego is having a field day.

- Where in my life am I continuously generating a negative conversation, either internally or with others? What are these conversations about?

- Where am I repeatedly complaining, dramatizing my feelings, or proclaiming how I have been victimized?

- Where am I punishing others or myself? Where am I being mean or unkind to others or myself?

- Where or when in my life am I being adversarial toward others? Where and when do I make myself or others wrong?

- Where am I blaming others and seeing them as the problem? Who am I trying to change and what am I trying to change about them?

- Where am I being hyper-protective, constantly in fear of being let down, hurt, or betrayed?

- In what situations am I defensive, despite my best efforts not to be?

- What am I trying to manipulate others into doing, and when am I using force instead of making a straight-up (clear and clean) request?

- Where do I feel less than, inferior to, or not good enough? Where do I feel better than, superior to, or self-righteous about something?

- Where am I being consistently mistrustful, cynical, or skeptical?

- Where am I telling lies and fabricating an alternative reality? Where, and about what, am I being deceitful?

- Where am I sabotaging myself?

- What am I addicted to or compulsive about? What do I *have* to have or do, or think I can't feel OK without?

- Where am I settling for short-term solutions and instant gratification to avoid uncomfortable or painful situations, even when I know that doing so will only create additional, possibly worse, pain in the future?

Steps for Getting Free of Your Negative Ego

1. *Shift into observer mode.* This is always the first step to relaxing the grip of the negative ego. Notice and be awake to when your negative ego has taken control. Often this is when you feel bad inside, not OK, or in disequilibrium. Remember that you *have* a negative ego, but you are *not* your negative ego.

2. *Assess your authentic needs.* Are there any legitimate needs (those of your three selves) that you can take responsibility for getting met? For example, if you can make an assertive request for an authentic need to be respected, then your interpersonal dynamics will immediately shift toward mutual respect and mutual benefit.

3. *Accept responsibility for not being present and for having had your ego do the wrong job, forcing it to become a negative ego.* Thank it for delivering its cautionary information whenever it kicks into dictator mode and is shouting at you inside your head, telling you what to do or how messed up you are. Tell it very firmly to quiet down because you're now present and accounted for: your conscious self is now in charge of the show.

4. *Make assessments and choices from your conscious self when it is time to act.* Ask yourself, "Will this action feel really good and be enduringly beneficial to me, others and the situation?" and "Do I feel like I am taking responsibility and taking back my personal power and autonomy?"

5. *Actively listening for guidance from your superconscious self.* Slow down, meditate, sit in silence, breathe deeply, or employ some other contemplative practice that helps you quiet your mind. It is in stillness that you can best hear the voice of your superconscious self. Be intentional about listening for intuition, insight, and guidance about the ways in which you can go about taking back your power and strengthening your autonomy. Be wary of taking advice from the voice of your negative ego, which will usually encourage you to punish yourself or others in some way. The guidance of your superconscious self is always consistent with mutual benefit.

6. Be willing to let go of self-pity and feeling self-righteous, revengeful, helpless, petty, or wronged. Be willing to stop putting yourself or other people down. When the voice of the inner critic starts to get loud, the voice of your conscious self needs to get louder. This is the inner version of "When they go low, we go high."

Taking Charge of Lower-Self Subpersonalities

Overview

We all have times when we are stressed, and the ways in which we show up in relation to others are not consistent with how we would want to be. At these times, we are most definitely *not* being our best selves. In certain recurring situations, specific buttons get pushed and we find ourselves flying off the handle, often in predictable ways.

Whenever this happens, our negative ego gets engaged and we unconsciously jump onto the drama triangle, embodying the roles of victim, persecutor, and rescuer. We start operating from the defensive needs of our negative ego and are in the grip of a lower-self subpersonality. Remember that these characters usually were created when we were in a situation in which we had a need that didn't get met. We felt wounded in some way, experienced pain, and formed a coping strategy to deal with that situation to the best of our ability at that time.

After you've been caught up in acting out a lower-self character and have returned to a state of equilibrium, it can be illuminating to create an illustration of that persona. By using this technique to personify a lower-self subpersonality, you can get to know and understand what part of you keeps showing up. You can then reparent that part of yourself and help it to relax, mature, and become more integrated.

As always, when working with your subconscious self it is critical to hold an attitude of loving kindness and self-acceptance, and to remember that your subconscious is devoted to having you survive and thrive. By understanding what this part of you is trying to accomplish, you can be more compassionate and forgiving toward yourself. Remember that healing can only happen from a place of love and acceptance, and it is impossible to integrate the parts of yourself that you are adversarial toward.

Managing Lower-Self Subpersonalities

Following is a quick three-step process for managing lower-self subpersonalities when you are in the middle of a stressful situation. [xx]

1. Recognition. *The first step for working with a lower-self subpersonality is the recognition of when you are caught up in one.* Awareness is always the first step to getting free. When you are stressed and in the grip of a lower-self reaction, often the first and best thing you can do is to shift into observer mode by metaphorically taking an inner step back to assess what is going on.

2. Lower the Stress Level. *The second step of working with a disintegrated subpersonality is lowering your stress level.* This is usually achieved through a practice such as resonance breathing. Paying attention to using your breathing is one of the easiest and most potent tools available for interrupting yourself whenever you're feeling stressed, and when you feel yourself starting to slip into the grasp of reactive behavior patterns. The great thing about a breathing exercise is that you can do it without anyone else noticing.

One of two things happens when you get stressed: either your sympathetic nervous system kicks into gear, and you expand energetically to fight or flee, or your parasympathetic nervous system kicks in, and you contract energetically to withdraw or freeze. You overcompensate or undercompensate. Either one of these states dramatically affects your breathing, usually making it shallower. Sometimes it is possible to even forget to breathe at all when you're feeling frozen.

The simplest thing you can do when you're feeling stressed or upset is to remember to breathe. Just take several deep, calming breaths. Slow your breath down. The hardest part is remembering to do it. Find techniques you can do easily, and then practice them until they become second nature and part of your automatic default reaction. The breathing techniques we recommend are the resonance breathing technique, which was covered at the end of the chapter 6, or the centering breath technique, which was covered in chapter 7.

3. Return to Your Conscious Self. *The third step of working with a lower-self subpersonality is using your intention to shift your awareness away from your subconscious self and return it to your conscious self.*

Remind yourself that who you really are is your conscious self. Find affirmations that work for you or create your own. Here are some examples:

- I am a centered, conscious self.

- I am a grown-up, and this is a part of me that needs the help of my inner adult to become more integrated.

- I am more than the reactions and actions of this subpersonality and my negative ego.

- I have this subpersonality; it doesn't have me. I am not my subpersonality.

- It exists in my space. I'm bigger than this reactivity.

- I run it; it doesn't get to run me.

- I get to choose how I think and respond.

Remind yourself that you are a capable adult and can handle this situation from a place of respect and responsibility, with an intention for mutual benefit. Remember to hold a loving attitude toward this less mature part of yourself, so that you can reparent this disintegrated aspect of your subconscious self.

Healing and Integrating Lower-Self Subpersonalities: The Subpersonality Drawing Exercise

The Two Steps of Subpersonality Drawings

In addition to the preceding three steps for managing lower-self subpersonalities when you are under stress, if you want to really heal, integrate, and relax the grip of a specific recurring subpersonality, then there are two additional steps you can take.

1. Spend a few minutes getting to know and understand whatever persona keeps showing up by creating a subpersonality drawing. This is best done when you are calm and not in the middle of an upset and is an easy way of getting familiar with this part of yourself. Although it can be amusing to do, this exercise also can be incredibly effective in helping to integrate and mature these subconscious parts in a healthy way.

2. Once you have completed a subpersonality drawing and have gotten more insight into this part of yourself, have a conversation with that lower-self subpersonality to let them know how you, as a conscious self, are choosing to act henceforth. The best way to communicate with your subconscious self is in a meditative state, where you can meet it in its own vibrational realm.

Step One: Create a Subpersonality Drawing

Drawing has proven to be an excellent way of revealing subpersonalities. The quality of the artwork is irrelevant to the quality of insight, so just relax and have fun with it. The idea is to take a nonjudgmental, neutral, and kind approach to personifying these parts of yourself, so that you can own them without being critical or hard on yourself. This is a very effective way of bringing an unconscious part of yourself up to your awareness, so that you can observe and get to know it. Then you will be able to practice self-parenting to help that part of your subconscious become more integrated with the rest of your psyche.

When you do a subpersonality drawing exercise, you are creating a cartoon character to represent a persona you have, one that shows up most vividly in your relationships with people that you really care about. Your subpersonality is often a persona or role you unconsciously assume that is getting in the way of having a great relationship with others.

Remember that these lower-self subpersonalities show up most often when you are stressed and feel that you have a lot at stake or feel threatened in some way.

A. *Draw a picture to answer this question:* Who is that part of myself that most gets in the way of having a positive and productive relationship with this person [fill in the name] whom I care about?

How does this subpersonality look and act? Try to capture visual elements such as posture, facial expressions, and trademark gestures. What does it say? Does it have any catchphrases? Put classic comments and catch phrases in a dialogue bubble above the character's head.

These drawings are usually caricatures or exaggerations of some part of yourself. Get into your mind an image of a stress-driven, lower-self persona that is not your best self. This is something that you do or some way that you become that gets in the way of having a great relationship with someone you respect or love.

The example question posed at the beginning of this section (Who is that part of myself...) is a good one to ask yourself when first learning how to do subpersonality drawings. You can come up with additional questions to help personify lower-self characters that emerge in other stressful situations that are unhelpful. For example, "Who is the part of me that gets in the way of having a productive and positive relationship with money?" and "Who is that part of me that gets in the way of sharing leadership roles with my colleagues at work?"

B. *Get to know this subpersonality by reflecting on these questions and answering them on another sheet of paper:*

- How old is this part? When did it first get created?
- What are the body sensations and postures that go with it?
- What emotions is it feeling? What is the fear that is driving this part?
- What does this persona think? What are its beliefs or attitudes?
- What inner critical voice or parental injunction is it listening to?
- Does it speak softly or loudly?
- What does this subpersonality think it needs?
- What is it trying to achieve?

C. *Name the subpersonality and add some dialogue bubbles to your drawing.* It can be helpful to have the name of your subpersonality be an alliteration, such as Helpful Hanna, Polly Pleaser, Anxious Annie, or Angry Arnold, if you like, so that you can remember it with some humor. Fill in a couple of dialogue bubbles on your drawing with comments that you either say to yourself or out loud to others when you are in this persona.

Step Two: Have a Conversation with Your Subpersonality

It is important to let your subpersonality know that you, as a mature, capable conscious self, are present and accounted for and that you trust yourself to be able to handle this situation from now on.

A. *Close your eyes and focus on your breath.* Give yourself time to relax into a meditative state and then imagine your subpersonality. Remind yourself to hold a loving attitude toward that subpersonality. Take the time to reconnect with that part of yourself. Allow yourself to experience how that subpersonality feels in your body.

When they are sufficiently present, let them know that you would like to have a conversation with them. Ask them what they need to say to you about the following:

- What authentic need do you have that they were trying to get met?

- What is it that they have been trying to accomplish?

- What are they afraid will happen if they don't take charge of a situation?

- How hard have they been struggling to protect you and make things work?

B. *Remind yourself that everything your subconscious does is an expression of self-love.* Its goal is to have you survive and thrive, but sometimes the way it expresses this goal is not very effective. Like a child, it needs the help of your inner adult to help it get untangled and integrated.

C. *Reparent your subpersonality by letting it know what the program is going to be henceforth.* What do you need to say to yourself whenever you feel this persona arising within you that would help it relax? Often these parts want to cling to control and need to be dealt with in a very firm and kindly manner.

Tell them that it is okay for them to take it easy and to go have a good time. Thank them for working so hard to have you survive, and let them know that you are a grown-up now and can deal with the situation. They don't need to worry about it anymore. In other words, reaffirm your inner adult.

Lower-self subpersonalities are always fear-driven, and you can address and assuage their fears and concerns. Let them know that this is not a life-and-death situation and that you know what to do to have it work out for the best—that you can handle it.

If appropriate, then it can be particularly valuable and illuminating, and often quite amusing, to share your picture and insights with the person you had in mind— the one who was negatively affected by your subpersonality—when you did your drawing.

Summary of Self-Empowerment Tools and Practices

Give up any attachment to negativity (surrender your negativity), and refuse to generate a negative conversation about yourself, others, or a situation.

Recognize when you are operating from the fear-driven, defensive needs of your negative ego versus the authentic needs of your three selves.

Relax the hold of your negative ego by choosing to respond to challenging situations from your conscious self.

Personify your lower-self subpersonalities through practices such as subpersonality drawings and journaling. Take charge of them and practice self-parenting.

PART IV

CHOOSING HOW YOU SHOW UP IN LIFE

Building Blocks of Emotional Literacy

Understanding how the defensive needs of the negative ego drive the dysfunctional patterns of behavior that get played out in the drama triangle.

Understanding the two fundamental operating states of being human.

Understanding how your conscious self is the ground of being from which you can initiate the functional patterns of behavior that get played out in the empowerment dynamic.

Understanding what it means to be heart-centered and to gain access to your true core of power.

Core Competencies of Emotional Intelligence

Being able to recognize when you feel OK or not OK, and what that might reveal about your current state, especially regarding any unconscious losing dynamics you might be caught up in.

Being able to identify in yourself and others the unfulfilled needs driving self-defeating unconscious behavior patterns.

Being able to consistently operate above the line. This includes being able to recognize and own the payoffs and costs of your unconscious, unworkable behavior patterns and trade them for more functional and mutually beneficial outcomes.

Demonstrating the willingness and ability to take responsibility for your circumstances (to operate as if you are at cause), while modeling self-respect and respect for others.

Chapter 11
REVEALING UNCONSCIOUS
LOSING GAMES AND DYNAMICS

Overview

In this chapter we will be exploring more deeply how the defensive needs of the negative ego get expressed in our day-to-day lives. We'll dive more deeply into unconscious losing games and dynamics, which will include reviewing and expanding upon some of what we covered in chapter 1.

To be empowered to intervene in the downward spiral of destruction and dysfunction that occurs when our ego has gone rogue and becomes a negative ego, we need to understand more fully how these losing dynamics play out in our relationships with others. We will do that by examining the cognitive map of the drama triangle in greater depth, and investigate the unconscious roles we play in life whenever our negative ego is in charge.

The main defense mechanisms and survival strategies of your negative ego get expressed through the disintegrated parts of your subconscious self. When you're in a state of waking sleep, feeling bad or not OK, and your negative ego starts driving your reactions, it can create all sorts of problems by having you default to unconscious losing games and dynamics. Whenever we are caught up in these lower-self dynamics, it is referred to as either playing a losing game or running a racket.

The use of the term *game* here does not equate with the fun versions of games and is in no way meant to trivialize the significance or painful impact of these problematic patterns. A game in this sense is about acknowledging that there are parameters and rules regarding how something is being played out. *Running a racket* usually means playing out an unconscious set of behaviors we created to avoid being responsible for some aspect of ourselves. Although we get some interim payoffs from this avoidance, we are also causing ourselves unnecessary suffering.

We all learned as young children to play these defensive losing games in an unconscious attempt to get our needs met. When you are caught up in your negative ego, it plays these losing games *at* or *all over* you, and has you play them *at* or *all over* other people. Sometimes you can get entangled in a losing game that someone else (who is in the grip of their negative ego) is playing *at* or *all over* you.

Finite, or win-lose games, are dynamics in which the scoring of the game is set up so that there is a point in time when a winner and a loser are declared. The most common finite games are war, sports, elections, and contests of all kinds. Unconscious win-lose dynamics in everyday interactions are a particular type of finite game. They start when your negative ego persuades you that acting in a certain way will make you feel superior or have you win over someone else.

However, these dynamics don't stay feeling good for very long, if ever, because the win is so interpersonally destructive. Unconscious dynamics may start out as win-lose, but they always devolve into lose-lose, zero-sum outcomes. Therefore they are referred to simply as losing games. When we look at human relationships, win-lose always ends up being lose-lose. This includes neighborhood, workplace, marital, and family battles for supremacy.

When playing a losing game, there's usually a sense of being caught in a downward cycle of bad feelings, no matter the actual outcome. A contentious divorce, especially when there are children involved, is an apt example of this. At the end of the day, no one feels truly good inside: not the parents and certainly not the children who have been traumatized during the process. In any interaction in which there is a power struggle over who gets to be right or gets to dominate the other, there is going to be ample opportunity for the so-called winner to experience guilt later on or be the target of reprisals.

Playing losing games leads to playing more losing games, as everyone tries to get to a place where they feel as though they're the one who's winning over everyone else. It is impossible to get a full-on sense of having won a losing game—where we feel OK and good about ourselves and our relationships—because they always devolve to zero-sum outcomes. They go on and on without any satisfactory conclusion.

When confronting a losing game, knowing what *specific* game is going on is of secondary importance to being able to recognize that a game is, in fact, occurring. Once there is awareness, you can empower yourself by examining the underlying needs that aren't getting fulfilled and affirm that you have other ways to get your authentic need taken care of, options that are more satisfying than continuing to participate in a losing game.

Characteristics of Unconscious Losing Games and Dynamics

1. *Unconscious losing games and dynamics are repetitive patterns of dysfunction, usually with the concealed motivation of creating an advantage for oneself and a disadvantage for another.* Most of these games started when we were very young, in the theta sponge-brain state. We didn't have a choice about what we were learning and thought we could get our needs met through playing out these win-lose scenarios. These reactive games just happened to us, and we were swept up into unconscious, codependent cycles of losing dynamics with our family members, teachers, and other caretakers.

2. *Unconscious games always have payoffs and costs.* We get habituated to playing losing games because they satisfy the defensive needs of our negative ego. There is a voice in our heads exhorting us to keep playing losing games so that we can keep being a winner. The interim satisfaction of feeling like we are winning is a form of instant gratification and is one of the payoffs of continuing to play the game. Of course, this is a false sense of winning, as these dynamics always become lose-lose scenarios eventually.

Our negative ego is certain that the interim payoffs that come with engaging in these dynamics are essential to our survival. These are payoffs such as being right, getting attention, being in control, feeling dominant or superior, or any of the other defensive needs of the negative ego covered in the previous chapter. As a result, these payoffs keep overriding the multiple costs that accompany the playing of any losing game, especially in the absence of a more satisfying and viable alternative.

The costs of losing games encompass every unpleasurable aspect of life you can think of, such as *disconnection, breakdowns, antipathy, humiliation, guilt, depression, pain,* and *alienation.* Having these sorts of feelings is a big clue that you're caught up in some form of losing dynamic.

3. *Losing dynamics are rooted in victimhood and create more victimhood, usually in the form of self-pity, feeling like you are a wrong sort of person, or that you've been wronged by others in some way.* Playing at being a victim embodies a lack of respect and responsibility toward oneself and others, and is antithetical to expressing our conscious self.

We feel like victims because we have legitimate needs that have gone unmet, and we don't know how to go about getting them taken care of. Often we're afraid to ask for what we really need and don't know how to express our reactive emotions and feelings constructively, so we resort to playing losing games instead. We tried to get our real needs met. When that didn't work, we settle for second best—catering to the defensive needs of our negative ego—because at least that meant we were somehow surviving.

No one ever wins these losing games because they are based on being a victim, which, by definition, is not a winner. Self-pity over the costs that accompany game-playing, as well as the general feeling of never quite getting a full-on win, keeps us repetitively engaging in losing dynamics. The game keeps going as we obsessively but unsuccessfully keep trying to make ourselves feel good by attempting to be superior to or win against others.

4. *The bottom line of any losing dynamic is always a feeling of "I'm not OK" or "I don't feel good."* Most losing dynamics also involve "You're not OK" and "You don't make me feel good." Losing games always leave everyone involved feeling bad in various ways: *confused, dissatisfied, manipulated, left out, thwarted, helpless, discounted, controlled, at the effect, ignored, dominated, angry, hurt,* or *anxious.*

5. *All losing dynamics are unconscious and fear based.* Mostly, we aren't even aware that we're entangled in them, except for maybe wondering why we feel bad.

We begin a losing game because we somehow feel not OK and are afraid we'll stay in that place. We may be anxious about confronting or expressing the difficult emotions we're feeling. Or we avoid delving deeper to figure out what our real needs are because of the disturbance this might cause. We might resist having to face the embarrassment that we've been involved in these sorts of petty dynamics. Desperately, we attempt to get away from feeling like a loser or a failure, from being dominated or getting rejected. We unconsciously and mistakenly think the losing game will get us to where we want to go.

You will find some examples of classic losing games at the end of the next section.

The Drama Triangle

Overview

In this section, we are going to review and build upon some important distinctions about the drama triangle that were covered at the beginning of this material. We will be delving more deeply into these dynamics to create a greater understanding of how they occur.

Remember that all unconscious, losing games and dynamics are played from the three positions, or roles, of the drama triangle: victim, rescuer, and persecutor. All the roles of the drama triangle are played from the subconscious self and are aspects of the negative ego. As has been stated several times, these roles are fundamentally adversarial and are based on an attitude of you *or* me, or you *versus* me.

A key thing to remember about the drama triangle is that each role is based on disrespect and a lack of responsibility. Whenever you're caught up in an unconscious dynamic, you embody at least one of these three roles. Often while playing a losing game you shift around from one position to another, as you keep failing to find an OK outcome.

The drama triangle is a fear-driven defensive structure, which became a default strategy in the process of growing up. The three positions of the drama triangle are learned when young and are continually reinforced by family members and other sources of cultural conditioning. As young children, we witnessed the people around us sliding around from position to position in their all-too-human efforts to feel OK in difficult situations. These dynamics are extremely common and are mostly invisible to us, leaving us confused, frustrated, and feeling not OK.

Key Characteristics of the Victim

- Victims don't respect or own their true selves—their inner strength, power, or autonomy—in the present moment. Instead, they keep reliving past hurts, upsets, and wounds, or get caught up in fearful imaginings about the future and impending harm. They try to fend off past and future pain by engaging in the self-limiting behaviors of losing games and defensive mechanisms.

- Playing the victim is a way to avoid taking responsibility. When you succumb to the temptation of playing the victim, you give up your power. Ultimately, the victim role is a mental construct that is about internal oppression, as opposed to being oppressed by external forces. In other words, playing the losing game of being a victim is distinct from actual victimization at the hands of others.

- One of the payoffs of playing at being a victim is getting taken care of by others. Victims manipulate with their inability and weakness so that things will get fixed or handled for them. Or they're looking to get sympathy and support from others who will hopefully feel sorry for them. Or they get to blame others for how badly things are going.

- Playing the victim is the opposite of being responsible. Ultimately, playing the victim lets you off the hook for having to be responsible for yourself and accountable for your life. Acting like a martyr is a classic example of playing at being a victim. "Poor little me," "alcoholic," and "addict" are other compulsive, self-harming behavior patterns that are common victim games.

- Victim is the central role of the drama triangle. Whenever we get engaged with the drama triangle, no matter what role we start from, the reason we're playing at all is because we feel like a victim somewhere in our lives.

- Other people, in the roles of rescuers or persecutors, often react badly to us when we're being a victim. Then they, in turn, feel at the effect of or victimized by being on the receiving end of our victim racket. Their negative responses leave us feeling even more like a victim. Our real needs don't get met when we're dependent on someone outside ourselves to make us feel OK, and that has us sliding into the victim role yet again. In other words, everyone ends up feeling like a victim in some way.

- All we basically want is to get our underlying needs fulfilled and to not feel so uncomfortable and distressed. Not knowing how to do this in a mutually beneficial way has us feeling like a victim from the get-go. We play manipulative, losing games, unconsciously hoping they'll work and give us some relief from feeling bad.

- The drama triangle is called that because it is emotionally dramatic to lose and end up in the victim spot again. We all hate being in the victim position and have big emotional reactions to it which are often very intense, even if we're suppressing these emotions with all our might.

Key Characteristics of the Rescuer

- Rescuers usually come in with an overt, and apparently sincere, agenda to help others and to make a positive difference in someone else's life. However, when playing the role of rescuer, a person assumes a superior position in which the underlying assumption is that others are incapable of helping themselves: they *need* the rescuer to help them. This leaves those people being rescued feeling disrespected because they're being treated as though they're inferior, weak, stupid, or incapable.

- This form of rescuing isn't the same as offering genuine help when it is requested. Instead, it is an ego-driven way of feeling superior and indispensable to others. The main attitudes of this role are, "I am more knowledgeable and capable than you," "I am important because you need me," and "The more you need me, the more important I feel."

- Following are some unconscious motives of the rescuer:
    - I need the validation of being needed.
    - I need to be a savior by saving people who can't save themselves.
    - I need to take care of others to feel worthy or be superior.
    - I need to play the hero so I can feel good about myself.
    - I need to fix this myself to feel like I have control of the situation and I don't trust the other person's ability to do it.
    - I don't have the patience to let others do something for themselves when I know that I can do it more efficiently.

  It is worth noting that these motivations of the rescuer are all versions of the defensive needs of the negative ego.

- The relationship between the rescuer and the person being helped is often one of codependency. The rescuer tries to keep the victim dependent on them, needing the helplessness or neediness of the other to keep the game going. This also allows the rescuer to feel indispensable. The victim, by definition, wants to avoid responsibility and have someone take care of them or the situation. Usually, what is going on is that both parties are playing the game by agreement, albeit unconsciously, and are in some form of collusion. This is the most classic example of the typical double-victim games that rescuers play.

- All forms of being a rescuer are ultimately disempowering, rather than empowering, to the person the rescuer is attempting to help.

- You can also play at being the rescuer toward yourself. This happens when you try to save yourself from feeling not OK, but you do it by going for an instant gratification payoff, without responsibility for your long-term well-being. Although being an addict is very much a victim dynamic, *addiction* is probably the ultimate rescuer game that we might engage in with ourselves.

Key Characteristics of the Persecutor

- When we persecute someone—oppress, victimize, blame, dominate, berate, control, ignore, reject, or otherwise harass a person—we discount them. We don't respect them enough to let them be who they are, what they are, or the way they are.

- Whenever we slide into the persecutor role, we are unconsciously and profoundly fear-driven about something and are trying to protect ourselves by dominating others or the situation and being in control.

- Persecutors disrespect other people's values, choices, and boundaries, and are in denial about the hurtful impacts they have on the people around them. They are seemingly uncaring about the negative effects they have on others or the larger situation. They are afraid that if they were empathic, then they wouldn't be able to force people to be a certain way or do things a certain way.

- The key motive for playing from the persecutor position is to be the one with the power and control, so that no one has power or control over you. Persecutors may seem fearless, but in fact they're trapped by the fear of being in someone else's power in a negative way.

- A basic attitude of the persecutor role is, "I'm right and you're wrong." It might even be, "I don't know how you're wrong; I just know that you are. Oh, and by the way, I'm right."

- Persecutors have a hard time listening to others because they're afraid they won't like or can't control what they hear.

- Persecutors need to win at all costs. They're willing to be manipulative, dominating, and controlling, and are usually aggressive and on the offensive. They defend the defensive needs of their negative ego, with the best defense being a good offense, in order to stay in control and to take care of number one.

- Sometimes persecutors take a more passive stance and can make others feel bad and at the effect of them by stonewalling, withdrawing, or otherwise refusing to communicate respectfully.

- Although this role is usually played by a person, the persecutor role can also be any situation, condition, or circumstance that has you feel like a victim. It can be anything that has you feeling out of control and out of touch with your sense of responsibility and personal power. Unfair rules, prejudice, ignorance, technological and mechanical failures, viral epidemics, and natural disasters are a few of the types of situations you might feel persecuted by.

- You can play at being the persecutor toward yourself. This looks like being self-punishing, self-critical, self-blaming, or self-denigrating in any way. When you are defending the lie of your lack of worthiness you are persecuting yourself, which then has you feel like a victim and a loser.

- The most common, everyday forms that persecuting takes are judging, belittling, criticizing, making someone wrong, and casting blame.

Sliding Around the Drama Triangle

The following is a description of how it is possible to slip around from one position to another on the drama triangle, always ending up in the victim position:

1. A person starts out playing the role of the saintly rescuer, trying to feel important, superior, or valuable, and ends up with their help being rejected by the person they're trying to rescue, who feels denigrated in some way.

2. This causes the rescuer to feel at the effect of the other person's rejection, and feel they are an unappreciated and disappointed victim.

3. That has the original rescuer turn around and criticize or be angry at or persecute the so-called victim they tried to help.

4. Now the person they were trying to help gets mad or self-righteous about the rescuer's criticism or anger and walks away, turning into a persecutor. In other words, they are persecuting the rescuer, who is now a victim again.

5. Alternatively, the person they were trying to help feels too guilty to reject their help and stuffs their feelings of anger. They accept the original offer of help (which feels denigrating and inauthentic to them) in an attempt to prevent or rescue the original rescuer from feeling the pain of feeling rejected.

There are many reasons why a person attempts to be a rescuer. They might want to be a hero or to feel needed. They might be driven by a defensive need, such as wanting to be in control or feel superior somewhere in their life, so they choose to rescue others that they deem to be less able than they are.

What is happening when you are trying to be a rescuer is that you're denying that the other person has the capability to help themselves. Everything short of life-and-death circumstances or other kinds of serious physical harm generally do not require a rescue. What might make a difference instead is some form of support or empowerment, given from a place of partnership, with respect for who that person is and their strength and capability.

How can you tell if the assistance being offered is a rescue or not? Rescuers don't usually ask permission before they jump in, and they don't listen to any refusals of their help. Also, their habit of jumping in to fix things or help is compulsive and happens again and again—in other words, way too often.

Following are some examples to illustrate more clearly how these dynamics work in our day-to-day lives.

Rescuer to Victim to Persecutor

The drama triangle's version of the rescuer position refers to someone who treats another person as if they were a victim, as though they were incapable and needed the rescuer to save them. The rescuer assumes that certain people don't have the capacity to take care of themselves, or the rescuer has decided to step in to keep a situation from going badly. They do this even when the other person would have been capable of acting appropriately if they were either left to their own devices or were empowered to take care of themselves.

One of the most common examples of fear-driven rescuing is the parent or caregiver who overprotects a child and does things for them that the child could be learning to do for themselves. This leaves the child feeling incompetent, put down, discounted and disrespected. Now the victim (the child) turns to persecution of the parent as an attempt to get out of the game, acting out and rejecting the rescuer's efforts, and perhaps rejecting the rescuer (the parent) as well.

Taking the time to coach a child in how to do something and challenging them to persist in their learning process, instead of rescuing them by doing it for them, is a very respectful and beneficial practice. Unfortunately, parents' fears and their defensive personality traits, such as impatience, arrogance, or martyrdom, can come up so strongly that parents can slip onto the drama triangle without even realizing it. This is a fast route to having children come to resist and resent their parents.

Persecutor to Victim to Persecutor

The slide from persecutor to victim is perhaps the simplest to explain. This is the format that most recurring arguments take. If you feel persecuted by someone, then chances are that you will feel victimized and will want to persecute them back. You lash out and make them your victim. They then turn on you and persecute you back whenever they get the chance, either overtly by fighting with you, or attempting to get even with you covertly or anonymously.

Whenever a victim slides into the persecutor role by turning against the persecutor, the persecutor will return fire by criticizing, blaming, accusing, or sabotaging (either covertly or overtly) the other person—or by severing the relationship. They may remonstrate them by proclaiming, "You can't treat me like this," "I am going to make you pay," or "There is no chance of my forgiving you for the damage you have caused." Whether the persecution comes in the form of control, domination, character assassination, blaming, bullying, or passive-aggressive behavior, both individuals end up in the victim role.

By this stage, usually some amount of hatred and disgust has set in. Both parties are caught up in the drama triangle, losing and experiencing being harmed over time. Almost all unwilling victims of a persecutor will find that their feelings about being treated disrespectfully come to a boiling point and they reject the persecutor. It doesn't matter whether that person is a parent, friend, boss, coworker, spouse, or stranger: when the pain becomes too great to bear, the relationship will be broken and destroyed.

Types of Losing Games

Classic Losing Games

Poor Little Me: This is a classic victim losing game that we play to get attention, sympathy, and help, without having to take responsibility for our own lives, reveal our own real needs, or make clear, assertive requests. When a victim starts to own their feelings and takes personal responsibility for getting their underlying needs taken care of, the victim game ends.

Bully: This is a perfect example of the false winning of a persecutor game. Bullies are childhood victims who were usually abused themselves and who, because they are lacking in true inner self-esteem, bully weaker people to feel superior to or better than others. As is true for any classic persecutor, the bully's thrill of winning is very temporary. The bully doesn't really feel like a confident, superior winner in real life: in fact, they feel not OK inside.

A bully's negative ego needs them to dominate everyone else in order to win, thus protecting themselves. They keep on bullying as a way to cover up feeling like an abused victim inside and to avoid being exposed as a loser. And of course, none of this is conscious: not to them, not to their victims, and not to most observers.

Becoming conscious of the dynamics and working to heal the underlying wounds or unmet needs of the bully can blow apart the game as a survival strategy.

Here, Let Me Do That for You: This is one of the most common, everyday rescuer games. We often unwittingly play this game with anyone very young, very old, very small, or in some other way apparently weaker. It differs from being of assistance in an empowering way, in that rescuer games always insist that the person cannot do it for themselves, which has that person feeling disrespected, weak, stupid, helpless, and inferior.

A straight-up, clean offer to be of assistance is respectful of the other person and allows them to accept, refuse, or make a counteroffer. They might do it themselves or they might gladly accept some assistance, which does not imply that they are incapable or inferior in any way.

Losing Games by Role

Victim Games

Self-Deprecation and Chronic Self-Doubt: The victim stays stuck in these debilitating patterns in which their thoughts and emotions are obsessively focused on what is wrong with them, what they don't do well, and how they are not good enough. This lets them off the hook for having to show up and be successful in the world.

Self-Destruction: The victim is so far down the rabbit hole of thinking they are worthless that they are reckless, addicted, and chronically failing to affirm that they have any redeeming value. This lets them off the hook for ever growing up and becoming a responsible adult. They get to avoid the challenging work of reparenting and healing themselves.

I Am Unlucky: Whether in life or love or physical well-being, this is another version of "Poor Little Me," which lets the player of this game have an external excuse for failure, saying, "It's not my fault: I can't help it that fate is against me." Because life is clearly out to get them, this is a great excuse for being depressed and unable to get motivated or do what it takes to have life or love turn out well.

Permanently Dependent: "I can't get it together; I don't know what to do for a living; I am a mess and need your help." This is an excellent way to never be expected to grow up and become capable of independence or success in anything.

Rescuer Games

Bail Them Out: Saving others from themselves and the natural consequences of their actions by always showing up for them before they have a chance to take care of themselves. Not allowing others to experience the consequences of their actions.

Helicopter Parent: Obsessively hovering over the child to protect them from experiencing any pain, disappointment, failure, or difficulty. This can result in children staying dependent and emotionally immature.

Savior: Showing up to rescue someone from their state of victimhood and feelings of being lonely, overwhelmed, or helpless by taking over the situation for them.

Codependent Enabler: A person whose cycle of sympathy, caretaking, forgiveness, and misguided expressions of love encourages another to stay locked in a detrimental and compulsive behavior pattern, such as substance abuse, violence, or chronic failure. Someone who feels compelled to keep enabling an obese person to treat themselves by overeating huge quantities of unhealthy food or encourages an alcoholic to have fun by partying with them are examples of this.

Persecutor Games

Control Freak: When someone dominates other people and situations by thinking their way of doing it (whatever *it* is) is superior. Often this involves micromanaging.

Character Assassin: This is when someone persecutes others with a barrage of criticism or put-down humor, either in private or by forms of public humiliation. This is often done covertly.

Flaw-Finder: This persecutor game occurs when someone is committed to generating negativity by finding fault with the situation or person and by playing the blame game, which allows them to feel superior or right.

Uproar: An aggressive losing game in which the defensive strategy is to have a good offense. The persecutor always gets so loudly upset that they totally manipulate the entire situation, dominating everyone in it.

Tiger Parent: A parent who ruthlessly demands perfection of their child as a way for the parent to look good and be superior to other parents, because they believe that an accomplished child will reflect well on them.

How Losing Games Play Out Over Time

Within the various branches of psychology there are a number of different names for, and ways of describing, how losing games play out over time. For our purposes, to make this as simple and as empowering as possible, we will be using the term *life script* as the overarching designation. We will delve into the various ways that life scripts play out in life—as complexes, false personas, archetypal characters, lower-self subpersonalities, and personality disorders—to give you a number of ways of recognizing them in yourself and others and determining how to best deal with them.

Although life scripts may seem complicated, they are also extremely common. You will discover them in yourself and in everyone you know. According to disciplines such as cognitive psychology, *everyone* has some sort of life script that determines how they interpret and interact with their reality. Some examples of life scripts are the romantic dreamer, the lazy goof-off, the Don Juan, the temptress, the rebel, the good little girl or boy, the addict or alcoholic, the tyrant, and the narcissist.

Life scripts are incredibly powerful in shaping how we show up in life and have a tremendous impact on intimate relationships. When unconsciously acted out, they are a huge factor in the breakdown of all kinds of partnerships, from marital relations to business collaborations.

In the preceding section we covered some examples of common losing games. The bad news is that people seldom play just one losing game at a time. Often they will play out a cluster of interwoven losing games. Whenever a person plays out a cluster of losing games over a significant period of time, it becomes a type of life script that is called a psychological complex.

The martyrdom complex is one cluster of losing games that many of us are familiar with. Some other well-known examples of complexes are the guilt complex, the superiority complex, and the inferiority complex. Many of the less extreme psychological disorders listed in the Diagnostic and Statistical Manual of Mental Disorders (DSM) could also be thought of as complexes or clusters of losing games. The point here is that we don't need to know all the types of complexes, but we do need to understand that they are everywhere, and they are negatively impacting our lives.

The good news is that no matter what games are being played, or how many of them are being played simultaneously, the principles of getting free of them are still basically the same; there is just more to unravel. Also, multiple games will often originate from the same core wound, so doing the work to heal a particular wound can oftentimes untangle a multitude of losing dynamics.

What all life scripts have in common—whether they are an individual losing game or a complex—is that they get played out on the drama triangle. Ultimately, they all devolve to the victim position. Getting free of any losing game always starts with self-awareness and having the intent to reconnect with the conscious self and be in observer mode. It requires self-acceptance, self-love, and working to heal the core wounds of pain and shame that are at the heart of losing, dysfunctional dynamics.

Life scripts are often associated with a primary, fear-driven, unconscious belief we have about ourselves, such as, "I don't belong," "I don't trust myself," "I'm not good enough," "I don't deserve it [whatever *it* is]," or "I can't trust other people or the situation to be supportive of me." We desperately and unknowingly spend our lives trying to hide this shameful "truth" about ourselves from others. One reason that personality typing tools such as the Enneagram are so useful is because they can help to illuminate these fear-driven unconscious beliefs, personality drives, and self-defense structures.

Having a false persona is another way that we express our life script. This false self or persona got created when we were children and felt overwhelmed by life in a harmful way. We developed a negative ego, and with the formation of any negative ego comes the development of an unconscious, self-protective mask. We created a set of defense structures which we internalized as a survival strategy, and then we became identified with our wounds and our strategies about how to protect ourselves from further harm.

Because we felt so vulnerable, we created this act, or role, that we could hide our authentic self behind, which we then completely bought into and embraced. We may have hidden our authentic self from others, but we also hid it from ourselves and then forgot about its existence. We began expressing our false self, with all of its defensive needs, into the world through a complex of losing games. When our persona, with all of its attendant losing dynamics, became an ingrained, long-term, fundamental way of operating in life, it turned into our life script. By now the terms *life script* and *persona* have become interchangeable.

There are many roles or false personas one could potentially adopt. A few more examples, in addition to the ones listed previously as life scripts (the rebel, the Don Juan, and so on) are the bully, the chronic complainer, the ghost (withdrawn and shy), the know-it-all, the entitled prince or princess, the miser, the dilettante, the robot (unfeeling), and the savior. These personas could also be thought of as archetypal characters.

Our life scripts and the personas that we present to the world are also congruent with our lower-self subpersonalities. We unconsciously live out our lives in ways that are consistent with being a Polly Pleaser, a Disappointed Donald, an Angry Annie, a Needy Ned, and so on. These become our self-fulfilling prophesies, and we then wonder why people don't like us, we never seem to win, life is constantly frustrating, and no one really loves us the way we think they ought to.

A person's public persona and life script can overlap or even be the same, but it is likely that the dysfunctional life script is more noticeable in private, as it is usually operating underneath a more acceptable public persona. When this private versus public persona differs, it can be like dealing with a split personality. There is a charming public version and an abusive private one, which is tragically inflicted upon family and intimate loved ones. This is a common dynamic with domestic abuse, in which the perpetrator may seem to be an upstanding citizen in public but is an abuser in the privacy of their own home.

When life scripts become more extreme and dysfunctional, they can be labeled a personality disorder. Narcissism, for example, is a life script that, when extreme, can also be a personality disorder. Someone who has adopted a narcissistic personality will go about getting the defensive needs of their negative ego met by playing a combination of persecutor games, such as the ones listed previously: control freak, character assassin, flaw-finder (the blame game), up-roar, and others. Usually, these are all dysfunctional ways of dealing with a core wound of shame or abandonment from childhood.

The more entrenched a life script is, the harder it can be to deconstruct, heal, and get free of. Life scripts are complicated in a very subterranean way. When people are playing out an unconscious life script, it can become deeply ingrained into their everyday lives and become their dominant way of operating. If they *are* aware of the costs of their behavior, then they often feel hopeless about stopping it.

Trying to relate in a positive way to someone who is caught up in an entrenched, unconscious life script can be enormously frustrating. Unlike when dealing with a simple losing game, straight talk about confronting their game playing is usually insufficient to break open the dynamic. The denial and defensiveness can become so deeply entrenched that it can be extremely difficult to reach that person's inner, authentic being.

Although it *is* possible to heal life scripts, it can be a challenging process when they have become highly dramatic, defensive, and ingrained. Interventions, such as facilitated communication or therapy, even if done over a long period, may not seem to stick or make a permanent impact. These interventions can also fail when they don't empower the person to rebuild their connection with their authentic self or go deep enough to heal the pain and trauma that is driving the dynamic.

Sometimes these interventions can result in the person digging in their heels and becoming more defensive. There are various reasons why this resistance can occur. One reason is that the person's negative ego is in charge and has convinced them that denying their woundedness and pain is the only way they can survive. Admitting they are wounded looks too much like admitting that something is wrong with them, which would leave them feeling unbearably vulnerable, embarrassed, or ashamed. Or perhaps they haven't yet made the choice to end the interim payoffs they are getting from their life script.

You can never force another person to do the work of getting free from their life script, no matter how obvious it is to you that it would be in their best interests. As difficult and as frustrating as it may be, it is important to remember the "you do you and let them do them" rule. Usually the most impactful action you can take is to model your own internal emancipation and be an inspiration to others in their journey.

A critical factor in someone becoming more authentic and evolving beyond their life script is the degree to which they genuinely desire and are committed to their own healing, personal growth, and freedom. They must make an autonomous choice to work on their own emancipation, and they will either be ready, willing, and able to make this choice, or they will not be. This choice *must* be made freely, because they want it, not just because others want them to.

Some other important factors in healing a life script are a person's willingness to:

- Recognize, accept, and own that they have been operating in life in ways that have been generating dysfunctional losing games and dynamics.

- Allow the discomfort and feelings of vulnerability that letting go of these self-protective defense mechanisms engender.

- Let go of the payoffs they have been getting from their life script and losing games while recognizing and owning the costs of their behaviors.

It is important to remember that life scripts get created out of being wounded, and a good rule of thumb is that the more entrenched the life script is, the greater the woundedness and the amount of pain, fear, and shame that is attached to it. Whenever you, or someone you know, is caught up in a life script, it helps to find some compassion for how not OK you or they feel inside. It is also helpful to practice disidentification to remember who you, and they, really are as conscious beings, so that you can affirm everyone's self-worth. Remember that you are not your life script. You are the being, the consciousness, that is the space in which your life script exists. You have a life script; it doesn't have you.

It takes a great deal of personal commitment to heal the pain and shame of life scripts and get free of them. It requires becoming aware of their devasting costs and making a choice to work for internal emancipation. Getting free of the entanglement of life scripts requires self-advocacy by committing to waking up and by being centered in the conscious self. It requires the relentless application of self-love, healing practices, and the principles of operating above the line.

It is good to remember that any progress you make toward your personal emancipation is *always* worth the effort, and that the bigger the challenge, the greater the opportunity for transformation.

Summary of Self-Empowerment Tools and Practices

Recognize when the dynamics of the drama triangle are at play and understand how they turn into losing games.

Recognize when you are caught up in playing a losing game, and know how to distinguish between simple losing games and more complicated dynamics, such as complexes or life scripts.

Have compassion for the woundedness that is underneath unconscious losing games and dynamics.

CHAPTER 12
ENDING UNCONSCIOUS LOSING GAMES AND DYNAMICS

Ending the Drama Triangle

In this section, we cover some best practices for how to prevent yourself from getting on the drama triangle in the first place, or if you do find yourself caught up in drama triangle dynamics, how to stop perpetuating them. What actions you take depends upon whether both (or all) parties involved are willing to stop playing losing dynamics—or if only you are.

Prevention

The best way to escape the drama triangle is to be conscious enough to not let yourself slip into any of its roles, no matter how much you might be feeling provoked to do so.

1. Avoid surrendering to negative thoughts that have you identifying yourself as a powerless victim. Take responsibility for what is occurring so that you can take back your personal power.

2. Be sure that you are not being passive when someone accuses you or blames you for their feelings of victimization, trying to place you in the persecutor role. Clearly state your intentions to respect and empower them, rather than cause them harm in any way.

3. Be self-reliant and resist allowing others to rescue you from your problems or help you when you don't need it. This is especially important when you suspect that they are on an ego trip of needing to feel superior and you could end up feeling wrong, incapable, stupid, or diminished.

4. Be mindful when offering help to others if you haven't explicitly been asked for support in assisting them with something. If they have requested your help, then focus your assistance on enabling them to be self-sufficient.

When Both or All Parties Are Willing

Trying to escape the drama triangle by avoidance or denial will not solve the problem of ending up sliding around the roles of the drama triangle repeatedly in the future. When you are willing to end a losing game, and you have a sense that the other parties are willing as well, there are several actions you can take that will result in benefit for all.

1. Be awake to and acknowledge the fact that you are both caught up in playing the roles of a dysfunctional dynamic. Agree that the drama is sufficiently unsatisfying, uncomfortable, or disturbing that both of you are motivated to get free of it.

2. To identify the roles everyone is playing, there must be some meta-communication, which means looking at the bigger picture or the context for why this situation is occurring. Being in observer mode can help you discover in a nonjudgmental way who is playing what role and how the interactions are occurring. This sort of communication, which brings clarity to the dynamics driving the situation, usually needs to be done when everyone has sufficiently calmed down.

3. Use methods such as validating underlying needs or searching for positive intentions beneath the roles. Or use humorous play-acting to allow each party to lighten up and take responsibility for the role, or roles, they keep playing. Ask them what their underlying needs, concerns, or feelings of discomfort are that keep having them land in certain spots on the drama triangle, and be sure to examine yours.

4. Once everyone is awake and owning their part in the dynamic, make agreements that will serve both your and their needs for being in a mutually respectful and beneficial relationship.

5. Over time, anchor these agreements through check-ins with yourself. Make sure that being awake, responsible, and respectful are consistently present in your interactions.

When Only You Are Willing

The preceding steps are difficult, if not impossible, to do when the other person (or persons) involved feel defensive, are stuck in victim mode, or are unwilling or unable for some reason to stop acting out the roles and dynamics of the drama triangle. When this is the case, you can begin by employing self-reflection and self-scrutiny to recognize and own any part that you have played in perpetuating dysfunctional dynamics with them. See if you can identify any pain or woundedness that is driving this losing dynamic and if you can have compassion for yourself and the other person.

Recognize that at least by knowing the other person is currently stuck on the drama triangle, you can reorient yourself to a more appropriate dynamic with them. Determine what would be healthy boundaries to set with yourself and with the other person and make assertive requests to do so.

You can do this kind of inquiry by yourself or with the help of a friend, a counselor, or therapist. Even if you cannot imagine the other person ever doing this kind of meta-communication work with you, it can be invaluable to do it for yourself. This frees you up to invest your energy in prevention, which you can do by setting healthy boundaries and making amends for any part you have played that resulted in you or others feeling like a victim. You can forgive and move on.

You can then concentrate on practicing how to respond to others from the roles of the empowerment dynamic: creator, coach, and challenger. From your conscious self, you can hold an attitude of understanding, empowerment, and compassion, regardless of what roles on the drama triangle the other person might slip into.

Freedom from Losing Games

We have just covered several practices for how to prevent or escape from playing the dynamics of the drama triangle. This section covers how to do the deeper work of getting free from losing games and dynamics on a sustainable basis. This is about what you do in those moments when you are caught unawares and end up in the grasp of unconscious dynamics and constrictive emotions.

Best Practices for Getting Free of Losing Games

1. *Find your center.* The place to begin is always to remember that you are not your reactions or your emotions. You have them, rather than they have you. In other words, you begin by shifting into observer mode and disidentifying from your reactivity. You can remind yourself that your reactions and emotions are not who you are as a conscious being: they are things that you have.

2. *Remind yourself that most of the reactivity and negativity in life is generated from old wounds and are forms of self-protection.* These are usually outdated, unhelpful ego defense structures, ones which no longer empower you and which you can deconstruct and let go of. You can accept and take responsibility for your thoughts, feelings, and reactions, which allows for greater access to your autonomy and

personal power. You can choose to own your reactions and author your responses in ways that are consistent with your best self.

3. *Remind yourself that you can't end a losing game and get free of the roles of the drama triangle from within it. Instead, you must transcend it.* You can rise above acting out the roles of the drama triangle and return to being heart-centered and in your conscious self. From there, you are free to exercise your will and choose how to respond constructively to the situation. There is nowhere to go. There is only waking up to what is occurring.

You need to be in your centered, conscious self to confront game-playing. Only then can you break free of habitual losing patterns. When there's a sufficient sense of your conscious self present, there's no need for you to continue to attempt to get your needs met by engaging in unconscious, losing dynamics. Once you wake up, start being self-reflective, and take responsibility for your circumstances, you can apply your conscious will and free choice to your own dynamics and be able to say, "I'm back, present, and fully accounted for."

4. *Have some self-compassion.* It is often uncomfortable and embarrassing when you start waking up to how you've been involved in unconscious losing dynamics. It can help to just accept that you learned these games long ago and that self-blame isn't necessary or helpful. It was inevitable that you kept trying to make these losing dynamics work, and it doesn't mean that you're a terrible, wrong, or bad person.

5. *Figure out what needs you have that aren't getting met.* From a place of self-awareness and observation, you can look at whatever your underlying, genuine needs are and dialogue with yourself about how you can best go about getting them met. Then you can determine what needs you can fulfill for yourself and what assertive requests you might need to make. You will need to keep making choices about how to act and react that are based on responsibility and mutual respect.

6. *Examine any unconscious fears or concerns you might have.* Your real self—your soul-oriented, conscious self—is always present and available to you at any moment. However, it is easy to abandon yourself when you replay reactive stories of past wounds or get caught up in fears about the future. These fears include any worries you might have about being at the effect of another person in an unpleasant way by becoming entangled in the drama of their dysfunctional dynamics.

Ask yourself if your fears are valid. Often you will find that they are leftover fears from when you were younger, but if they are relevant in the current situation, then that points to specific actions to take and requests you might need to make. You can speak to whatever subpersonality has been reactivated, and let that part of you know that you are an adult and can handle whatever arises.

7. *Practice self-inquiry.* A substantial clue as to whether you're playing a losing game is your level of discomfort in looking at your reactions and actions. Once you own up to the discomfort, it is possible to say, "Aha! I'm feeling defensive and uncomfortable, so I'm probably engaged in some unconscious game-playing that I don't want to face." This is a powerful step in the direction of self-respect and responsibility.

8. *Tune into how you are feeling physically, emotionally, and mentally.* Another tip-off that you're engaged in unconscious, losing dynamics is when you're aware that you're feeling constricted, contracted, tense, stuck, aggravated, or some other version of not OK.

9. *Remind yourself that everyone is losing, not just you.* Even if they are acting like they are scoring points in some way, no one is experiencing authentically winning. Everyone feels not OK and is getting hurt by the negativity that is being generated. Nobody wins from within losing games and dynamics.

How to Be Great with Yourself

The following are best practices for dealing with your own unconscious, losing games and dynamics.

1. *Choose to be functional, rather than dysfunctional.* Start cultivating ways to bring or hold your reactivity within the space of your more centered, conscious self. Remember to be in observer or witness mode about your reactivity and own your emotional reactions.

2. *Be kind to yourself.* Remember to have some self-compassion. Remind yourself that most reactivity comes from old, unprocessed wounds. Accept what is going on and then adopt a friendlier attitude toward your reactions, upsets, foibles, and limitations. In other words, be a more loving parent toward any immature, wounded, or disintegrated parts of your subconscious self. Use self-parenting to help these parts heal, grow, and evolve.

3. *Take responsibility for your feelings, and make a choice to heal and grow.* Work on resolving old negative thoughts and unresolved feelings, wounds, and issues, rather than trying to operate on top of them and ignoring your pain-body. Refuse to carry around old emotional baggage.

4. *Assess what needs you have that are not being taken care of.* Look for authentic heart-centered needs underneath the defensive needs of the negative ego. Validate these needs and see how you can best take care of meeting these needs for yourself. Sometimes you might also need to make assertive requests of others.

5. *Assess what payoffs and costs you might be getting from dysfunctional behavior patterns.* Assess what the potential benefits could be if a situation were approached from a more conscious, heart-centered, and functional place.

6. *Practice self-care and self-parenting to process whatever hurt feelings or anger you might have about your needs not getting met.* If your feelings seem too big, if they seem to run too deep, or are bringing up more unresolved pain than you feel you can deal with, then get some empowering therapeutic support for yourself. You may need to work with a trauma specialist to release old emotional wounds and triggers. Trauma healing therapy is a rapidly expanding area and there are now a number of effective modalities available.

7. *Develop practices that appeal to you to help strengthen your connection to your conscious self.* Meditation, exercise, mindfulness, contemplation in all its various forms, and remembering to breathe when you're feeling reactive are but a few of the many practices that work for expanding your experience of being fully present with your inner being.

How to Be Great with Others

The following are best practices for dealing with other people's unconscious, losing games and dynamics.

1. *Remember who people really are.* A person is a conscious self, even if they're not awake to it. The more you can relate to that place in them, the better your interactions will go and the more likely it is that they will wake up and choose not to engage in losing dynamics.

2. *Practice acceptance and neutrality.* Do everything you can to avoid relating to people as though they are the problem, or to yourself as though you are the problem. Practice disidentification: they may *have* an issue, but they *are not* their

issue. The same goes for you. Give other people the benefit of the doubt instead of making assumptions about where they are coming from or what they mean.

3. *Remember the "You do you and let them do them" rule.* How you choose to utilize your personal agency to grow and evolve is your responsibility. How they choose to grow and evolve is their responsibility. Avoid trying to fix or change others, force them to be a certain way, or get them to respond in a certain manner. It is their responsibility to say how and when they are ready and willing to grow.

It may be challenging to just let them be, but trying to rescue them or force them to change their dysfunctional behaviors won't work. Let them take care of themselves in whatever way they choose or choose not to. No matter how empathic we may be, we can never really stand in another person's shoes. Every person's path of evolution is unique, and it would be self-centered and presumptuous of us to think that we know better than they do about how they should be moving forward in life. In wisdom traditions this is called the law of noninterference.

That doesn't mean that we can't, from the role of being a coach, challenge and support a person in being their best self—but only if there is a request. You can coach someone *only* when they have a request for it. Plus, you can only coach another when you are being heart-centered and holding a loving, nonjudgmental space. Stay focused on your own needs and keep being authentic about what is occurring for you, what your needs are, and what works for you. You do you and let them do them.

4. *Set healthy boundaries and have respect for yourself, as well as for them and their boundaries.* Make clear, assertive requests about having these boundaries respected and getting your needs met. Remember that allowing others to violate your boundaries doesn't serve them or you in being your authentic selves.

Understanding and being firm about your boundaries is especially important when someone is caught up in a losing dynamic that is impacting you in a negative way, but they are not willing or able to shift to healthier, more functional ways of operating. When this is the case, the best you can do is accept the truth of the situation and then orient yourself toward them in a way that is a more appropriate dynamic for maintaining your well-being. Sometimes this requires removing yourself from their sphere of influence.

5. *Remember that the fastest way to bust game-playing is by being authentic and telling the truth about what you are feeling and observing.* Be sure to use responsible

"I" statements, such as, "When you did or said X [fill in the blank], this was how I felt, and this was how it affected me." As challenging as it might be, if you come across as judgmental or defensive, then you are only going to escalate the level of conflict. Centering yourself in the neutrality of your conscious self is essential for being authentic and assertive and creating mutual benefit.

It can be helpful to give the other person the benefit of the doubt by saying something like, "I don't think this was your intention, but when you speak to me with that tone of voice and say X [fill in the blank], I feel hurt, and I feel as though there is nothing I can do that will work." And then you can describe, in a nonjudgmental, nonadversarial way, how they are affecting you, what you are feeling, and what the dynamics are that you are observing. Avoid making assumptions about what they are thinking or feeling. Remember that it is not in anyone's best interests to be caught up in a losing game.

6. *Have compassion for others' underlying needs when they are acting out.* Ask them if there is something they need, and actively listen for what their legitimate needs might be, to the degree that they can discern and voice them. If they can't voice their genuine needs clearly, then respectfully ask questions to support them in looking more deeply. Offer support in this inquiry if that feels true for you.

7. *Remind yourself that whatever you or anyone else is experiencing is valid.* Recognize that you can't change anyone's feelings, and remember that emotional reactions are not logical and using reason to attempt to control them doesn't work. You don't have the right to ask people to change how they feel, nor do they have the right to demand it of you. Trying to deny or change how anyone feels only leads to resistance rather than authenticity, to separation rather than connection. Allow space for feelings to be acknowledged, experienced, and processed, so that they can be let go of.

8. *Own your impact on others and make amends as necessary.* Take responsibility for whatever you may have done or not done that contributed to another person being in the grip of reactivation. Ask for forgiveness and be forgiving. Practice the art of making authentic apologies. Be willing to stay in the process with them until everyone gets to a place that feels better.

9. *Remind yourself that understanding is an essential component of compassion.* The more you can understand the fears, wounds and unmet legitimate needs driving losing games, the more compassion you can have for yourself and others.

Summary of Self-Empowerment Tools and Practices

Prevent yourself from getting engaged with the roles of the drama triangle. If you do find yourself caught up in drama triangle dynamics, then wake yourself up and do whatever is needed to stop perpetuating them.

Do the inner healing work to get free from losing games and dynamics on a sustainable basis, and be great with yourself and with others in the process.

CHAPTER 13
CREATING WINNING GAMES
AND DYNAMICS

Overview

Winning games and dynamics are infinite, win-win interactions based on mutual benefit. There is a sense of being in an upward or beneficial cycle when playing this sort of game. These are dynamics in which everyone wins, because they are experiencing greater love, connection, success, and partnership.

The goal of a winning game is to keep it in play with no fixed end point. Scoring is all about how enjoyable you can make the interactions and how well you can foster a sense of co-creative partnership, because you want to keep the exchange going. The way to ensure that the game stays in play is to strive for having everyone feel great about their participation, express their best self, and experience making a difference—all while feeling enlivened and connected.

These kinds of interactions allow for the participants to have grand fun in life. No one wants to call an end to a game that is enjoyable and beneficial to everyone involved, one in which everyone is having a wonderful time and from which they are getting tremendous value.

> "There are at least two types of games. One could be called finite, the other infinite. A finite game is played for the purpose of winning, an infinite game for the purpose of continuing the play. The rules of the finite game may not change; the rules of an infinite game must change. Finite players play within boundaries; infinite players play with boundaries. Finite players are serious; infinite games are playful. A finite player plays to be powerful; an infinite player plays with strength." —James P. Carse, *Finite and Infinite Games*

Friendship is an infinite game if there is mutual respect, caring, and acceptance. Partnerships at work, if conducted with respect for the players' personal and professional needs, can be played as infinite games. Parenthood can be an infinite game when there is unconditional love and acceptance of who each child is. When conflict occurs between a parent and child and there is an environment of mutual respect, they will be able to move beyond the upset or breakdown by making amends and finding forgiveness, thus continuing the infinite game.

Fundraising and contributions aimed at making a positive difference in the world can be an infinite game when the players are coming from sufficiency, rather than a mindset of scarcity. The Olympics are an infinite game, with every event set up as a finite game played within the larger games, which are meant to go on and on, ad infinitum.

The Empowerment Dynamic

Overview

"The Creator Orientation challenges every assumption and attitude that the Victim Orientation holds to be true. By assuming the Creator Orientation, you enter a whole new set of dynamics that support rather than sabotage your happiness." —David Emerald, *The Power of TED (The Empowerment Dynamic)*

The empowerment dynamic and living above the line are concepts that, in addition to the drama triangle, were introduced at the beginning of this volume. Now that you have a stronger foundation of understanding about how you (as a human being) operate in life, we will be reviewing and expanding upon these concepts. The intent is to give you a fuller grasp of these distinctions and assist you in anchoring them more deeply, so that they are more integrated into your ground of being. As with everything that is covered in this program, the goal is to empower you to be able to generate these positive dynamics in your own life.

The empowerment dynamic is the basis of all infinite, winning games. The three roles of the empowerment dynamic are the creator, the coach, and the challenger.[xxi] The roles of the empowerment dynamic provide excellent, above-the-line replacements for the roles of the drama triangle. When you are present and in your conscious self, instead of being a victim, you become a creator. Instead of being a rescuer, you become a coach. And instead of being a persecutor, you become a challenger.

The most important thing to know about the empowerment dynamic is that all the roles originate from the conscious self and are the embodiment of taking a heart-centered approach to life. The outstanding characteristics of the roles of the empowerment dynamic are personal responsibility, self-respect, mutual respect, self-trust, mutual trust, and mutual benefit. These roles and the attitudes that accompany them are powerful ways to gain access to and express your conscious self in action. All these roles are based on a fundamental attitude of you *and* me, and are an expression of true partnership. It takes willingness and commitment to keep choosing these roles.

The empowerment dynamic could also be called the partnership dynamic. You cannot create real partnership unless you are centered in your conscious self and are choosing to operate above the line. It is impossible to create partnership from an adversarial, below-the-line, negative-ego-driven place. For example, if you try to be a challenger when you are in a below-the-line state, you will end up persecuting others.

Key Elements of Partnership Dynamics

- *Co-creative:* Acting in ways that are inclusive, collaborative, and supportive. Actively listening, rather than dominating, being right or self-righteous, or having hidden agendas. Looking for shared interests and needs.

- *Nonadversarial:* Adopting an attitude of you *and* me, rather than you *or* me, or you *versus* me. Affirming that everyone is on the same side of the issue, facing the problem together. Being nonjudgmental and letting go of positions that are based on assumptions, resentments, or biases.

- *Nonabusive:* Practicing respect and nonviolation of boundaries. Refraining from insulting others, making harsh verbal criticisms, or putting others down.

- *Respectful:* Honoring and appreciating the worthiness of others. Creating win-win outcomes, which are mutually beneficial. Not objectifying or demonizing the other or making assumptions about their motives.

- *Responsible:* Willingness to take ownership of whatever dynamic is occurring while intending to create mutual benefit.

- *Authentic:* Creating a foundation of honesty, integrity, and trust. Being trustworthy and continuously building trust by honoring promises and agreements. Willingness to be vulnerable and to be seen and known.

All three roles—creator, coach, and challenger—are part of an infinite game, free of losing dynamics and liberated from both domination and anti-domination tactics. By returning to the roles and attitudes of the empowerment dynamic, you are lifted on an upward spiral of workability. Your interactions with others are more successful, feel better, and are more satisfying and fulfilling.

Key Characteristics of the Creator

- Just like the victim is the central role of the drama triangle, the creator is the central role of the empowerment dynamic.

- The essence of being a creator is responsibility. There is no access to personal power without responsibility. It is possible to instantly move from being a victim to being a creator by finding ways to take responsibility for yourself, your relationship with others, and whatever dynamic or situation is occurring.

- Creators *choose* to not consider themselves to be victims.

- Creators are self-generating and self-initiating. They are willing to hold the attitude that they are responsible for playing a causal role in their lives and experience. They refuse to give away their personal power or agency.

- Being a creator means imagining and bringing something into being or causing something to happen. It means being led by vision and motivated by purpose and passion.

- Self-respecting creators reassure themselves: "Even if I fail or get hurt, I will be fine and I will have learned something," and "I can handle this."

- Creators are really co-creators because they see others as creators as well.

Key Characteristics of the Coach

- Being a coach is a role based on empowering individuals to be self-reliant, resourceful, and successful in reaching their goals. Coaches are respectful and provide empowerment only when there is a request for it.

- Coaches see others as whole and complete human beings, not people who are inadequate, incompetent, or broken and need to be fixed. Coaches work in co-creative ways to create opportunities for people to flourish and be their best selves.

- Believing in other people's innate worth and intelligence, the coach supports and facilitates other creators in realizing their dreams and potential.

- The essence of being a coach is respect. Having respect for the person you are assisting and a regard for their strengths and talents allows you to move from being a below-the-line rescuer to being an above-the-line coach.

- Coaches often act in catalytic ways. They listen closely to the needs of others and then work in partnership with them to provide or unlock whatever is missing for their success.

Key Characteristics of the Challenger

- The challenger has mastered the art of self-advocacy. In other words, the challenger has an active commitment to being their best self. This gives them the gravitas to exhort others to rise to the occasion, do their best, and be their best selves. Through their own magnanimity, they bring out the magnanimity of others.

- The challenger calls forth the will in others to be creators. They challenge others to be more conscious and responsible, from a belief in and respect for other people's inherent ability and intelligence.

- The challenger can be a person, but it can also be a circumstance. For example, depending on how you approach problems and breakdowns, they can be seen as opportunities that empower you, rather than as circumstances that persecute you.

- The essence of being a challenger is trust in self and trust in others. Having trust in who you are and who other people really are—their authentic selves—allows you to move from being a persecutor to being a challenger.

Results to Expect from the Empowerment Dynamic

One of the main outcomes of embodying the empowerment dynamic is a sense of vitality, of feeling fully alive. When interactions are characterized by responsibility, respect, trust, and mutual benefit, everyone involved feels good about themselves and their interactions with others.

For example, when people in a work environment are operating predominantly through the roles of the empowerment dynamic, they experience a great deal of fulfillment and purpose. This creates a sense of aliveness, as if each person had a dialogue bubble above their head that said some version of "I feel good," or "This feels great."

By being co-creators who are committed to an overall mission, there is an elevated sense of appreciation for the essential role that each person plays in the success of that mission. Individuals are empowered to express their leadership from whatever position they hold within the group.

Conversely, when responsibility, respect, trust, or a commitment to mutual benefit are missing, there are usually bad feelings and a sense of feeling not OK, of something being off. This often feels like a pervasive sense of anxiety and a lack of alignment, which can lead to hierarchical thinking, objectification, and denigration.

The dialogue bubbles above people's heads in this organization would be "I don't feel good," "This doesn't feel right," or "This doesn't work." This way of operating creates a toxic work environment, which negatively impacts morale and productivity.

Following are some examples of ways to approach various situations when you are operating from the roles of the empowerment dynamic.

1. I am committed to my colleagues' success, but I don't need to save them. If they are interested, then I will offer to pass on some ways of looking at the situation that have worked for me, or I will offer to problem-solve with them. This means thinking it through with them and discovering what feels like an opening, instead of acting like I know better than they do about what they need to do to address the situation.

2. Instead of complaining or blaming others about something that isn't working, out of my commitment to our mutual success I will take action to bring some clarity and accountability to the situation. Or I might request that others join me in co-creating a workable strategy.

3. I will challenge myself to find better ways to make a positive impact and find mutually beneficial outcomes.

4. When I feel the inclination to control a family meeting by talking over my relations, I will instead be curious, ask questions, and listen. When I feel the urge to dominate the decision-making process, I will instead make sure I solicit ideas and suggestions from others.

5. I will give my intimate partner the benefit of the doubt when they say or do something that I don't agree with or find upsetting *before* I start acting out my reactivity. I will ask questions to find out what their thinking is behind what they are saying or doing, so that I can understand their motivation and goals. I will look for the deeper needs that I, and they, are attempting to get met.

Embodying the Empowerment Dynamic

In this section, we will delve into several distinctions about how to embody and consistently operate from the empowerment dynamic in your life. Being present in your conscious self and embodying the roles of the empowerment dynamic creates a pathway to a life that is rich in happiness, fulfillment, and self-mastery. You are expressing the language of your conscious self in your reality and relationships. This is what living from your best self and reaching for your highest ground looks like in action; it is a real, accessible, and practical way of operating.

A key to being your best self is understanding the interaction between your will and your three selves, as well as the role of will in making the choice to operate from the empowerment dynamic. This understanding is strengthened by examining and leaning into what it means to take a heart-centered approach to life and how to gain access to your true core of power by bringing love and will together.

Operating Above the Line

Following is a quick review of what was covered in the first chapter with regard to the distinction of operating above the line. We will be expanding upon what it means, how to recognize when you are above or below the line, and how to become more skillful at being above the line on a consistent basis.

Remember that the line between the top of the subconscious self and the bottom of the conscious self is the demarcation of the arenas of life that are called above the line and below the line. The roles of the empowerment dynamic originate in the conscious self. The unconscious roles of the drama triangle originate in the disintegrated aspects of the subconscious self, specifically the negative ego. This diagram also appears at the beginning of the book but is included here so that you don't have to go back to find it.

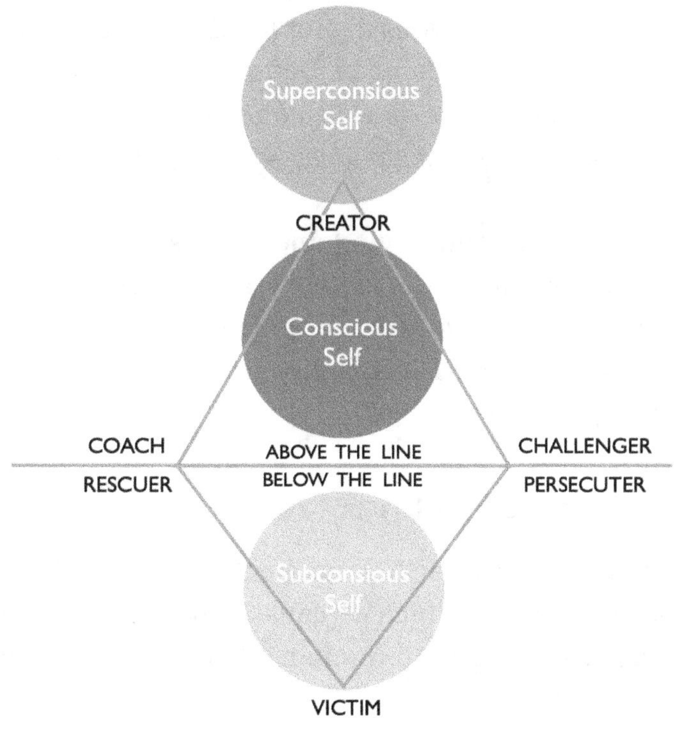

The terms *operating above the line* and *operating below the line* are simply a way to describe methods of operating in life that are functional versus those that are dysfunctional. Operating above the line requires actively making the choice to be functional instead of dysfunctional, by moving your inner orientation from your subconscious self (centered in your solar plexus) up to the wisdom of your conscious self (centered in your heart). When you are operating above the line, you are awake. When you are operating below the line you are on autopilot, in a state of unconsciousness or waking sleep.

Remember that in wisdom traditions the line of demarcation between these two states is called the altar of sacrifice. What this refers to is the understanding that you need to be willing to sacrifice, or give up, the payoffs or false sense of winning you're getting from acting out unconscious, losing games and dynamics. You can then replace these payoffs with the much greater benefits of taking a heart-centered, conscious approach as you rise above the line and into your heart.

The rate of change and growth in your life is a direct function of how willing you are to give up the payoffs of your losing games and self-defense mechanisms. Being above the line means moving away from being motivated by the fear-driven, defensive needs of the negative ego—such as self-protection, control, being right, and looking good—toward being motivated by authentic needs, such as being heard, making a contribution, and being understanding, loving, and respectful.

A measure of character is the extent to which you consciously create your ground of being and choose to operate from your higher principles and your conscience. This is especially true when feeling challenged. Depth of character is about choosing to be functional and heart-centered, especially when it is not easy. It is about making the choice and taking a stand to banish negativity from your life.

When you are committed to embodying and expressing these qualities of self-empowerment, your entire life becomes your practice. Your life is your meditation, and everything that occurs for you is an opportunity for you to strengthen your practice of being your best self. The number one question in life is, "How am I showing up right now, in this moment?"

The Two Fundamental Operating States

Operating either above or below the line can be thought of as the two fundamental operating states of being human, which we constantly slide back and forth between. These are the two basic paradigms or domains that are available to us from which to approach life.

Each of these domains is a ground of being, or the place from which you move toward life that shapes and influences everything that occurs in your reality. One ground of being is fundamentally nonadversarial (you and me), and the other ground of being is fundamentally adversarial (you or me). At every moment you have a choice about which domain you are showing up in.

It bears repeating that embodying emotional intelligence means *consciously choosing* to be heart-centered. Remember that being emotionally intelligent is not a destination: it's a moment-by-moment practice of constantly bringing yourself back to your most centered, grounded sense of self. It requires practicing self-advocacy by becoming a staunch advocate for your inner being.

The process of operating more and more above the line requires waking up and taking responsibility for healing and integrating the wounded, defensive, fear-driven parts of your subconscious self. In the process, you learn how to reparent yourself and become your own healer. No one else can do this inner work for you, and no one gets a free pass. Self-mastery, which is your personal power and agency, is reflected in the speed with which, and the degree to which, you choose to do this inner clearing up work.

It is important to remember that these modes of operating are not just conceptual: there is a visceral feeling that goes along with each one. They are energetic states, which are primarily made up of either positive or negative energy. One way to recognize which state you are in is by tuning into your body and becoming more aware of how this energy manifests physically for you. How does it feel when you are reactive? What physical sensations do you experience? How does calmness and being in equilibrium feel in your body?

Being aware of when your current state is disordered and below the line is the first step to being able to shift to a more positive, better feeling place. The playwright Eugene O'Neill sums up this below-the-line, unconscious operating state: "There is no present or future, only the past happening over and over again." Staying in this state costs you your creativity and spontaneity. The diagram that follows contrasts key elements of each operating state.

Above the Line	Below the Line
Heart-Centered	Centered in the Solar Plexus
Functional and Integrated	Dysfunctional and Disintegrated
Awake, Conscious	Waking Sleep, Unconscious
Oriented toward the Present and the Future, Mindful, Creative	Driven by the Past, Automatic, Predetermined
Centered in the Conscious Self	Centered in Disintegrated Aspects of the Subconscious Self (Especially the Negative Ego)
Connected, Empathic	Disconnected, Alienated
Autonomous	Codependent
Positive Energy, Expansive	Negative Energy, Contracted
Loving, Self-Assured	Fearful, Self-Protective
Nonadversarial, Nonjudgmental	Adversarial, Judgmental, Critical
Dominion, Co-creative, Skillful Means	Domination, Power Over, Force
Me and You	Me or You, Me versus You
Do No Harm	Wounding to Self and Others
Equilibrium, Calm, I'm OK	Disequilibrium, Reactive, I'm Not OK
Mutual Benefit, Win-Win	Losing Games, Rackets
Vulnerable, Open, Authentic, Honest	Defended, Closed, Inauthentic, Manipulative
At the Cause Of, Creator, Responsible	At the Effect Of, Victim, Blaming
Challenger, Self-Advocacy, Self-Affirming	Persecutor, Self-Punishing, Self-Negating
Coach, Respectful	Rescuer, Disrespectful
Trust of Self, Others, and the Universe, Feeling Secure	Fear-Driven, Survival-Driven, Distrustful, Feeling Threatened
Open-minded, Flexible, Accepting	Cynical, Rigid, Denying, Rejecting

Making Conscious Choices

You have a choice about where you operate from in life. When you notice you've slipped below the line and catch yourself entangled in playing losing games in some area of your life, you can rechoose to operate above the line. This choice is within your grasp, right this moment.

You don't have to be different from the way you already are. It is a matter of changing your perspective and choosing to take a more heart-centered approach to life by replacing old, habitual, and dysfunctional patterns with more functional ones. Remember, there is nowhere to go; there is only waking up. You must lift yourself up out of negative dynamics by becoming aware of them.

Being "at choice" happens from the conscious self. It is a thoughtful, above the line way of expressing your agency and responsibility. It involves creating and holding a context for the content you're dealing with and seeing the potential future you want to create. This in turn allows you to discern your course of action. Making a real choice requires a certain level of awareness. It involves seeing the possibilities and having the willingness to make the call on how best to move forward. Usually, this includes weighing the pros and cons (the benefits and costs) of the various alternatives.

Choice requires that you exercise your will and call forth your commitment. It means standing for the choices you've made and being responsible for your actions, rather than having regrets or second-guessing yourself after the fact. Sometimes it requires self-forgiveness, especially when you discover in hindsight that you didn't make the optimal choice or that your choice had unintended consequences. Being responsible for your actions allows you to discern and integrate lessons learned from your successes *and* failures, so that you can grow in positive directions.

Being at choice allows for greater expression of personal power and authenticity. Rather than feeling restrictive, once a true choice has been made there is an inherent sense of freedom that comes with making it. It allows for new pathways to unfold that are consistent with who you really are and where you want to go in life.

We tend to make decisions about the content of our plans. We make choices about our overall vision and program. Exercising your will by being at choice is a key to living a transformational life, meaning that you have the power to choose how you respond to the things that affect you. You may not be able to change the circumstances, but you can own your reactions and choose how you intend to respond.

> "Be miserable. Or motivate yourself. Whatever has to be done,
> it's always your choice." —Wayne Dyer

Imagine living a life where you never hang on to feelings of regret, where you never torture yourself with "what-if" or "what could have been." How conscious would you need to be about the important decisions you make? What would it take for you to have your decisions be empowered choices? Can you own your choices and forgive yourself when mistakes arise, as they invariably will? Rather than bemoaning the vagaries of fate, can you take responsibility for your choices and their impact, and integrate the lessons and learning that come out of having made those choices?

While we all have regrets about things that we wish we would have done differently, hanging onto regret is a way of persecuting ourselves. It keeps us stuck replaying the past and feeling like a victim of our actions. Regrets and guilt are similar, in that they are both mental constructs and not true emotions. For the purposes of self-empowerment, try substituting genuine remorse for regret and guilt. Then strive to do better, make the necessary amends, integrate the lessons, forgive yourself, and let it go.

> "Human beings were given a left foot and a right foot to make a
> mistake first to the left, then to the right, left again and repeat."
> —Buckminster Fuller

Exercising Your Will

Will is a somewhat mysterious yet very important subject. Making conscious choices in life requires that you exercise your will and utilize the power of your intention. Therefore it is useful to have a deeper understanding of what will is, how it manifests, and most important, how to work with it in ways that are empowering.

The concept of will has had its cultural moments. For example, it was very popular in Victorian England and then later devalued in modern psychology. In our daily lives, we tend to have a very real and ongoing struggle with having the willpower to practice better habits and achieve our goals, no matter how mundane they may seem. In this section, we have synthesized the aspects and role of will into distinctions that we think are the most useful in terms of self-empowerment.

Will is defined as having resolve, strength of character, commitment, dedication, purposefulness, and drive. When will is expressed, it can look like concentrating on something with an intensity of focused intent.

When people are being motivated by a disintegrated part of their subconscious self, their will can get expressed as willfulness or stubbornness. They might be narrow-minded, positional, self-righteous, or dominating. They might use force or impose their will on a situation in ways that lead to unhealthy outcomes. Willingness and flexibility can look like being a pushover, being weak, or too accommodating. All of these examples are below-the-line ways of expressing will.

When you are expressing your will from your conscious self, it can look like adhering to healthy boundaries and being intentional about taking actions that are consistent with your principles. It can be expressed as taking a stand for something to which you are deeply committed. It can include being passionate and inspiring and having an enlivening energy. Needless to say, this is an above-the-line expression of will.

Choosing to operate from the roles of the empowerment dynamic is an act of will, as is owning your reactions and authoring your responses. Instead of weakness, willingness now looks like strength and a readiness to engage in becoming more integrated through healing and letting go of old, dysfunctional ways of being. When people get stuck in a state of unwillingness it is often because they have unacknowledged fears. Becoming more willing to engage with what is fearful often requires calling upon your courage and your commitment to getting free.

One way you can look at will is in terms of levels or types. In our current culture, there is an existential debate going on about the relationship between spiritual will and individual or free will. Do you simply surrender to the call of your spiritual will and chalk this up to being your destiny? Or can you be self-determined by exerting your individual free will? By looking at will through the lens of the three selves, rather than seeing spiritual will and individual will as oppositional forces, we can discover that there is another, much more co-creative, dynamic possible.

The Four Main Types of Will

Following is a description of four main types or qualities of will. This is not necessarily a definitive list; rather, it is a way to begin to discern how will is related to your psyche and how it might play out in your life.

1. *The spiritual will of your soul, which is sometimes called true will.* This is the innate drive you have, which is at the core of your ultimate needs and desires for the presence of love—both giving and receiving it—and your desires for happiness, illumination, self-actualization, and integrity. This type of will gives rise to adhering to your most deeply held principles and your conscience. This is the will that comes to you from your soul and is stepped down through your superconscious self.

2. *The reflective will of your superconscious self.* This sort of will has to do with manifesting your dreams and visions. You need to be self-reflective to discern what these dreams and visions are. This is the will of your superconscious self. You can gain access to both your spiritual will and your reflective will by being contemplative and actively listening for your intuition.

3. *The active will of your conscious self.* This type of will is about fulfilling your desires and needs beyond your most basic ones and is also known as individual or free will. This sort of will determines what your heart's desires are. This could be your desire or need for beauty, knowledge, or connection. Active will is associated with the conscious self and is also known as having personal agency.

The conscious self is also where all the various types of will get synthesized and from there get expressed in your life. Reflective will and spiritual will can be received and expressed only through the conscious self. The act of being actively receptive to the voice of your intuition is a function of the will of your conscious self.

> "Everyone who wills can hear the inner voice.
> It is within everyone." —Mahatma Gandhi

4. *The automatic or instinctive will of your subconscious self.* This type of will has to do with carrying out what is necessary to respond to your basic needs. It can be as simple as deciding what to wear or what to eat. This sort of will is most closely associated with the subconscious self, which is the vast filing cabinet of all your preferences, routines, and rituals. Thankfully, this sort of will requires very little thought or effort while assisting you in navigating all the minutiae of your everyday life.

The Three Main Stages of Will

It can also be useful to look at the three stages of will,[xxii] which includes being lacking in will, and how these stages get expressed.

1. *Lacking will (having no will).* This is an unconscious, below-the-line condition. Usually, this looks like being in a state of passivity or victimhood, where you feel at the effect of other people, your circumstances, or life itself. This can look like playing out the roles of the drama triangle. Sometimes this can also look like being willful, by acting in a fear-driven, unconscious, passive-aggressive way.

"People do not lack strength; they lack will." —Victor Hugo

2. *Being willing.* Being willing means recognizing the possibility that you have a choice in the matter, that you can take responsibility for yourself and your experience and can engage in a meaningful process to create growth and integration.

3. *Exercising will (having a will).* This is a conscious, above-the-line state, which is about having agency, making choices, and taking actions consistent with your principles and intentions. It can look like making a choice or taking a stand to be more integrated, responsible, and purposeful. One way that it gets expressed is by choosing to embody the roles of the empowerment dynamic. Self-advocacy occurs as a function of this kind of will.

The most powerful thing you can do to motivate yourself to exert your will is to recognize the benefits of taking a conscious, heart-centered approach to a situation or person. These benefits far outweigh the negative ego payoffs you've been getting, along with all their accompanying costs. Another way to say this is that when it's clear to you that the costs of *not* ending your losing games have become too great, you'll choose to give up the old payoffs and replace them with the much greater benefits of conscious, win-win dynamics.

A clear example of this is what happens when an addict hits rock bottom and is finally motivated to become sober. Awareness of the tremendous costs of their addiction and the desire to feel better become the motivating factors for change, and key to their successful recovery is exercising their will and practicing self-advocacy.

"Willpower isn't something that gets handed out to some and not to others. It is a skill you can develop through understanding and practice." —Gillian Riley (author)

Taking a Heart-Centered Approach to Life

For millennia, the concept of the human heart has been rich in symbolic meaning. In Christianity, the heart symbolizes the core of a person's being, the place from which love, prayer, and a sense of morality emanate. The word *heart* is mentioned nearly 900 times in the bible.[xxiii] In Buddhism, the Heart Sutra is the most well-known text and is said to be a pure distillation of wisdom.

In yogic traditions, the spiritual heart *is* God. It is our essential and ultimate nature. The heart chakra is the synthesizing center of the body, harmonizing the three chakras below it with the three above. In esoteric philosophy, it is said that knowledge without an awakened heart is just information, but when the heart and the mind are connected, the result is illumination and wisdom.

The symbology of the cross is also connected to the heart center. The ancient Gnostic cross represents the intersection of a vertical (spiritual) orientation with a horizontal (physical) orientation. The center of the cross symbolizes where the spiritual and material worlds meet. The shape of the cross suggests the form of a human being with arms extended. The vertical and horizontal axes meet in the heart center. It is in the heart that a person centers in their conscious awareness and synthesizes their inner, spiritual life with how they express themselves in their outer, physical life. When this synthesis occurs and there is congruency between the inner and outer worlds, a person is being sourceful and has the potential to become self-actualized.

Embodying the empowerment dynamic, being your best self, and living your life above the line requires a heart-centered approach to life. This means taking a stand to locate yourself in the loving awareness of your heart. You consciously choose to have that metaphorically be your center of gravity, the place you have as your default position in life. It means committing yourself to a practice of strengthening your connection to your inner being and becoming more present and awake.

When you take a heart-centered approach to life, choosing to live above the line and be your best self, you are practicing self-empowerment. You are empowered to accelerate your personal evolution and to strengthen your ability to create everyday transformation. You are empowered to shift from dysfunctional to functional dynamics.

Taking a heart-centered approach also means being self-accepting, even with all your perceived foibles, and loving yourself enough that you can love others. It means exercising your will to consistently express your best self and take an active, loving, and compassionate approach to life. A heart-centered approach looks like owning your reactions and authoring your responses, rather than being reactive. It requires being respectful and responsible, and is a powerful, courageous, magnanimous, thoughtful, civil, and principled way of living.

The Two Main Components of a Heart-Centered Approach

1. Be Present in Your Conscious Self

If there is only one thing that you could take away from this curriculum, then the most important and empowering distinction would be how to cultivate and live more fully from your conscious self. Although this point has been made many times and in a number of ways, it still bears repeating.

Being heartful or wholehearted means having your focus be within your heart, the energetic center of your conscious self. It involves tuning into your experience of loving awareness and allowing that to shape your actions toward yourself and others. Genuine love from the conscious self gets expressed in action as respect, compassion, understanding, caring, kindness, and a commitment to mutual benefit. This in turn creates resilience and greater trust. It engenders intimacy and the experience of being known. It also leads to a feeling of emotional safety by decreasing the fear of loss and increasing everyone's sense of security and pleasure.

This stance in life automatically brings you into alignment with your superconscious self and your soul. When you combine the knowledge in your head with the love in your heart, the natural result is intuition and wisdom. You are more in touch with your sense of responsibility, authenticity, and integrity. You become sourceful in life and more skillful at expressing these qualities in every aspect of your daily life.

You can't get to being wholehearted through your subconscious self or the machinations of your negative ego. It is *easy* to indulge in acting out reactivity, being petty, and hanging out on the drama triangle. It is much more challenging and requires strength of character and commitment to do the inner work necessary to be your best self. However, the benefits of this approach far outweigh the effort required.

2. Combine Love with Will

Will is what makes love powerful. Continually choosing to be present and accounted for is an exercise of will. Directing your actions in mutually beneficial ways requires using your will. For example, when you do your work because you care (love) and are committed (will) you can move mountains. Love combined with will grants focus, clarity of intent, and impact.

What happens when love and will aren't combined? While love without will might be warm and soft, it can also be weak and insipid. Will without love can be cold and dangerous. When we are lacking in love and will, we devolve into taking a victim role in life. When we attempt to express love from this victim role it becomes twisted and deteriorates into fantasies, with all the attendant melodrama. It leads to pain, apathy, and codependence. Likewise, when we attempt to exercise our will selfishly, without loving awareness, it can become manipulative, domineering, passive aggressive, forceful, controlling, and destructive.

When you combine will with love, you gain access to your true core of power: your authenticity and creativity. Love grants self-acceptance and self-affirmation, whereas will grants presence of self and the power to be self-aware. Love grants you the ability to be fulfilled, but it is will that brings creativity by focusing your intent and directing you in that fulfillment. Love and will together grant individuality, agency, and self-confidence. They are at the core of your personal power and what it means to be a conscious self.

Summary of Self-Empowerment Tools and Practices

Choose to create infinite, win-win, partnership
dynamics in your personal relationships.

Embody the above-the-line roles of the empowerment
dynamic (creator, coach, and challenger) to replace the roles of
the drama triangle (victim, rescuer, and persecutor).

Use responsibility and respect to empower you to shift from being a
victim to being a creator.

Recognize which of the two fundamental operating states you
are in at any moment, and choose to be above the line.

Use your spiritual, reflective, and active will to generate partnership
(co-creative) dynamics in your relationships with others.

Exercise your will to align your desires in life with your higher principles.

Move through the stages of will so that you get to a place of
exercising your will when faced with new challenges or obstacles.

Take a heart-centered approach to life: combine love
and will in order to gain access to your true core of power and
reach for your personal highest ground in any situation.

CHAPTER 14
LIVING ABOVE THE LINE

Overview

In this chapter, we will cover some self-empowerment tools that, when incorporated as practices in your daily life, enable you to shift dysfunctional, reactive, adversarial dynamics to functional, respectful, mutually beneficial ones. This includes the principles of creating positive change (and why it can be difficult), the stages of personal growth around any issue, how to turn breakdowns into breakthroughs, and successfully navigating upsets.

Remember that a key to accelerating your personal growth is to empower yourself by developing your own set of practices for staying awake and being heart-centered in life. As was discussed at the beginning of this volume, practices can take many forms and are often tailored to specific situations or goals. An obvious one is using regular meditation to strengthen your connection to your inner being. Using coherent breathing when you are stressed can help you stay calm in challenging circumstances. Disidentification is a powerful exercise for remembering who you and other people truly are. Creating context and reframing situations are transformative skills that can profoundly alter how situations unfold.

Many practices are simply part of your inner conversation—things you tell yourself that are empowering, such as, "I am worthy" or "I am enough." Or they might be attitudes that you are committed to holding that are positive, such as, "What is in my way, *is* the way." They might be a strategy of not buying into the negative conversations of your inner critic. What is important is that they are ways of being, thinking, and acting that resonate with you, feel authentic and positive, and enhance your experience of being OK.

Principles of Creating Positive Change

Overview

As we have discussed numerous times, the most fundamental core competency of skillfully navigating life and causing positive personal growth and change is strengthening your connection with your conscious self by developing metacognition, your ability to be in observer mode. Change in the form of personal growth naturally occurs as you build up your muscle of being in witness mode, which allows you to relax the hold of your negative ego. The more you do this, the freer you become from old limitations, unprocessed constrictive emotions, habitual patterns of losing games, and other behaviors that are self-sabotaging.

As you consciously work to replace these dynamics with more functional and positive ways of operating, you become more accomplished at creating upward cycles of workability and mutual benefit in your life. Things feel better and work better for you and for the people around you. This sort of change is the work of *clearing up* and is about radical acceptance and a process of inner transformation, rather than trying to force things to be different from what they are.

Why Behavioral Change Is Difficult

To understand how behavioral change happens, it is helpful to first understand why change can be challenging to achieve and so often *doesn't* happen.

Lack of Self-Trust

We don't trust our own ability to cause real change in our lives based on our track record of failure in a particular area. We think we *should* change but quickly fall back into old patterns of self-gratification and defensiveness, blaming our inability to change on our lack of willpower.

Short-Term, Superficial Change Is Easier than Lasting Change

We suffer from an illusion that we can make big changes without doing the necessary internal work. We *can* change almost anything temporarily, just because we say we want to. We attempt to make these types of changes because it seems like they shouldn't be very difficult.

But if we are still operating on top of unconscious dynamics and unprocessed emotions, then it becomes very difficult to make and sustain a lasting change. Emotions, especially repressed or unprocessed feelings and the negative thoughts that are associated with them, have a big role in sabotaging change. This is the main reason why almost all diets, exercise programs, and other types of New Year's resolutions fail.

It Can Take a Breakdown to Get Our Attention

Although it isn't necessary to approach change in this way, permanent and enduring change of an individual's character or way of being often comes only when there is some sort of disaster or breakdown. This is often true for dealing with addictions; hence the cliché about needing to hit rock bottom. This means that when we have an addiction, we come to a place where the interim payoffs from our behaviors are creating too great of a cost to our well-being and relationships. We can then replace these payoffs with the greater benefits of lasting change. Part of developing self-mastery is learning how to create the life we want without needing to wait until we are in the drama of being in a breakdown.

The Negative Ego Is Never a Source of Positive Change

Mistakenly, we try to berate or shame ourselves into changing, but this doesn't work in any comprehensive or lasting way. Negative feelings and thoughts might get you to consider changing, but "shoulds" (when you have competing wants or desires or are guilt-tripping yourself) are never helpful in the long run. The negative ego, once it is engaged, is too defensive to be able to bring about a lasting and positive transformation of your attitudes and your patterns of thoughts and behaviors.

Fixing something inside yourself that your ego has labeled as wrong doesn't really have a big enough payoff to stick. Making yourself wrong feels punishing rather than beneficial. Most of us are used to responding to self-punishment by making temporary changes, but we usually rebel against this punishment later by going for instant gratification, undoing any changes in the process.

What everyone really wants is to feel good inside, and when we do, we're motivated to keep doing whatever creates that feeling. Being transparent, taking responsibility for making healthy choices, making a contribution, empowering others, and rising to challenges are all serious, meaningful actions that can be challenging yet feel great.

Causing Enduring Change

Only the conscious self can provide the ingredients for lasting change, and these qualities already exist within you and need to be cultivated. Enduring change requires generous quantities of self-love, patience, assertiveness, and forgiveness. You cannot change who you basically are as a being or a self. In fact, you don't need to, because your conscious self already contains the you that you want to become, the you that is already all right or OK. Enduring change is more like a metamorphosis: the caterpillar turns into a butterfly.

In a manner of speaking, lasting change isn't change at all, but rather a day–by–day revealing of the real you, out from underneath the masks of unconscious dynamics and the dictates of your subconscious and negative ego. Change can be more accurately described as becoming an unfaltering advocate of your conscious self and placing your agency squarely behind the steering wheel of your life. How this gets expressed is in consistently and reliably shifting from states of dysfunction to states of functionality, from disequilibrium to equilibrium.

Remind yourself what it takes to shift from unconscious, losing games to conscious, win-win dynamics. To get free of playing an unconscious, losing game you must treat it like any other addiction or habit-forming activity. Remember that we all have a tendency to get addicted to the payoffs when we habitually engage in unconscious losing dynamics. Finding bigger and better benefits by engaging in conscious, empowering win-win dynamics is the pathway to freedom.

Trying to just stop playing out a negative behavior pattern usually doesn't work: you need to replace it with something that feels better in some way. You can't just stop doing something. Notice how impossible it is to *not* think about a purple bunny once you have read the words "purple bunny?" If you think it, then it exists in your psyche.

Instead, you will need to replace negative patterns with something better, something compelling enough to empower you to make a lasting shift to healthier behaviors. This is what is meant by the term *creating a positive addiction*. After a while the old unhealthy behavior, if you leave it behind for something that feels much better, will just wither away from lack of attention and energy because you have successfully moved on.

Creating Positive Patterns of Behavior

Human Nature Does Not Register a Negative

As referred to in the preceding example about a purple bunny, the mind does not register a negative, an "it" that does not already exist in your reality. For example, the habitual mind does not really recognize the command to stop smoking. Rather, it focuses on the "it," which in this case is the reality of smoking. You need to give the mind a new "it" to focus on that is better than the old one, such as being healthy and vital or able to participate with your children and be a positive role model for them.

Another example of this is when the mind cannot do anything with the command to lose excess weight: it just fixates on the reality of having the excess weight. The only thing you can tell it that works is something clear and specific, such as seeing food as fuel, eating lightly and deliciously, being strong and limber, and feeling physically light. You need to know what the feel-good benefits are—the greater benefits that you will become positively addicted to—that will replace all the old instant gratification behavior payoffs.

Choose to Listen to Your Positive Inner Voices

It won't work to just tell yourself that you are going to stop the negative, self-sabotaging voices in your head: rather, you must actively and consciously *replace* and *displace* these voices with the ones you want. The critical voice of your negative ego may say, "I'm going to let everyone down and feel humiliated, so I should just give up now." You can replace this with the voice of your conscious self, which says, "I'm really good at what I do. I'll give it my best shot, and no matter what the outcome, I intend that everyone will receive some benefit from it."

Another method is to actively turn the volume down on the negative voices so low that you can barely hear them. Do this by refusing to believe in them or give them any energy. In Buddhism, this type of method is consistent with the practices of *cultivating right thought* and *developing mental discipline*. Alternatively, you might listen to your inner nurturing parent's voice of reassurance, validation, and loving respect.

New Behavior Patterns Are Built Over Time

All behavioral change requires three main things:

1. Having sufficient motivation.

2. Possessing the ability to do the steps and actions that are required.

3. Putting into place the necessary practices, prompts, and reminders.

Create empowering practices that are easy to do and that remind you of what your intent is. These practices will become your new rituals and routines. This includes changing your environment so that you have embedded positive prompts and have removed any reminders, or triggers, that you find disempowering.

Everyone needs ways of reminding themselves to actually do the new behaviors they haven't yet integrated, and a key to success is setting up your environment to support you. For example, moving your alarm far enough away from your bed that you can't keep hitting the snooze button and having your exercise clothes already laid out are simple ways of changing your environment to support you in your workout goals.

This process works best if you don't delay starting to feel good: enjoy yourself now, in the present moment. Feel the enjoyment and pleasure that comes from true self-care. Celebrate and feel gratitude for any positive, interim outcomes on the way to reaching your big goals. Don't sabotage yourself by being self-punishing for not having reached where you want to be yet. Feel good right now.

Plan to engage in any newly chosen behavior for at least three weeks, preferably longer, to anchor it as a new habit. It won't work to only say, "I'm going to stop sabotaging myself by doing X [fill in the blank]." You will need to create new neural pathways by replacing the old, habitual patterns with new, more beneficial ways of operating. Make choices, identify new rituals and routines, and take actions consistent with your conscious self that feel good, week after week, month after month, until they become a consistent habit.

Causing Personal Growth

Overview

Now that we have covered the principles of creating positive change and some of the things that get in the way of being successful, you can build upon this understanding to enhance your personal growth. This section is about understanding how to do self-therapy. When you want to get free of the grip of unconscious dynamics that are holding you back, there are four basic stages that comprise the process of causing personal growth and development. Each of these stages is important. To get the most out of this section and to internalize this process, try choosing an issue you would like to change about yourself and apply the following four stages of personal growth.

Often, people are stronger or weaker in one of these areas than the others. The area of weakness is most often the follow-through stage, and this is something to keep in mind when working on your issue. You may need to ask for extra support and be extra-vigilant when working with this stage.

These stages are not entirely linear. You might get partway through and discover something new that you need to go back and incorporate into a previous stage. Be sure to include each stage, at least to some extent, so that you don't undermine your success. As you move through the stages, you will gain more insights, which will upgrade your process and help you revise your plan. This is a key element of the follow-through stage, which helps to ensure maximum success.

The Four Stages of Personal Growth

1. Awareness Stage

This first stage is about illuminating the dynamics of whatever is not working that you want to change, identifying the interim payoffs you have been getting that have been keeping you stuck, and clarifying your goals. This is the "what's so stage," where you get really clear about what is going on regarding the current issue or dysfunctional behavior pattern that is getting in your way. It helps to take a kind, compassionate, and nonjudgmental approach when doing this sort of self-scrutiny. Reaffirm that you are a conscious self and that you are bigger than whatever is occurring: "I am not my behavior pattern."

2. Emotional Commitment Stage

This is also known as the acceptance and motivation stage. This is where you get clear about your current level of willingness, commitment, and readiness to replace the old pattern or patterns with something new. This involves coming to terms with the costs of keeping the pattern around and creating a vision of what the positive benefits would be of shifting it. It requires understanding what might be needed to complete the past so that you can get free of its influence. It also involves clarifying what your genuine needs are that would be fulfilled by making this change.

Dysfunctional behavior patterns always have a price to your sense of self, your self-respect, and to other people's respect for you. That price includes the cost of the time and energy it has consumed, which could have been devoted to something more beneficial. The costs of unconscious losing games and dynamics encompass every unpleasurable aspect of life we can think of. This includes disconnection, breakdowns, antipathy, humiliation, guilt, depression, pain, and alienation. The costs may include indirect or direct harm to yourself or others and hamper true creativity, spontaneity, and self-expression.

This step is about creating a vision of where your life is heading, and what it will look like when you have made the change you are seeking. It is about identifying what the benefits and positive addictions are: the self-respect, good feelings, and positive outcomes, which will replace the old compulsive pattern. Imagine all the potential benefits and how you will feel once you have accomplished your vision. It is also important to identify more empowering attitudes and beliefs to replace the old, unworkable ones. One of the outcomes of this stage is to have a clear sense of your purpose or reasons for evolving and what your intended outcomes or goals are.

3. Behavioral Practice Stage

In this phase, you create your action plan—the structure for fulfilling the desired changes that you're committed to—and begin to implement actions. The bigger the changes are you want to make, the more detailed this plan needs to be. This is also referred to as conditioning a project, which means breaking your goal down by identifying and fleshing out the elements needed to shape, mold, and guide what it is you want to turn into reality. These factors include identifying the key elements of success (things that must happen or resources that are needed), important people and their roles, timeline, budget, and any major milestones.

For example, if you want to make a change in your physical well-being, then this stage is where you do the research, make appointments for tests, get advice on your diet and supplement program, and so on. This step is also when you need to put new actions into practice over time to create new neural pathways and habits.

Whether you are working on an inner issue or one that is occurring in your relationships with others, this is when you figure out what practices you are going to incorporate into your life. You assess areas of weakness and set inner boundaries. You create clear goals for who you are becoming and develop affirmations. There is a lot of strength available in community and you might put into place a support team of friends and counselors. You don't just have some nebulous idea of how you might want to evolve: you make it real in your everyday life, and live as if it were already real and happening.

4. Follow-Through Stage

This stage is about feedback, reassessment, revision, and recommitment. Every time you want to create something new, you need to breathe life into it—or it disappears. As you carry out your action plan over time, this is when the rubber really hits the road in terms of creating enduring change. During this stage, you will need to continually review where you are regarding achieving your goal. Keep assessing what is working and what is not working and adjust accordingly. Be sure to acknowledge and celebrate the incremental changes you have made and any territory you have taken.

A potential pitfall to watch for is that once you have created an intention and launched a program or project, it is normal to feel at the effect of what you have created. There is a gap between where you are and where you want to be, and that can feel frustrating or uncomfortable. It is easy to slide into being overwhelmed, which can rapidly turn into a victim game in which whatever you are creating feels bigger than you are.

This overwhelm is one reason why people so often flounder in the follow-through stage. The only thing to do is to recognize and acknowledge when this arises, and then intentionally bring yourself back to your conscious self. Remind yourself that this is occurring in your space and that you need to practice persistence and have patience and fortitude. You could create a motto, such as "Evolution, not revolution," to remind yourself that processes take time.

Chances are that whatever condition you are working on took far longer to become an issue than the short amount of time you have dedicated to changing it. Be vigilant about reinspiring yourself with, and re-enrolling yourself in, the value of what you are creating. Keep making the necessary revisions to successfully step your change process down into achievable actions that fit within the demands of your life.

Navigating Challenging Circumstances

There are two common types of difficult situations that require additional understanding and skill to shift them from dysfunctional to functional dynamics. These two types of circumstances are breakdowns and upsets. Everyone experiences these two situations from time to time, and they are fraught with the potential for wreaking havoc in our lives if not handled well.

Specifically, we will look at how to turn breakdowns into breakthroughs, and how to successfully navigate upsets so that you can return to feeling OK about yourself and the situation as quickly as possible. By adopting these practices, you will be empowered in transforming these situations from being potentially damaging to being mutually beneficial.

From Breakdown to Breakthrough

Overview

> "What if the worst thing that happened to you turns out to be the best thing that has ever happened to you?" —Dr. Joe Dispenza

Strictly speaking, breakdowns don't necessarily occur as a function of unconscious losing dynamics, but when confronted with a breakdown, often the main default is to slide into feeling like a victim or wanting to be rescued. Or people may find that their fear causes them act to out like a persecutor, trying to dominate everyone and the situation. By reacting unconsciously, they end up sliding right onto the drama triangle, casting blame, being judgmental, trying to control, or making others wrong.

The most empowering attitude you can adopt when faced with a breakdown or significant challenge in some area of your life is understanding that inherent in every breakdown is the possibility for a breakthrough. Embracing this attitude creates a powerful context for generating workability and success, one that incorporates breakdowns as key opportunities for causing accelerated growth.

Breakdowns only show up against a background of commitment to making something happen. If you didn't care, then it wouldn't be a breakdown. Breakdowns are a *natural* occurrence in the face of most commitments. True innovation *requires* failure that is held with responsibility, and therefore becomes an opportunity for growth.

Breakthroughs, on the other hand, are defined as the act of producing unpredictable, discontinuous results. This is when strikingly important advances or discoveries occur.

Following are the main characteristics of breakthroughs. They are:

- unprecedented and unpredictable; discontinuous from the past.

- an interruption in the status quo or business as usual.

- a manifestation of agency or assertiveness that forwards a positive vision and breaks with past expectations.

- illuminating in terms of what isn't working or what is missing.

Another empowering attitude to adopt is that breakdowns are major learning opportunities. When a breakdown occurs, you're faced with a critical choice. You can either use this breakdown to return to the status quo or you can use it as an opportunity to move yourself forward in your commitment in a significant way.

Without taking sufficient responsibility for the breakdown and taking a stand for the commitment it is showing up against, it is impossible to create a breakthrough. Owning any mistakes that have been made, without adding blame, shame, or guilt, is an essential component for integrating the lessons that are being learned.

Steps for Transforming Breakdowns into Breakthroughs

1. *Accept and own the breakdown.* Recognize when something isn't working or is dysfunctional and choose to use the breakdown as an opportunity to create a breakthrough (with all the actions that this will entail), rather than letting things drift along.

2. *Declare a breakdown.* Someone who is empowered with the authority or responsibility for the endeavor declares a breakdown with the key players involved. This is like a coach declaring a time-out: current action is suspended and a new process is put in place.

3. *Look at the big picture.* Identify what the larger background commitment is, the one against which you have declared a breakdown in its achievement. Reassess that commitment, revise it if necessary, and reaffirm it.

4. *Get clear about what is really going on.* This is also called getting clear about what's so, which is a process of bringing to awareness all related content and telling the truth about the current reality. Bring to the surface and illuminate what has occurred regarding the original vision, intentions, and strategy—as distinct from interpretations, assessments, or good ideas. Do this by using inquiry and acceptance, instead of judging, blaming, shaming, or finding the situation or people wrong. Identify what didn't work, what was missing, or any mistakes made regarding the declared commitment, and take full ownership of them.

5. *Have a conversation for possibility.* Re-envision what your endeavor might look like if it were really working.

6. *Have a conversation for opportunity.* Identify what is needed to allocate the necessary resources, and take the necessary actions that flow from your commitment. Assess any changes, corrections, or refinements that need to be incorporated into the procedures, protocols, or overall structure of your project.

7. *Have a conversation for action.* Strategize tactics to put the new plans into action, with clear accountability regarding who, what, where, and by when.

"Success is moving from failure to failure with no loss of enthusiasm."
—Sir Winston Churchill

"There is an easier way, called 'not do it at all.' I don't see a big, big, big success without a lot of missed targets, without a lot of 'I wished I hadn't.' It comes with the territory, and all the big people I know have

made huge errors—appropriate to their bigness—but they don't get out of the dance. It is just having the courage to keep on dancing."
—Joan Holmes (founding president of The Hunger Project)

Managing Upsets for Positive Outcomes

Overview

Another way to look at unconscious, losing games and dynamics is through the lens of the emotional upsets they create in your life. No matter how emotionally intelligent you are, it is inevitable that you will experience being upset from time to time. Either you will get upset with yourself or others, or you will be dealing with someone who is upset with you. The world is fraught with upsetting situations that need to be navigated.

Some common causes of upsets include expectations that are unmet, feelings of being disrespected or betrayed, concerns that seem unmanageable, or a sense of being on the losing end of something. Upsets are the emotional reactivity that goes along with these situations. When you have been overtaken by an upsetting emotional reaction, how can you best manage it? What matters is how you approach handling the upset, and having the intent to create positive, mutually beneficial outcomes.

The following is a description of what we've noticed happens during an upset and we get in the grip of our negative ego or a reactive, lower-self subpersonality. We've written this as a formula that illustrates every step of the process, so that you can refer to it for support in coming up with your own best practices. You may find that you do some of these steps but not others, or that you do them in a different sequence.

Have compassion for yourself when you get taken over by an upset. No matter how much work you've done on yourself or how much personal growth or experience you've had, upsets will always be a part of life. Being caught in an upset doesn't mean anything about who you are as a person or how emotionally intelligent you are: it just means that you are human.

Steps in the Process

1. Recognize that you just got grabbed by or are in the grip of an upset. Something isn't working and you have a definite feeling of emotional reactivity and of being not OK. "I'm not feeling so great; something isn't right here."

2. Breathe and recenter yourself. Get back to your conscious self by using the centering breath technique, resonance breathing, or another method that you can count on to work for you.

3. In a way that is loud enough to override any negative inner voices, tell yourself whatever will help you remember who you really are and that you have sufficient personal power to handle the situation. Use phrases such as, "I am bigger than this upset," "It is happening in my space. I am not happening in its space," "I have this. It is not who I am," or "I can handle this."

4. Allow yourself to take responsibility in some way for the upset. Remind yourself, "This is showing up in the face of my commitments. This means that there is some sort of opportunity in this, even if I don't like the way this is feeling right now."

5. Review the situation. Walk yourself through what is true about you, the other person, and the situation. For example, the negative ego likes to amplify danger, so it is helpful to step back and realistically assess any possible risk to yourself, rather than buying into the fears playing on the loudspeaker in your head.

6. Examine your unconscious assumptions and expectations about how you thought the situation would go or how the other person should be. Often unconscious expectations are the source of an upset and need to be adjusted.

7. De-escalate the situation and create space for reflection by physically removing yourself from the environment for some time. Keep breathing and give yourself the necessary time to talk yourself down off the pinnacle of reactive feelings before you reengage.

8. Discharge your emotions in a safe and responsible way, so that you can release enough of the energetic charge of the upset to become calmer and less caught up in the swirl of your negative ego.

9. Once you have discharged the energy of your emotions and feel more centered, ask some questions so that you understand where the other person is coming from and what their authentic needs might be. Listen to the other person in a way that they feel heard. Use reflective listening to ensure that you aren't misunderstanding them and that they feel known.

10. Taking total responsibility for your experience, use "I" statements to make heartful, authentic, and clean communications about how you are feeling, without

any shaming, blaming, or making wrong. The less defended you are, the less defended they will need to be. Remember that honesty is best served up with a dose of kindness.

11. Examine your underlying authentic needs, being sure to carefully filter out any defensive negative ego needs that you might be unconsciously trying to meet. Ask yourself, "What real needs do I have that are going unmet?" See if there are any assertive requests you can make about getting your needs met. Then make these requests.

12. Set healthy boundaries. Examine if you have any physical, emotional, or psychological limits that have been violated by others, and make assertive and nonadversarial requests about having your boundaries respected. Assess to make sure that your boundary requests aren't coming from an unconscious, fear-driven, defensive need for control. Healthy boundaries are usually negotiated, not unilaterally imposed. They require being respectful of yourself *and* the other person.

13. Remind yourself that it's not about being perfect: it's about being authentic. Any responsible communication that you are courageous enough to deliver, while simultaneously revealing yourself, being vulnerable, and maintaining healthy boundaries, will feel good and probably dissipate a lot of the upset.

14. Accept and forgive. Complete and fully integrate the experience by calling up some acceptance of the situation, forgiveness of the person involved, and gratitude for the growth and lessons learned on your continuing journey.

Summary of Self-Empowerment Tools and Practices

Use the four stages of personal growth when dealing with areas of your life you would like to change or evolve.

Motivate yourself by owning the payoffs and costs of any losing dynamics you have been caught up in and replace them with the potential benefits of shifting to a mutual benefit, win-win approach.

Adopt the attitude that breakdowns are opportunities for breakthroughs.

Navigate upsets successfully by discharging any reactive energy responsibly and returning to feeling OK as quickly as possible.

CHAPTER 15
CRAFTING YOUR GROUND
OF BEING

Overview

"Life isn't about finding yourself. Life is about creating yourself."
—George Bernard Shaw

The following is a summary of the basic premises for understanding and developing integral emotional intelligence. Some of these ontological distinctions have already been covered to some degree in this material, some can be inferred from what has been covered, and some are new. Working with ontological distinctions can be like peeling an onion. There are deeper and deeper levels of understanding available the more you work with them. These deeper levels of understanding can sometimes be abstract and hard to hold onto. Often they need to be revisited multiple times and looked at from various angles to tease out their nuances.

Now that we have covered so many building blocks of emotional literacy, this is an opportunity to look again at some of these key concepts to see if you can gain deeper insight into how they play out in your life. It is also an opportunity to build upon this foundation and introduce some new concepts. The intent is to empower you in anchoring them more strongly within, so that they show up as needed as you go forward in your daily life.

Although these premises are contextual in nature, they are also meant to be practical concepts regarding how to successfully navigate life. When adopted as personal operating principles, they contribute to creating a framework, or ground of being, from which you can approach yourself, your relationships, and your world; one that allows you to accelerate your journey of personal growth.

You are always operating from a ground of being: it is what shapes and filters how you approach everything in your life and how you show up on a moment-by-moment basis. It defines where you come from, and to a great degree is synonymous with your motivation. Your character, integrity, principles, beliefs, attitudes, and conscience are all part of your ground of being.

Mastering the art of everyday transformation requires that you consciously create your ground of being. You can do this by thoughtfully embracing a set of attitudes, principles, empowering beliefs, and practices that are closely aligned with your inner being. When you do this, you are being sourceful in life. As you strengthen your ground of being, you naturally begin to eliminate negative self-talk and relax the hold of your negative ego.

Unless you consciously create your ground of being, it will be to a great degree composed of your unexamined beliefs and attitudes. These tend to shape behaviors in ways that are driven by the past and aren't always in your, or others', best interests. Often these unconscious beliefs and attitudes are fear- and survival-based, and lead to playing losing games and being adversarial. In other words, your unconscious beliefs and attitudes can have you unwittingly take a victim approach to parts of your life and operate below the line.

Any individual who is committed to their own personal growth is already working on upgrading their ground of being, perhaps without realizing it. This is a natural part of working toward being centered in your authentic self, feeling good inside, and having your life work for you. By naming this process and bringing your awareness, commitment, and intention to it, you can empower yourself in greatly accelerating your journey of growth.

Several of the following premises are attitudes of the conscious self that, when taken on board, help you to lift from being in victim mode. You can shift from feeling like you are at the effect of whatever is occurring in your life into being more responsible, at cause, and in creator mode. By making this shift, you have greater access to your personal power and agency in effecting positive change and creating mutual benefit.

This review of basic premises is being provided as a resource for you in your work to develop your ground of being. You are encouraged to review these premises with that in mind as you work to formulate a set of operating principles and practices that resonate with you and are an expression of your commitment to who you are being and becoming. This process includes identifying elements of your current ground of being that are working for you that you wish to affirm, as well as ones that aren't working that you want to let go of.

The work of crafting your ground of being is an ongoing, even lifelong, process. It is an infinite game with no end point, only expanding states of awareness and fulfillment. There is no condition of perfection to achieve. Instead, what is required is a commitment to excellence and impeccability. You are not fixing yourself: you are evolving who you are being and how you show up in all the moments of your everyday life.

Summary of Foundational Premises

Understand, Recognize, and Use Ontological Distinctions

"Light is not recognized except through darkness." —Jewish proverb

In esoteric philosophy, the understanding of ontological knowledge is referred to as the science of the soul. Great ontological distinctions have a quality of being illuminating and revelatory. They empower you in your journey of acquiring self-knowledge by enabling you to observe and sort out your reality with fresh eyes. Being able to recognize ontological distinctions, recreate them, and use them in your life accelerates your growth and benefits you and the people you interact with.

Distinctions aren't about having to learn something new, which you must then impose on top of your life. Rather, they enhance your powers of observation and allow you to see more clearly and deeply, illuminating dynamics that are already occurring that you were previously unable to identify. The more you understand and anchor ontological distinctions within yourself, the less you need to try to remember them and the more they will show up when needed as you go about your daily life. The best way to internalize and anchor new distinctions is by applying them to your real-life issues.

The cognitive map of the three selves is a set of ontological distinctions. Understanding the nature of responsibility and what it means to be at cause and the creator in your life is a distinction. So is understanding discernment, practicing forgiveness, creating context, and being heart-centered. Almost all of the information in this first volume is comprised of ontological distinctions that help to illuminate the nature of your inner being.

Keep an Open Mind

In terms of maximizing the value you create for yourself as you go through life, it is essential to be willing to keep an open mind and try on new concepts as if they were true, so that you can experiment and see what occurs. Trust the voice of your intuition and your discernment to determine if something feels OK, resonates with you, and is aligned with your principles and integrity.

It's not necessary to believe in or agree with every new distinction, belief, or attitude you discover in life. The idea is to put on your researcher's hat and see what happens when you try on new concepts. You are responsible for adopting what works for you, disregarding what doesn't, and creating value for yourself in the process. Consider new information and concepts as opportunities for provoking deeper inquiry and bringing unconscious thoughts and dynamics up to the level of your awareness, rather than something you need to automatically endorse.

Reveal More of Who You Really Are

Remember that the process of growing and evolving isn't about fixing yourself: you are already deserving, competent, and worthy. It is not anyone else's job to handle, change, save, or rescue you in any way.

Engaging with developing emotional intelligence is a process of gaining techniques and tools that enable you to reveal more and more of who you truly are. It is about strengthening your connection to your conscious self, your sense of being and your inner magnanimity—your best self. It is a process of healing and integrating wounded parts of yourself and dismantling or dissolving old, fear-driven defense structures, which obscure your authentic self and hinder you in expressing your inner adult.

Make Your Spirituality Your Top Priority

Spirituality means cultivating the *being* part of what it is to be a human *being*. It refers to the inherent consciousness and intelligence that is present in all living things. Your spirituality is your relationship to consciousness and to who you are as a conscious self. It is not dependent upon any religion, religious theory, or dogma.

All the concepts in this material have been chosen to enhance and deepen whatever path you are on and whatever tradition you already practice, regardless of whether you take a secular or a nonsecular approach to life. This material is about who you are and what you bring to whatever path you are following.

Being on a spiritual path simply means having an intention to raise your awareness and become more present, awake, and heart-centered in life. This creates the context in which everything in your life occurs. No one else can do this work for you: it's an inside job. Make your spirituality a top priority because it will enhance, even transform, everything in your life.

Wake Up by Practicing Metacognition

Everyone goes through life cycling between stages of unconscious, waking sleep and being awake, which is also referred to as being present and self-aware. Your spiritual path, which is your personal evolution regarding the expansion of your consciousness, involves working with your awareness so that you can connect more and more fully to your sense of self—your inner being.

As humans, we are designed to be able to hold two levels of awareness simultaneously. We are able to be present to what is occurring while taking an inner step back to observe ourselves and how we are participating with what is occurring. This is called metacognition, and it is one of the most important skills needed for being emotionally intelligent.

By practicing metacognition, by using your will to continually remind yourself to be in observer or witness mode, you are developing greater presence while increasing your ability to be self-reflective and choose how you want to author your responses. When you approach life in this way, then even the times when you fall into a state of waking sleep and are operating out of reactivity will occur within the overarching context of becoming more and more awake in life.

Connect to Your Inner Knowing

One indicator of the efficacy of ontological material is having a sense of "already knowing" as you read it. Perhaps you weren't quite able to put your finger on a particular concept or articulate it clearly, but it seems familiar to your experience of life. You may have "aha" moments, or what are called blinding flashes of the obvious.

Another way to think about connecting with your inner knowing is that it is a process of being centered in your conscious self and actively listening for the voice of your intuition. It is about developing your sense of discernment and being able to recognize when something has the resonance of truth about it.

The process of tuning into your inner knowing is one of illuminating your authentic self. Instead of attempting to change what is so about you or making up some other, different way that you should be, you peel back the layers and go deeper within.

Look at Life from an Integral Perspective

Remind yourself that everything that happens in life has correspondences that occur simultaneously in all four areas of human expression: mind, body, emotions, and spirit or consciousness. For example, it is impossible to experience an emotion without having a related set of thoughts and physical sensations.

Conversely, your thoughts and your physical health have a direct impact on your emotions and mood. There is always a bigger context or purpose to an emotion and ways of working with it to create positive effects that can be discerned only through conscious reflection. Your spirit, or conscious awareness, affects all the other parts of your life by granting purpose and meaning,

You can't effectively engage with becoming more emotionally intelligent without taking all these areas of human expression into consideration. The more you continue to learn about how these parts work together in holistic, synergistic ways, the more empowered you will be in creating everyday transformation in your life.

Be Self-Reflective

The degree to which you are willing to be self-reflective and honest with yourself, which is otherwise known as telling on yourself, determines to a great extent the value you receive from your life experiences. The more you use self-inquiry to shine the spotlight of awareness on your inner dynamics and tell yourself the truth about what you observe in a kind and nonjudgmental way, the more you will be able to externalize and disidentify who you really are from whatever dynamic has had you in its grasp. In doing so, you can begin to relax its hold on you.

The more willing you are to scrutinize and own your hidden agendas and survival strategies, which are the defensive needs of your negative ego, the faster you can grow. Being self-reflective and practicing self-inquiry requires self-acceptance, vulnerability, and humility. Vulnerability is the willingness to express the truth of who you are, your authentic self, and what you are feeling at any given moment. It is a willingness to be seen and known for exactly who you are and what you are thinking and feeling. It can be both a scary and a liberating experience.

Cultivate Being Heart-Centered

Becoming more heart-centered and expanding the amount of love flowing in your life is an important part of being able to fully express your conscious self. Therefore, as you move through life it is necessary to inquire into and wrestle with the topic of love—what it means to you and any resistance or aversion you might have to giving or receiving it.

This includes examining your thoughts, beliefs, prejudices, and misconceptions about love. It also includes inquiring into what it means to hold a mature, loving attitude toward yourself and expanding your ability to experience yourself as loving awareness.

Everyone has wounds around love and constrictions around their hearts. This woundedness shows up as limitations that occur primarily in three ways: in our ability to discern and tune into the energy of love, in our experience of love for ourselves and others, and in the degree to which we are willing to allow ourselves to give or receive love.

Whenever there is a breakdown in life, it indicates that there is an insufficient amount of love being experienced and expressed. There is some sort of barrier or blockage that gets in the way of experiencing the love that is already and always present. This is the love that is our natural affinity with one another and is intrinsic to who we really are. Remember that all healing happens as a function of love: without love there can be no healing. There is no real safety without love, and the way to make something safe is to surround it with sufficient love.

"Love is the voice under all silences, the hope which has no opposite in fear; the strength so strong mere force is feebleness: the truth more first than sun, more last than star..." —E. E. Cummings

Practice Radical Acceptance of What Is

The practice of radical acceptance of what is occurring in your life is not only highly encouraged but is essential to integration. By owning what is occurring and where you are in relationship to it, everything, even what you perceive to be your mistakes or failures, can become opportunities for growth.

Accepting and embracing what is so becomes part of your practice of developing unshakable presence in the face of anything life might throw at you. Surrendering, which is another way of looking at acceptance, is not the same as succumbing, avoiding responsibility, or giving up.

By practicing radical acceptance, it is possible to find the grace—the learning, the gifts, the love that can lift you up—that is present in a breakdown. Often the bigger the breakdown, the fiercer the grace. There is no grace without love and acceptance that is expressed as responsibility, empathy, understanding, compassion, and forgiveness. When you can illuminate and accept what is so about yourself and the situation, dynamics can begin to shift and move in positive ways.

> "Life will give you whatever experience is most helpful for the evolution of your consciousness. How do you know this is the experience you need? Because it is the experience you are having at this moment." —Eckhart Tolle

> "You are ready. Face it. Your psyche will not give you any task that you cannot tackle. Difficult is not the same as bad." —Stanislav Grof

Practice Self-Love and Self-Acceptance

In addition to working with strengthening your attitude of self-acceptance, your practice of self-love is critical for developing self-mastery. By holding a loving attitude toward all parts of yourself, you are empowered to integrate and heal any blockages or barriers you might have that are limiting you in your ability to experience and express your best self.

There isn't a human being alive who doesn't have foibles or quirks. We all have wounds that we've developed unconscious ways of working around or on top of. Everyone has coping strategies and self-defense structures: it's how we're designed to survive childhood, when we didn't have the maturity or skills to deal with everything we were experiencing. There is no shame in any of this. There is nothing inherently wrong with coping strategies. They can be very useful. The real skill is recognizing when they don't serve you any longer and then dismantling them and letting them go.

It is easy to punish yourself when you feel like you are inadequate and don't measure up in some way. Self-flagellation is a practice that has, unfortunately, been seen as something exalted in many religions. Being hateful toward yourself might seem easier than being loving and might even feel like a default position in life, but not only is it unnecessary for development, it perpetuates shame and thus is an impediment to growth.

Being kind, nonjudgmental, and compassionate toward yourself requires intention, patience, and practice. You can become much more effective at letting go of attachment to your past and old, unhelpful ways of doing things by practicing acceptance and forgiveness toward yourself.

When you adopt an attitude of self-acceptance combined with self-love, it becomes possible to see that where you are on your journey of evolution is exactly where you are meant to be. Who you are and where you are is the perfect, and only, place from which you can grow and evolve. Intentionally engaging with whatever you have been given in life—your personal set of foibles, history, wounds, and defense structures—is your unique path to inner emancipation.

> "You took birth here because you had certain work to do. This is your curriculum. It's not an error. Where you are now, with all your neuroses and your problems, you're sitting in just the right place."
> —Ram Dass

Become Your Own Healer

Relaxing the grip of your negative ego and letting go of old, unhelpful defense mechanisms is all about integration and healing. There are two critical factors that make healing possible. First, you must realize that healing *is* possible and be willing for that healing to occur. Second, you must be determined to accomplish that healing. In the first step, you assess your willingness to be healed. In the second step, you take responsibility for your healing, call forth your will, and take a stand for it, telling yourself, "It will be done. I may not know how this is going to happen, but it *is* going to happen. I *will* achieve this."

Healing can happen only as a function of love. Practicing self-love and self-acceptance is the only place from which a successful healing process can be initiated. You can't heal what you deny or won't embrace. Being hateful toward ourselves in any way causes our disintegrated parts to persist and become more entrenched.

By learning how to integrate the areas where you are disconnected from your sense of self, you grow in your ability to heal. The more you do this healing work, the less your present is unconsciously driven by your past experiences and the more it is being consciously shaped by your vision of your future and your sense of who you are becoming, your future self.

It is important to remember that if you haven't healed a particular issue in life yet, it doesn't mean you have failed or are inadequate to the task. What it does point to is the need to bring more awareness to bear on the situation and the fact that there is still more value that you can squeeze out of it. In other words, there is deeper to go and more for you to reveal and understand about yourself.

Rather than throwing up your hands in frustration, you can choose to have patience and be persistent in reapplying your will and commitment to finding a way through. Whenever you hear the voice in your head telling you that life is hopeless and that you are helpless, recognize it as your negative ego and don't give it any energy. Replace that voice with positive affirmations.

You can adopt the attitude that there is always a solution and a pathway to greater wholeness. You can remember that you have never worked on this issue from who you are now, in this moment. You are more awake and mature, and you have more tools than you did when you last worked on healing this issue, even if it was only yesterday.

Create Your Reality

"We are what we think. All that we are arises with our thoughts. With our thoughts, we make the world. Your worst enemy cannot harm you as much as your own unguarded thoughts." —Buddha

Your attitudes, thoughts, and beliefs are some of the raw materials out of which you shape your experience and your reality. People always gather evidence to support their beliefs and attitudes, both their conscious and unconscious ones. They are convinced that their unexamined beliefs are the true and right ones to have, when actually, they are simply opinions that they hold with conviction. We often turn our beliefs and attitudes into rigid positions that we will defend at any cost. Out of fear, we get caught up in a negative ego need to have *our* beliefs be the "right" ones. This can hinder us in seeing other points of view, developing greater understanding, or having empathy for others.

"Almost all of what we demonstrate starts with a thought. But just because you have a thought doesn't necessarily mean it is true. Most thoughts are just old circuits in your brain that have become hardwired by your repetitive volition."
—Joe Dispenza

Part of the path of self-mastery is surfacing the unconscious beliefs and attitudes that don't serve you and consciously choosing to replace them with more empowering ones. It is possible to become more flexible and more in-tune with your reality by knowing when to change your mind and let go of old, self-limiting positions.

For example, when you choose to hold an attitude or belief that there are solutions to a situation, you are more likely to discover pathways through it, openings that you wouldn't have seen if you were stuck in a state of feeling hopeless. Out of your determination and commitment, new opportunities and solutions can arise. This is one of the meanings of the Latin motto *Credendo vides*, which translates as *by believing, one sees.*

Create Meaning and Value

"I am not what happened to me, I am what I choose to become."
—Carl Jung

Practice adopting a spiritual or yogic attitude, which can be stated as "You can't do anything bad to a yogi because everything that happens to them shows up as an opportunity." Things don't always happen for the best, but you can make them be for the best. When you bring your best self to a situation—your awareness, love, will, and intention to create something of value—you *make* it be for the best. Then obstacles do not block the path: they are the path.

"What stands in the way becomes the way." —Marcus Aurelius

You can create meaning and context, and you can use your will and determination to find the silver lining in any situation. You can look for potential lessons learned, use the breakdowns and challenges for personal growth, and in the process become more authentic, build character, and cause transformation. This spiritual or yogic attitude is foundational to the skill of being able to consistently cause breakthroughs from breakdowns.

"When you want, really want, answers—they are there. When you are ready, really ready, to change—the opportunities abound. When you are willing to listen and learn—even the stones speak." —Jach Pursel

Note that this attitude is not what is called conjectural optimism (or toxic positivity), which is being naively optimistic as a way of being in denial and ignoring or smoothing things over, or avoiding responsibility for dealing with what isn't working. This also doesn't take away from the fact that terrible, devastating things happen in life. Who you are, your personal agency in the face of these occurrences, is the most authentic power you have. Often the only way to get relief in difficult circumstances is by going deeper within to discover more of your authentic self, practicing nonattachment, and then choosing to show up more fully in life from that place.

> "In the midst of winter, I found that there was within me
> an invincible summer." —Albert Camus

> "The happiest of people don't necessarily have the best of everything;
> they just make the most of everything that comes along their way."
> —Anonymous

See Relationships as Opportunities for Personal Growth

If you accept that the overall goal of evolution is to grow and expand in consciousness, then it follows that the spiritual or overarching purpose of all relationships is to assist you in that growth and evolution. Indeed, it is possible to grow and learn only from someone, or something, you have a relationship with. We are often inexplicably drawn to people from whom we can learn more about ourselves, even when that relationship is difficult. The real challenge is in being awake enough to discern what these lessons are.

When you adopt this attitude, you can see others as the mirror they are for reflecting things that you haven't been aware of about yourself, particularly your blind spots. You can be grateful for the gift they are giving you, even when it is uncomfortable—perhaps especially when it is uncomfortable. You can create value no matter what occurs in a relationship, and you are empowered to know when you have integrated the lessons from that relationship and if, and when, it is appropriate to bless that relationship and let it go.

Focus on Your Own Growth and Internal Emancipation

"You do you and let them do them." What this means is that the *only* way you can gain access to your power and agency is by concentrating on doing your own inner work of personal growth. Rather than trying to change others, focus on your internal emancipation.

Just as this material isn't about fixing you, it is not meant to be used as a way of fixing or handling others. If this knowledge is used to be better than or superior to others in any way, then a fundamental point of this teaching will have been missed. Wanting to be better than or superior to another is a losing game and a very strong signal that the negative ego is engaged. It is also a covert way of shaming others.

The more you do your own work, the more you can model the insights and positive growth you are experiencing and inspire others on their journey. Only they can be responsible for their choices and behaviors, and you have no way of knowing what their spiritual path or soul's journey is. This is the practice of noninterference.

> "Until you can allow your own beauty, your own dignity, your own being, you cannot free another. So, if I were giving one instruction, I would say: work on yourself; have compassion for yourself. Allow yourself to be beautiful and all the rest will follow." —Ram Dass

Choose to make your growth, your well-being, and your spirituality—your consciousness and connection to your sense of self—your top priority, because it creates the container in which *everything* in your life occurs.

> "No effort that we make to attain something beautiful is ever lost."
> —Helen Keller

Work with Your Resistance

Noticing when you are experiencing resistance is a valuable tool on your journey of inner emancipation. Whenever resistance or defensiveness arises, it is a clue as to where deeper inquiry is needed and can bring to light parts of your subconscious self that need to be acknowledged and integrated.

Often when people experience resistance, their knee-jerk response is to push away from whatever they are resisting and go into denial about it. Usually they don't even realize they are doing this. Rather than resisting your resistance, you can lean into it and embrace it. Remind yourself that resistance causes persistence. Practice self-acceptance. You can't process and release something unless you lean into it and embrace it. This doesn't mean you have to act it out, but it does mean that you must process it in an emotionally mature way.

There are many possible sources of resistance that are useful to illuminate, untangle, and heal. Often they are irrational, unconscious, fear-based dynamics. Alternatively, your resistance might show you where your needs aren't being met or where you might need to be more assertive about setting boundaries. Sometimes, resistance can feel like an allergic reaction to something that feels off, which can provide contrast and help guide you away from unhelpful experiences and toward more beneficial ones.

Lay Down Your Arms

One way to think about doing the inner work of emancipation is that it is about disarmament: metaphorically relaxing the grip of your negative ego and laying down your weapons for wounding yourself and others.

This includes letting go of unnecessary self-defense mechanisms and the defensive needs of the negative ego: the need to be right and make others wrong, the need to be better than, the need to control and dominate, and so on. In the process of healing, integrating, and releasing these self-defense structures, you can discover more of your inner strength and become more present, awake, authentic, and resilient in life. You can discover more effective ways of getting your real needs met.

As a result of letting go of these defense mechanisms, you naturally become less adversarial and more skillful at creating dynamics of partnership and mutual benefit. You can become more comfortable with the discomfort of being vulnerable and become more transparent, open, and available in your interactions with others. More and more of who you really are as a conscious self is revealed as you release these old, unconscious ways of operating in life.

Do No Harm

Although we have not mentioned this concept previously, *do no harm* is an important principle for integral emotional intelligence and is related to the premise of laying down your arms. "With harm to none" is another way to say this principle, and it is a fundamental attitude of a spiritual approach to life. It is the basis of the Golden Rule, which is the essential teaching at the heart of all the great world religions.

> "This is the sum of duty: do naught unto others which would cause you pain if done to you." —The Mahabharata

Do no harm is a stance of not generating negativity in life. It requires letting go of punishing others and exacting retribution for perceived slights. Honest, assertive communication and setting healthy boundaries replace unconsciously lashing out as ways of getting your needs met. It includes having a firm commitment to creating mutual benefit and winning, infinite games in your interactions with others.

The very best way to avoid causing yourself and others needless harm is by practicing self-advocacy, choosing to be present in your conscious self and in observer mode, and operating from a functional, integrated, and heart-centered paradigm. In other words, by expressing your best self, being sourceful, and operating above the line in life.

Summary of Self-Empowerment Tools and Practices

Do the work of consciously crafting your ground of being by integrating and practicing the fundamental premises of integral emotional intelligence.

RECOMMENDED READING

Berne, Eric. (2004) *Games People Play: The Basic Handbook of Transactional Analysis.* New York, NY: A Ballantine Book, Random House.

Blandin, Brad. (1996) *Radical Honesty.* New York, NY: Dell Publishing, Random House.

Daniels, David D. and Price, Virginia. (2000) *The Essential Enneagram.* New York, NY: Harper Collins.

Davidson, Gordon. (2011) *Joyful Evolution: A Guide for Loving Co-Creation with Your Conscious, Subconscious and Superconscious Selves.* San Raphael, CA: Golden Firebird Press.

Emerald, David. (2010) *The Power of TED (The Empowerment Dynamic).* Bainbridge Island, WA: Polaris Publishing.

Lipton, Bruce H. (2011) *The Biology of Belief: Unleashing the Power of Consciousness, Matter & Miracles.* Hay House.

Marker, Sandra. "Unmet Human Needs." This is an article featured on the Beyond Intractability website. https://www.beyondintractability.org/essay/human_needs

Palmer, Helen. (1991) *The Enneagram.* New York, NY: HarperCollins.

Parfitt, Will. (1994) *The Elements of Psychosynthesis.* Rockport, MA: Element, Inc.

Riso, Don Richard and Hudson, Russ. (2003) *Discovering Your Personality Type.* New York, NY: Houghton Mifflin Company.

Riso, Don Richard and Hudson, Russ. (1996) *Personality Types.* New York, NY: Houghton Mifflin Company.

Stevens, José. (1994) *Transforming Your Dragons.* Rochester, VT: Bear and Company.

Tolle, Eckhart. (2004) *The Power of Now.* Novato, CA: New World Publishing.

Val-Essen, Ilene. (2010) *Bring Out the Best in Your Child and Your Self.* Culver City, CA: Quality Parenting.

Weinhold, Barry K. and Weinhold, Janae. (2017) *How to Break Free of the Drama Triangle and Victim Consciousness.* Colorado Springs, CO: CICRCL Press.

Endnotes

[i] See Ken Wilber, The Psychology and Spirituality Summit, Three Selves in the Journey to Growing Up and Waking Up, an online course offered by Sounds True. https://psychotherapy-and-spirituality-summit-sfm.soundstrue.com

There is also a video presentation of this material on the Integral+Life website, Wake Up, Grow Up: Enlightenment in the 21st Century. https://integrallife.com/wake-grow-edge-unknown-human-being/

[ii] See Daniel Goleman's article "What Makes a Leader?" Harvard Business Review, January 2004.

[iii] G. I. Gurdjieff, *In Search of Being,* page 35.

[iv] Gordon Davidson, *Joyful Evolution,* page 17.

[v] Bruce Lipton, *The Biology of Belief,* page 98.

[vi] Gordon Davidson, *Joyful Evolution,* page 23. The musical metaphors for the three selves are inspired by Gordon's description of them.

[vii] Eckhart Tolle, *The Power of Now,* page 36.

[viii] Gordon Davidson's book *Joyful Evolution* and his workshops have both been extremely helpful in distinguishing these subpersonalities.

[ix] The Enneagram Institute, the Riso-Hudson Enneagram Type Indicator (RHETI). https://www.enneagraminstitute.com/rheti

[x] David Daniels, the Stanford Enneagram Test and Guide. https://drdaviddaniels.com/stanford-enneagram-test-inventory-guide/

[xi] José Stevens, *Transforming Your Dragons,* page 4.

^{xii} See the Shalem Institute for Spiritual Formation's website for the article "What Is Contemplative Spirituality?" https://shalem.org/2004/03/01/what-is-contemplative-spirituality/

^{xiii} Go to The Center for Contemplative Mind in Society's website at www.contemplativemind.org for further information and for a downloadable copy of The Tree of Contemplative Practices.

^{xiv} Will Parfitt, *The Elements of Psychosynthesis,* page 37.

^{xv} Gordon Davidson, *Joyful Evolution,* page 221.

^{xvi} Go to the National Association of Adult Survivors of Child Abuse's website. http://naasca.org/2012-Resources/010812-StaisticsOfChildAbuse.htm

^{xvii} Bruce Lipton, *Biology of Belief,* page 98.

^{xviii} Jach Pursel (lecturing as Lazaris), audio recording *Negative Ego: Ending the Co-Dependenc.* https://www.lazaris.com

^{xix} Bruce Lipton, *The Biology of Belief,* page 132.

^{xx} The steps for working with lower-self subpersonalities and the subpersonality drawing exercise were adapted from Ilene Val-Essen's book about conscious parenting, *Bring out the Best in Your Child and Your Self,* page 60.

^{xxi} David Emerald, *The Power of TED,* page 99.

^{xxii} Will Parfitt, *The Elements of Psychosynthesis,* page 57.

^{xxiii} Wordwise with Robert Cottrill, see the article "The Human Heart (Bible Study)." http://wordwisebiblestudies.com/the-human-heart-bible-study/